The Definitive Guide to Windows Installer

PHIL WILSON

The Definitive Guide to Windows Installer
Copyright © 2004 by Phil Wilson

ISBN (pbk): 1-59059-297-2

Printed and bound in the United States of America 9 8 7 6 5 4 3 2

Lead Editor: Dan Appleman

Technical Reviewers: Chris Gouge, Carolyn Napier

Editorial Board: Steve Anglin, Dan Appleman, Ewan Buckingham, Gary Cornell, Tony Davis, Jason Gilmore, Jonathan Hassell, Chris Mills, Dominic Shakeshaft, Jim Sumser

Project Manager: Tracy Brown Collins

Copy Manager: Nicole LeClerc

Copy Editor: Susannah Pfalzer

Production Manager: Kari Brooks

Compositor: Vijay Nicole Imprints

Proofreader: Liz Welch

Indexer: Carol Burbo

Cover Designer: Kurt Krames

Manufacturing Manager: Tom Debolski

Distributed to the book trade in the United States by Springer-Verlag New York, Inc., 233 Spring Street, 6th Floor, New York, NY 10013 and outside the United States by Springer-Verlag GmbH & Co. KG, Tiergartenstr. 17, 69112 Heidelberg, Germany.

In the United States: phone 1-800-SPRINGER, e-mail orders@springer-ny.com, or visit http://www.springer-ny.com. Outside the United States: fax +49 6221 345229, e-mail orders@springer.de, or visit http://www.springer.de.

For information on translations, please contact Apress directly at 2560 Ninth Street, Suite 219, Berkeley, CA 94710. Phone 510-549-5930, fax 510-549-5939, e-mail info@apress.com, or visit http://www.apress.com.

The source code for this book is available to readers at http://www.apress.com in the Downloads section.

Contents at a Glance

Contents

About the Author

Phil Wilson graduated from the University of Aston, Birmingham, England, with a BSc in chemistry, but preferred computers to test tubes and eventually worked for 15 years on developing operating systems for Burroughs and Unisys mainframes. Phil started programming for Windows in the early 1990s and has developed in MFC, ATL, COM, Visual Basic, and C#. He has been involved in installation design and technology for about eight years, and became a Microsoft Most Valuable Professional for Windows Installer in 2003. To get away from computers, he plays and records guitar, and enjoys camping in the California desert. Phil works for Unisys Corporation in Mission Viejo, California.

Acknowledgments

Many thanks to the people at Apress for giving me this opportunity, especially Dan Appleman. Thanks to Tracy Brown Collins, Susannah Pfalzer, and Kari Brooks for getting me through it all. A lot probably goes on in this process that they kept me blissfully unaware of; all I had to do was keep writing.

My heartfelt thanks go to Chris Gouge and Carolyn Napier of Microsoft for their technical review. They patiently corrected my misunderstandings, and the book is much better for their review. I can't imagine what it must feel like to have someone write a book about the software that you work on every day, so to them and the rest of the Window Installer team: I hope I've done a good job.

Thanks also to R. Michael Sanford for his early review work.

Finally, thanks to my family for their patience while I was holed up evenings and weekends for the duration, and thanks to my friends M.G., A.K., and V.R. for believing in me.

Introduction

Installing new software is perhaps the most adrenalin-inducing experience you'll have on a computer, aside from whatever games you might play. It's not hard to see why. You give over control of the system to a program that often demands Administrator privilege and that then starts updating some of the most fragile parts of your system. You might know the actual product being installed quite well, but there's rarely any documentation about what the installation of it will do to your system. It might install kernel drivers or Services, it might alter your personal settings without your permission, and it might result in other applications on your system no longer working. For a company building and shipping software, the installation might be the first time the customer has seen your product or your company, and it's your opportunity to make a lasting impression one way or the other. An unreliable installation will affect the customer's image of you for a long time.

The goal of this book is to show you how to build safe and secure installations. Its focus is Windows Installer technology on the Windows NT series of operating systems for Windows 2000 and above, and you'll build example projects as Visual Studio Setup and Deployment Projects. Aside from the actual nuts and bolts of building Windows Installer-based installations, I'll offer advice on how to build a reliable installation and what you should and shouldn't do. The integration of installer technology as part of the Windows operating system means that the dividing line between an application and its installation has become much less sharp, and the book will cover how you need to design applications to integrate properly with Windows Installer.

The book starts with basic principles and drills down deeper in later chapters. I start with the installation equivalent of the "Hello World" program, and then gradually get deeper into the contents of installer MSI files, including installation in the .NET Framework world. Along the way I'll stop to look at best practices and how to keep your installation reliable. Where I show use of the installer APIs, I'll use VBScript for the sake of simplicity and clarity, but I'll also point you at the Win32 equivalents and show you a couple of ways to call them from the .NET Framework language C#.

As is often the case when you try to explain something, you find that you test your understanding, and if you're lucky you learn something new at the same time. I hope you learn as much from reading this book as I did writing it.

CHAPTER 1

Installations Past, Present, and Future

IT OFTEN SEEMS that the installation of a product is almost an afterthought. Developers spend hundreds of labor-months building that great new three-tier application. However, I wouldn't be surprised if you're reading this book because you're the person who has to figure out how to install the application while everyone else is out celebrating the fact that they've finished it. Of course, an application isn't actually finished until you can install it on your clients' systems.

Background

Many people see installations as a simple process of copying files to the client system, but in reality, copying files is probably the most straightforward part of the whole installation process. When installing a product on the Windows operating system (OS), you need to consider all the following areas, and this is not a complete list by any means.

Where the Files Go

It is not always obvious where files should actually be installed. The usual convention is that they get copied to the Program Files folder associated with your company name and product name. But this isn't always the case. For example, if your company has a set of component object model (COM) components, then you can't usually have your own private copy in each of the product's folders. There is only one set of COM registration entries on the system. If you install the component at one location in one product, then at another location from another product, the last copy of the component is the one that all the client programs will use. That's because the install marks the InprocServer32 entry to point to the last location the shared component was installed to. Uninstalling any one of the products breaks all the remaining products because the uninstall removes the registration data when the program is uninstalled.

Redistributing Supporting Files

Many products also need supporting software to be installed before they will function correctly. Sometimes this means a collection of supporting DLLs or OCXs, sometimes it means something rather complicated such as the Microsoft Database Engine (MSDE) software. Not only that, but different operating systems have different requirements. To show a couple of examples, Windows 2000 has many of the Visual Studio 6.0 support DLLs for Visual Basic, ATL, and MFC projects as part of the operating system, so they don't need to be installed. However, if you're supporting Windows NT 4.0, they do. Microsoft's Visual Studio .NET (VS.NET) has a new set of redistributables (ATL70.DLL, MFC70.DLL, MSVCR70.DLL) that always need installing, even on Windows 2000. This area can be confusing and contributes to the general expression for this situation— "DLL Hell."

Installing Windows Services

Windows Services sometimes depend on other Services that are already on the system. Installing a Service might therefore require stopping these other Services, installing yours, then starting up these other Services, and finally starting your Service.

Files in Use

The typical problem with in-use files is that you're trying to replace them with newer versions. It is good practice to attempt to shut down the application using these files. If the application is a Service or an application that has a user interface, you might be able to send messages to close it down (or prompt the user to do so), but some of these scenarios can be complex. You might be trying to register a COM DLL by calling its DllRegisterServer function (which is what REGSVR32.EXE does). However, that DLL might require a dependent DLL that could not be installed because an older version of that dependent DLL is in use. In these situations the only recourse is to arrange a reboot to get the files replaced. In the case of registering COM servers, you typically need to write an entry to the system Registry's RunOnce key to register the DLL, and then arrange the reboot.

Security and the Target User

Installations often have to be run with Administrator account privileges because they update parts of the system that require privileges to create or modify them. On the other hand, say you're installing on a shared computer and you'd like to install something on behalf of another user. Although you could go ahead and install it with an Administrator's account, it's not clear that you want this other user to have Administrator privileges. There is also a privacy issue on shared computers, perhaps not so much when one individual installs something for another, but in the corporate world where several users might be sharing one computer. Therefore, there is often a conflict between the security requirements of the installation and the security requirements of the installed product.

Maintaining the Product

It's a pretty safe assumption that sooner or later a product will need updates, whether they are bug fixes or feature additions. You need a mechanism that can identify where the existing files are located on the client system and replace them with new versions. This maintenance requirement has all the drawbacks you already looked at relating to files in use and so on, with the additional difficulties of working out what to do if the update fails. This can mean identifying the files that are to be updated, and backing them up somewhere. That way the user can restore them if the update fails or if the user finds that the updated product is broken and needs to uninstall the update. This is the model used with Windows Service Packs. Because of these possible requirements, this type of service pack installation is sometimes different than the original installation, and you may use a different tool to build it. It would not be unusual for an installation developer to need to understand at least two types of installation— the original product installation and the tools that build it, plus the tools to build service packs.

Environments

For example, if a product consists of three distinct tiers, there are likely to be three distinct environments onto which you have to install some piece of the application. Perhaps you need to divide the product into separate features, one per environment. Perhaps files or programs are common to some of the tiers, so you would need to break out these common files into some kind of separate feature (not visible to the user) that can be installed on all the tiers by default. Each tier might also be a different type of Windows environment. For example, the back-end tier might require a server operating system, so you probably don't want to allow it to be installed on a workstation. In other words, the application needs to be broken up into pieces and rebuilt as a set of features that can be targeted at the appropriate user or platform.

The One-Way Nature of Installations

Although you usually call an installation program a "program," it's not like other programs in a couple of interesting ways. If you have an application program that has a bug, you ship a fix to your clients, who replace the old version with the new one and start running the new version. Installation programs aren't like that. If you've shipped a broken installation, you can't just ship a corrected one to your clients and ask them to use it. That's because no program on the client's system can be replaced—it's not literally a program in that sense. In reality, an installation is a process, a sequence of actions that alter the target system, and once the installation has done its work you can't just replace it with a corrected (updated) version. There is also the uninstall process to keep in mind. Once the product has been installed, then so has the uninstall process, so it's essential that the uninstall process work properly. A product that cannot be uninstalled is potentially useless if fixing or replacing it requires users to uninstall it.

Development Ease and the Installation

Development tools make it easy to build programs. You use a wizard, add some code, and your system is already set up with the support necessary for you to test the program. I'm exaggerating somewhat, but the point is that when you install the program or application on a client system, you need to know about each file, supporting DLL, and Registry entry that the application needs for it to run. If you're communicating this to someone who's building the installation program, detailing everything that's needed is a nontrivial task.

Development Installs vs. Production Installs

Development environments and documentation frequently talk in terms of command-line programs that perform installation tasks. In COM, developers are used to the idea of running Regsvr32.exe to register COM DLLs, or a –Regserver command-line argument to register a COM local server. In the .NET Framework world you see references to running Regasm.exe, Gacutil.exe, and Installutil.exe to install assemblies for .NET COM Interop, to install assemblies into the Global

Assembly Cache (the GAC), or to register assemblies as .NET Windows Services. However, not one of these command-line programs is necessary for a Windows Installer–based installation because installer support is provided for the functionality offered by these programs.

Introducing Windows Installer

Before Windows Installer there was no specific Windows functionality supplied to install products. (Strictly speaking, there has always been the Setup API, but its main functionality is based on using INF files to perform installations.) The Windows programming environment happened to be rich enough that developers could use its APIs to perform installs. A major consequence of using the general-purpose Windows APIs was that there was no consistent integration between Windows and the installed product. For example, if you wanted to inventory the products installed on a system, you could enumerate the contents of the Registry area used by the Add/Remove Programs applet, but any number of different tools could have installed each product, and even a simple task such as finding where the product was installed was nontrivial.

Around the Windows 2000 timeframe, Microsoft supplied Windows Installer as the installation technology for Microsoft Office 2000. I'll take a brief look here at the problems it helps solve, and a more in-depth look in later chapters. Windows Installer provides a standard way to install, maintain, and uninstall software. However, that by itself is not justification, so let's look at what makes Windows Installer unique and how it addresses some of the preceding topics.

Transactional Behavior

Nobody wants an installation to get partially completed and then fail for some reason, leaving a system in some indeterminate state. Windows Installer turns product installations into an all-or-nothing proposition—the product is either successfully installed on the system, or the installation does not work and all the changes that might have been made to the system are backed out.

A large part of this transactional nature is a consequence of eliminating as much code as possible from the installation process. As you'll see later, Windows Installer offers features that mean you don't necessarily need to run custom code at install time. This is necessary because otherwise you, the installation developer, would be responsible for reversing any changes made to the system during the installation.

As an example, consider COM server registration. As I noted earlier, a COM server historically required its DllRegisterServer function to be called, and likewise the uninstall process would call DllUnregisterServer. This requires the COM server to initialize, where it might need a dependent DLL that isn't on the system yet. Windows Installer deals with this by storing COM registration data inside the actual installer package, the MSI file, so it doesn't need to call or run the COM server to install or uninstall the Registry entries. Windows Installer can add or remove the COM Registry entries whether the COM server itself is functional or not. Installing the COM server means copying the file to the system and writing the Registry entries from installer tables.

The same general idea applies to Windows Services (sometimes called NT Services). When they are installed with something like a –Service command-line argument to a run of the Service program itself, install and uninstall are dependent on the Service being functional. However, Windows Installer has support for installing Services directly from the installation package with no requirement to run the Service executable to install it. Consequently, installation and removal of the Service are controlled more safely.

Repair

It's not unusual for files that belong to a product to get accidentally deleted. Windows Installer has repair features that restore an application that is broken because of missing files or Registry entries. If the installation marks a file or a Registry entry as "key," Windows Installer has the capability to restore the file or entry automatically if it's missing. When you go to Add/Remove Programs, a Repair choice is offered, along with other choices to uninstall or modify the installed features.

Repair is probably the feature that most often surprises developers. They are generally familiar with the idea that a product can be installed and then manipulated afterwards by adding new files or removing unwanted ones, only to find that the repair mechanism restores the files or Registry keys to the initial installation state. Users too are sometimes surprised when they remove a shortcut and move it to some other location, only to find that Windows Installer restores it through a repair.

64-bit

There is support in Windows Installer for installing applications onto 64-bit Windows operating systems. This doesn't just mean that you can install 32-bit applications onto 64-bit systems, it means that Windows Installer is likely to be the only way to install 64-bit applications onto a 64-bit system.

Sharing Files

Sharing has always been an important aspect of installations. The sharing issues are largely responsible for the situation popularly (or unpopularly) known as "DLL Hell." You need to work out which Microsoft DLLs need installing to support your product, and consequently run the risk of creating an incompatible set of system DLLs. Or you might have shared components in your company's products that all need to be installed and managed correctly on client systems. This is becoming less of an issue since Windows 2000 introduced Windows Protected Files, a feature that prevents installations from replacing critical system files. Windows Installer does not even attempt to replace those protected files that are considered to be part of the OS.

Sharing in Windows Installer uses reference counts for each unique component. You still need to follow rules, as you'll see later, but the Windows Installer component sharing mechanism is much more robust than previous schemes.

System Integration

Products installed with Windows Installer are integrated into Windows. APIs and COM objects can report information about installed products to a detailed level. In addition, a Windows Management Instrumentation (WMI) provider reports the content and configuration of installed products. If you ever wondered whether there is a way to discover accurately what products are installed on a system, the fact that there are standard API calls is a vast improvement compared to prowling the Registry looking for products. These APIs not only return detail about potentially every file installed by a product, they also allow the application code itself to integrate with the installation and modify installed components on the fly. The APIs also allow access to installation packages (MSI files). For example, it's relatively easy to query the contents of an installation package and compare the contents with a version of that package that is installed on the system.

.NET

Windows Installer has built-in support for installing .NET assemblies into the Global Assembly Cache (GAC). This is likely to be the only way you should install assemblies into the GAC. Yes, Microsoft supplies the Gacutil.exe utility in the development environment, but this program knows nothing about the Windows Installer reference-counting scheme, so shared assemblies installed into the GAC require Windows Installer to maintain correct shared-installer reference counts.

For the System or for Current User

When you start installing a product you are often asked if it's being installed for you (private to your account on the system), or whether it's being installed for everyone. These generally affect whether, for example, certain Registry entries are written to the HKEY_CURRENT_USER (HKCU area) or to HKEY_LOCAL_MACHINE (HKLM). If you assume that the target user is in fact the current user of the system, this means that the application should not be visible to other users. But think about the mechanics of COM registration, where code in the DllRegisterServer entry point creates COM registration entries on the system. You'll realize that there is no way that the code in DllRegisterServer knows whether the installation is per-user or per-machine, so the registration code cannot know which Registry location is the correct one, HKLM or HKCU. The code in DllRegisterServer registers to the local machine Registry keys, so in effect an install for the current user leaves COM servers accessible to everyone on the system. It therefore makes a lot of sense to get COM servers out of the business of self-registration and have Windows Installer create the registration entries in the appropriate Registry location.

Security of Installation vs. Security of Product

When trying to install a product for a user who might not have the security privileges to install the product, there needs to be a way for this user to install the product without requiring those elevated privileges on a permanent basis. Windows Installer provides some ways to deal with these issues. One reason it helps with these issues is because it runs as a Windows Service and doesn't need to be constrained by the privileges of the current user. Another reason is because policies can be configured so you can perform an installation with elevated privileges on behalf of a user who is not privileged.

Updating and Deploying New Versions

Before Windows Installer, when you wanted to ship corrections to a product, perhaps you simply rebuilt the entire installation setup and sent it to your clients. However, you can't just ask your client to install the product, because you'd end up with two copies of the product on the system. However, if you're supplying a fix or an update you need to replace the existing installed product. Generally speaking, the incoming new installation would detect the existing one and uninstall it, or perhaps even arrange to completely install itself on top of the existing product. Another choice would be to produce a service pack to update the product, often requiring use of a separate tool to install the updates to the client system. To summarize, there have been a number of ways to deal with these maintenance issues. Windows Installer has some formal mechanisms for installing product updates and fixes.

Advertisement

You can think of advertisement as installation-on-demand. It can be particularly useful in corporate environments—you can have practically everything installed (shortcuts, Registry entries, and so on) except for the files. When you reference the advertised product, the installation starts installing the files from a network location onto the client system. Even after a product has been installed, perhaps some of its features will be advertised, so that when the advertised feature is first used this feature is installed.

The idea of advertised features is that you install a hook of some kind, typically a shortcut. Using this shortcut causes the feature to be installed. If the advertised feature consists of one or more COM components, there is a similar advertisement installation step that causes the component to be installed.

Running Your Own Code

Many of the observations made in this chapter might give the impression that you can't add your own code to the installation process. In fact you can—when you do this it's called a custom action. Many types of custom actions allow you to run VBScript, executables, and call into a DLL, to quote a few examples. So that changes to the system can be provided with transactional behavior in mind, you can associate these custom actions with the install, the uninstall, and also the rollback process that occurs when an installation fails and everything done to the system is being undone to restore the system to its original state.

The Tools

Windows Installer packages have the MSI file extension, and the Windows Installer Service installs these packages. You can use an SDK here, just like in many other aspects of Windows programming. In this case, you use the Windows Installer SDK, which is part of the Platform SDK. This contains documentation, tools, and sample code to create and modify installer packages. VS.NET offers wizards and a development environment to build installation packages.

Third-party vendors who provide tools to create installation setups have been around for a while (for example, InstallShield Software). These companies' tools historically have built installation packages that differ from one another, although most generate a wizard-based approach to the installation process. The inner workings of the install—the code, the log files and so on—are all proprietary.

After Microsoft introduced the Windows Installer Service, these vendors introduced tools to create installer packages (MSI files). Apart from companies and products such as InstallShield, Wise, OnDemand Software's WinINSTALL, Zero G Software's InstallAnywhere.NET (formerly ActiveInstall), and Corner House Software, there are open source and free tools that you can use to build installer packages. Although this book uses VS.NET extensively for its samples, it is important to realize that Visual Studio Deployment Projects provide just a basic authoring tool for creating packages compared to some of the more advanced third-party products. It's quite likely that you or your company will want to build installer packages using features that Windows Installer provides but that are beyond the capabilities of Visual Studio Deployment Projects. Although this book will help you build and use installer packages, you'll find it much easier to build more complex installation packages using a fully featured tool with support for your required functionality built into its Integrated Development Environment (IDE). Everything you learn in this book about Windows Installer will be useful no matter which tool you eventually decide to use, but you'll find that the right development tool makes the process of building installer packages easier and faster.

Summary

Perhaps the most important characteristic of an installation package (installer terminology for an MSI file) is that it is a database. This is not loose terminology; it really is a database with tables organized into columns and rows. As you'll see later, you can even use SQL-like statements to query or update the installation package. The tables in the package describe the files, features, shortcuts, Registry entries, COM classes, and your custom action code, to name some of the content. Even the order in which activities occur during the installation process is determined by tables that contain each action and its order relative to other actions.

As you'll see as you progress through the following chapters, Windows Installer supplies a framework for installations. Like most frameworks, it works best when you don't bend it. When you design and develop applications, you're almost certainly aware of the limitations and capabilities of the implementation you're going to use, and you take these into account when you design the application. The same is true of Windows Installer. If you come to design a product installation, you must be aware of the direction that the technology would prefer you to take. It's probably no exaggeration to say that most installation problems are the result of a preconceived design or implementation plan that doesn't fit the framework.

You'll see how all these examples work using actual examples of installation packages, so let's get going and build your first installation package.

CHAPTER 2

Building an MSI File: Visual Studio and Orca

IN THIS CHAPTER, you'll build an installer package using a VS.NET Setup and Deployment Project and look at it with a tool called Orca, part of the Windows Installer SDK.

Background

First, some history and an overview of VS's capabilities in the installation area.

Microsoft has often added capabilities for building installations in VS—perhaps you've used the Visual Basic Package and Deployment Wizard. If you've used VS 6.0, you might have used the first version of Visual Studio Installer, which was available as a free download for VS licensees. VS.NET is the first release of VS that integrates the ability to build Windows Installer packages with the IDE. However, VS.NET's installation tool comes with some limitations and restrictions that become apparent as you use it. This doesn't mean that Microsoft did a bad job, but it does mean that if you want to use a substantial set of Windows Installer's features, you should look beyond VS.NET's installer tool. Look in Chapter 16 for a list of some of the vendors that supply fully featured tools to create installer packages.

One of the tools that Microsoft supplies to view and modify installer packages is called Orca. You can find it in the Windows Installer section of the Platform SDK; the installation package is (what else?) an installer package called ORCA.MSI. After you've installed it, you'll find that the right-click context menu on Windows Installer files (notably packages, MSI files and merge modules, MSM files) allows you to open and edit them. You'll be using Orca later to view and modify installation packages.

I'll describe everything I cover here regarding Windows Installer concepts in more detail in later chapters. In this chapter, you'll build an installer package so that you can look inside the actual MSI file; that's when you'll use Orca.

Building a Package

The first package you build is a simple one—this is the "Hello World" program's equivalent in the installation context. You'll install Notepad (NOTEPAD.EXE) and a text file, together with a shortcut to run the installed Notepad against the text file. Note that this project is supplied with the book, so you can build it yourself or use the one provided.

You start by running VS and choosing the New Project from the File menu, selecting Setup and Deployment Project, and then Setup Project. Once the wizard has completed, select the Project icon in the Solution Explorer. The Edit menu has drop-down choices for View ➤ Editor ➤ File System. When you're in this File System view, you can then select Application Folder. Then you can right-click in the file pane and select Add, then File. Add NOTEPAD.EXE and SomeTextFile.txt in that pane. Because you'll need a shortcut to NOTEPAD.EXE for the Programs menu, right-click NOTEPAD.EXE in the file pane that you just added it to, and choose Create Shortcut. At this point you should see something like Figure 2-1. Notice that this view also shows the Properties window for the Application Folder, where ProgramFilesFolder, Manufacturer, and ProductName are enclosed in square brackets. These are three standard Windows Installer properties. You'll see more of these later because properties are the variables that drive the behavior of an installation. For now the important thing to know is that the value of [ProgramFilesFolder] is resolved when the installation runs and is replaced with the Program Files path on the system. Those square brackets mean that the identifier they contain is a Windows Installer property.

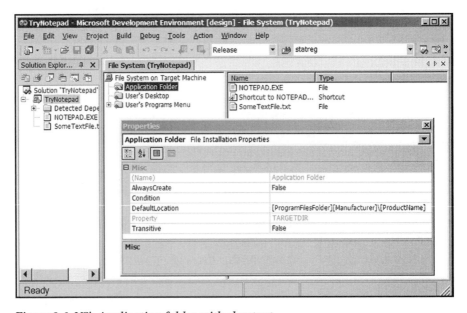

Figure 2-1. VS's Application folder with shortcut

You need the shortcut to Notepad for the User's Programs Menu, so right-click that shortcut and select Cut. Then right-click the User's Programs Menu item, select Add ➤ Folder to add a folder and a subfolder (I called it Phil and TryNotepad), then use Paste to get the shortcut into the pane. You'll see something like Figure 2-1.

Before you do a build, right-click the Project in the Solution Explorer and set the build properties to package files "In setup file." Options are here for bootstrappers (in other words, making sure that the Windows Installer engine is installed on the target system), but you'll just be building the installer package, an MSI file. See Figure 2-2 for an example of the property pages for the build.

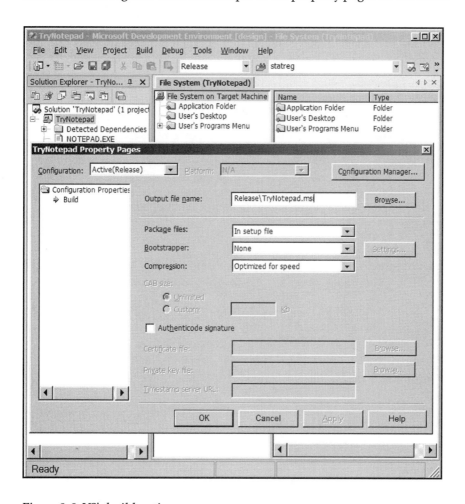

Figure 2-2. VS's build options

Now if you do a build it should create an installer package: an MSI file containing everything needed to install your Notepad application. You can now double-click the package and the installation starts. After the Welcome screen, you see a Select Installation folder that's got some notable features (see Figure 2-3):

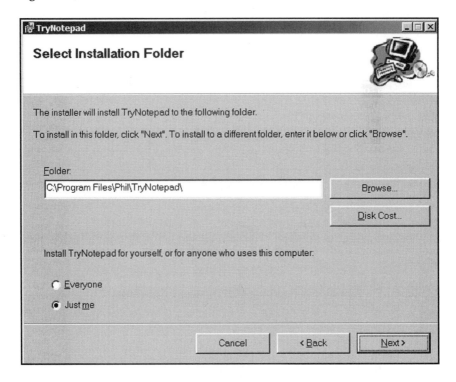

Figure 2-3. Selecting the installation folder

- The installer has resolved the ProgramFilesFolder property and the Folder box shows the actual path on the target system. This is a key feature of Windows Installer properties—not so much that they are resolved but that you can use them in square brackets in places such as folder names and Registry entries. I should point out that this folder isn't always C:\Program Files, which is why Windows Installer supplies a variable property.

- The dialog wants to know whether you want to install this application for Just me or for Everyone. In other words, should this be installed for the current user or for all users of the system? This choice affects an important Windows Installer property that you can control—the ALLUSERS property you'll look at later.

Select Everyone and continue. The installation should complete normally, and the Start Menu should now have the shortcut to initiate Notepad. You can uninstall the product in the usual ways via Add/Remove Programs, or by right-clicking the package and selecting Uninstall. However, you're going to look at the content of the package, so after you've installed Orca, right-click the package and select Edit with Orca. What you see is a screen like Figure 2-4, where Orca shows each installer table in the left pane and the rows and columns of each table on the right. (Figure 2-9 shows a view with more tables shown.) In the case of Figure 2-4, Orca is showing the File table because it's a useful place to start dissecting a package.

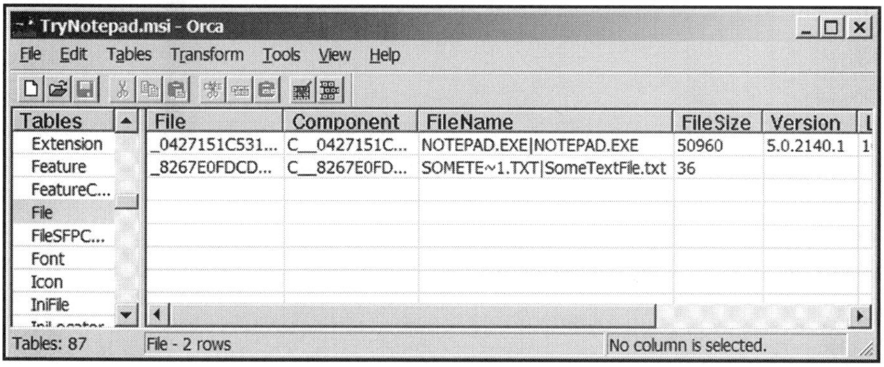

Figure 2-4. The File table

Before you go any further, the tables and their contents, including the details of each table and column, are documented in the Windows Installer section of the Platform SDK. I'm generally not going to repeat all that detail; I'll just point out how the tables work and fit together so that you can make more sense of the documentation.

Notice that there is a row for each file you're installing, and that each row has the name of a file in the FileName column. If you hadn't guessed from the format, the file name is shown in short file name and long file name format separated by a vertical bar. Perhaps more interestingly, the File table shows the version for code files in the Version column (which appears only if the file has a version resource). If you were thinking that Windows Installer uses this version value to decide whether to replace older versions on the target system, you're right, and you'll be using this value when you get to Chapter 6, which describes updating products.

An important item in the File table is the Component_ column. A Windows Installer Component is the key unit of an installation. There is a component reference at almost every place in the package where something is going to be installed onto the client system. VS has generated two components in the File table, one for NOTEPAD.EXE and one for the text file. If you've installed something and selected a "Custom" install, you're probably used to the idea of a list of features that can be selected or deselected for installation. The way this works in Windows Installer is that a feature consists of one or more components. In fact, if you look at Figure 2-5 you see the FeatureComponents table, which is where components get mapped to their owning feature. Notice that VS generates only one feature, called DefaultFeature. This is one of the limitations of VS: It has no capability to organize an installation into more than one feature. You also see more than just the two components in the File table here. It turns out that VS wants to be sure that the Program Menu folders get removed at uninstall time. It adds a component and some entries in the RemoveFile table to make sure that the Program Menu subfolders get deleted, and it creates a component because most activities done during an installation require an associated component. VS also creates a component to deal with some Registry entries it might create (more on this later in this chapter).

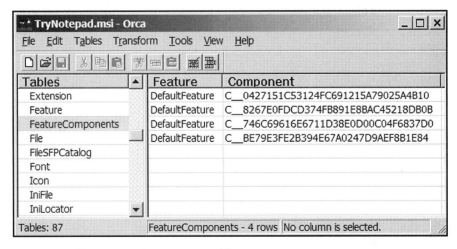

Figure 2-5. The FeatureComponents table

A First Look at Shortcuts

You installed a shortcut to Notepad in this installation. As you might expect, there is a Shortcut table in the installation package. Figure 2-6 shows the first few columns of the Orca view of the shortcut table and the entry for the shortcut to NOTEPAD.EXE.

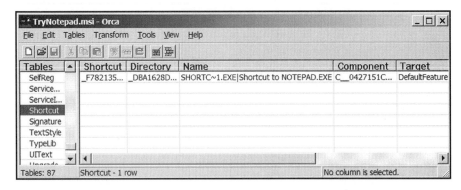

Figure 2-6. The Shortcut table

Note that the Component_ column contains the Windows Installer Component that the shortcut belongs to—exactly what you would expect knowing that all installed items belong to a component. There is also a Directory_ column, which effectively names the Program Menu folder and the subfolders that contain the shortcut. There is also an entry in the Target column that contains the name of the only feature in this installation. The fact that this is the name of a feature in the Feature table means that this is an "advertised" shortcut. Although advertised features are associated with the "install on demand" scenario, they have another interesting characteristic, which is that they verify the correctness of their associated installer components. In other words, using the shortcut triggers an automatic repair if the components are "broken." If you remove the file NOTEPAD.EXE from its installed location on disk and then use the shortcut, you see a Windows Installer dialog that restores the missing file.

Although the name of the shortcut is in the Shortcut table, there is no obvious reference to the actual target file—the installed NOTEPAD.EXE. That's because the linkage is indirect, through the component name in the Shortcut table. If you look at the Component table in Figure 2-7, the shortcut component is that top one, and that component has a KeyPath entry that is a key into the File table. Referring back to Figure 2-4, you can see that this File table entry is NOTEPAD.EXE. This is a specific case of a general principle in the installer—that a target file is indirectly referenced by naming a component that has a KeyPath entry referring to a File table entry for a file. In other words, the Shortcut table names the component (not the file), and the Component table's KeyPath entry points to the file. There's another subtle point to notice here about the Shortcut, which is that a shortcut file is not literally being installed. Although it might have looked as if you were installing an actual file in the IDE—a shortcut—the package contains no such file, just a table entry with the information required to create one.

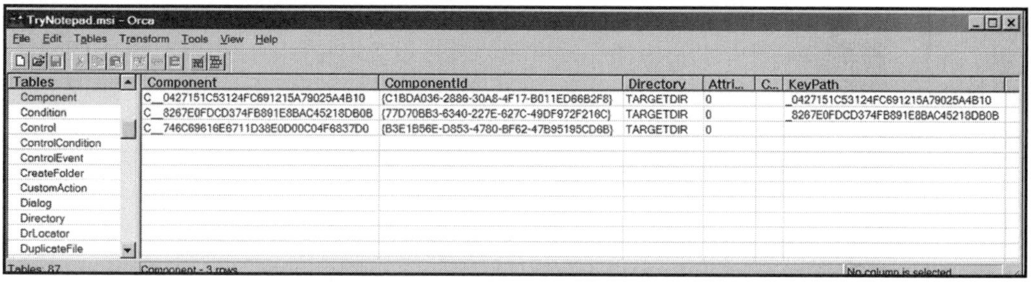

Figure 2-7. The Component table

If you look at this actual shortcut with Open All Users in Explorer, it looks like Figure 2-8. Compared to noninstaller shortcuts, the Target is grayed out and can't be altered. This is because this shortcut is encoded with the special behavior that causes Windows to verify the presence of the installer component.

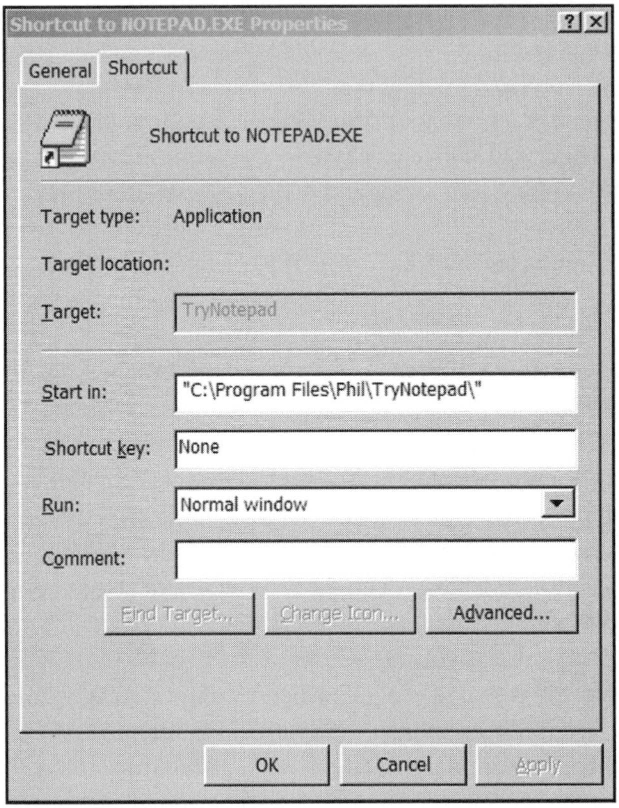

Figure 2-8. A Windows Installer shortcut

More About Properties

Windows Installer properties are the variables that you use to interact with the installation, such as the ProgramFilesFolder property I mentioned. They're somewhat similar to Environment variables in the sense that they are text-based variables that define other text, standard ones are provided by Windows, and you can define your own and sometimes set the Windows ones. You'll be looking at properties in detail later, but be aware that they have some important behaviors:

1. Properties are case-sensitive. If you create your own property name and refer to it later, be sure that you get the case correct.

2. A property can be public or private. A public property must be in uppercase. If it's public, you can specify it with a value in a command-line install of a package. Also, because of the way that installations work

internally, a public property that you create is also visible throughout most of the installation sequence. You cannot specify private properties in a command-line installation and you can't propagate them throughout the installation sequences (covered in Chapter 5).

3. You can treat properties as if they were logical values or data values. I'll use the built-in VersionNT property as an example. This property tells you whether the system you're installing on is in the Windows NT family (NT, Windows 2000, Windows 2003, Windows XP). For example, anything you do that depends on Windows Services can be conditioned on VersionNT as if it were a Boolean-valued attribute. It's not unusual to see VersionNT as a condition in these situations. However, if you look at the actual value of this property you'll find it returns the version of the NT family that is running. On Windows 2000 this property has the value 500, and on XP the value 501. In other words, it can be used as a Boolean True/False value even though it contains a version value. If you're a C programmer, you might be familiar with the idea that a value is True if it is non-NULL in spite of its actual value, somewhat like the behavior of some C language variables.

4. The data type of a property is vague. As you've seen, you can treat VersionNT as Boolean-valued even if the actual value of it is 500. If you wanted to check if you were running on Windows 2000 or later, you might check for VersionNT>=500. Does this mean it's a string or a Boolean or a number? In practice it usually doesn't matter because the context usually defines how the data type works, but this vagueness might well offend you if you are a programmer with a type-safe sensibility.

An installer package—a database—contains a Property table, which is where you can define your own properties if you need to give them default values, and also set values for standard installer properties. You aren't required to declare your own properties in the Property table. Declare them only if you need to give them a default value, because the act of programmatically setting a property name to a value creates the property on the fly.

Looking at Figure 2-9, you see the Property table of your Notepad package. The table in general is just a list of property names and property values, some uppercase and public, some lowercase and private. Because this list contains both user-defined (added by VS when it built the package) and Windows Installer–defined properties, there's no way to distinguish between what is a predefined installer property and what isn't, other than by looking in the SDK to see if it's defined there. ProductName and Manufacturer are among the standard installer properties that are defined here. Like many other properties, these two end up on the system, where they are available to be retrieved using API calls, or shown to the user in places such as the Add/Remove Programs Control Panel applet. ProductVersion is another installer property that you set, but unlike ProductName and Manufacturer, its value is more than just informational. When you look at upgrades and updating your product, you'll see that incrementing ProductVersion is a key step in the process.

Figure 2-9. The Property table

One of the key properties in an installation is the TARGETDIR property. This is the property that names the product's primary installation folder. It usually consists of a concatenation of other standard properties, such as [ProgramFilesFolder][Manufacturer]\[ProductName], which is what VS creates as the default location for the application folder.

GUIDs: Product, Upgrade, and Package Codes

You can see in Figure 2-9 that the ProductCode property is in fact a GUID, a unique identifier made famous by its use in identifying COM classes and interfaces. It's used here simply because it's a convenient mechanism to identify the product uniquely. It's in what is called the Registry format—text with curly braces around it. Windows uses the ProductCode property to identify this product uniquely, and the Windows Installer Service uses it to determine whether your product is already present on a system.

The UpgradeCode is also a GUID that you should not change within the lifetime of a product. The idea behind UpgradeCode is that you will have major revisions to a product over time, and each of these revisions is intended as a replacement for the previous version. The UpgradeCode is the constant that links these revisions together. You can think of an UpgradeCode as defining a product family. Windows can detect whether a product containing a particular UpgradeCode has already been installed on a client system. It provides a mechanism to uninstall the prior version as you install the new version, so that the replacement is a seamless process instead of a visible uninstall followed by an install of the newer product. Each version replaces the prior version until a product arrives that is completely independent of the previous versions. In practice, this might be a marketing decision as much as a technical one. For example, each new version of Microsoft Office that comes out is a replacement for previous versions. However, if you look at the VS product line, VS.NET was the start of a different product line—it did not replace VS 6.0 but could be installed alongside it. If you were designing these product lines, the versions of Microsoft Office would all use the same UpgradeCode, but VS.NET would have a different UpgradeCode than VS 6.0. The way you build an installation to perform a major upgrade of a previous version is covered in Chapter 6.

Each individual package—the MSI file—is also identified by a GUID—the PackageCode. This is used to distinguish between different builds of the same product. If you run Orca on an install package and choose Summary Information from the View menu, you see something like Figure 2-10. This shows the contents of the Summary Information stream for this package, and it includes the PackageCode. (You can also see a similar display when you choose Properties and Summary from the context menu when right-clicking a package, except that the PackageCode is reported there as Revision Number.)

The combination of ProductCode and PackageCode is the way Windows knows what to do if you try to reinstall the product. If you install your Notepad package that you built in this chapter, then try to install the exact same package again, you see that it shows a maintenance mode dialog. In this Notepad installation, this means that the setup shows a dialog with choices for Repair or Remove. Windows knows that this product from this package is already installed on the system, and the package itself is designed to go into this maintenance mode if the product is already installed on the system. By definition, the fact that you are attempting to install the same product (same ProductCode) from the same package (PackageCode) means that you either want to repair or remove it. No other choices make sense in this context—the product is already installed, after all! You can change the PackageCode by altering the Revision Number from Explorer (right-clicking, choosing Properties and the Summary tab) or in the Orca view of the Summary Information, then closing and saving the file. When you attempt to install this package now, you see different behavior. This time there is a message box from Windows saying that "Another version of this product is already installed" and suggesting that you reconfigure from Add/Remove Programs. In other words, you have to configure or remove the existing installed product before you can install the new one. The PackageCode determines the initial behavior here. If you change only the ProductCode in the Property table using Orca and then try to install the package, it would go into maintenance mode and ask for a Repair or Remove. If you change the ProductCode and the PackageCode, Windows thinks it's a totally new product and lets you go ahead with the installation.

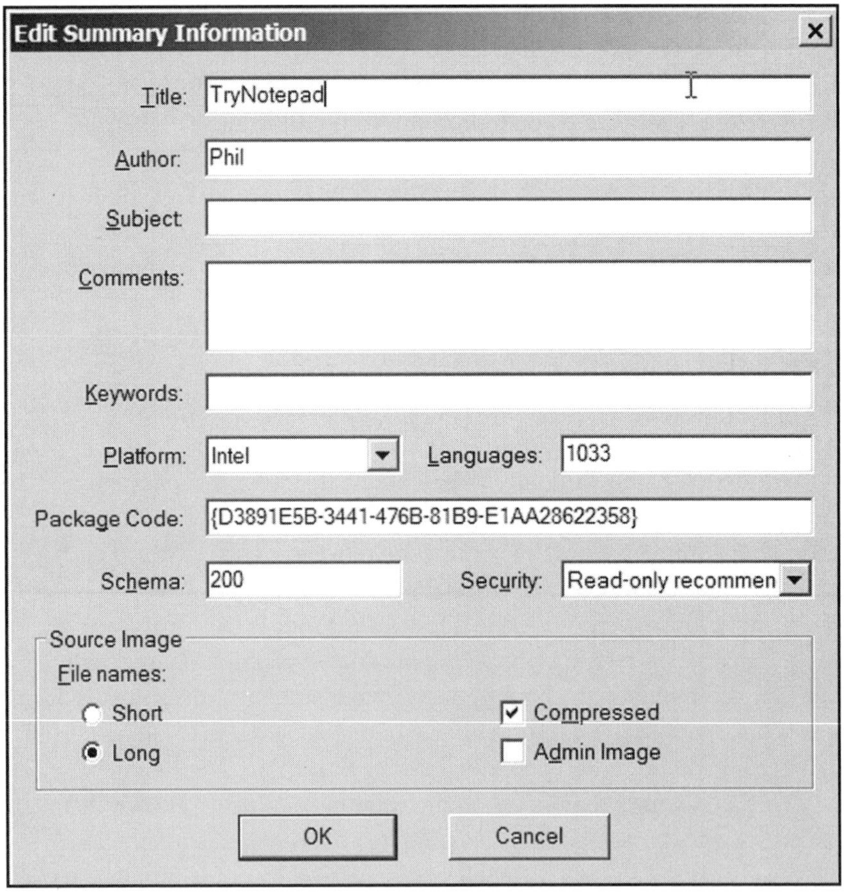

Figure 2-10. MSI file summary information

If you have built a genuinely new package containing new files, you've probably done so to have it update or replace the existing product on the system. This is the subject of Chapter 6. For now, the point of this exercise is to demonstrate the relationship between PackageCode and ProductCode.

Into the Package with Programming

Windows has a collection of Win32 APIs, all starting with Msi, that you can use on the contents of installation packages. Other APIs interface with Windows to interact with the products installed on the system. There's also a COM interface that is exposed mainly for administrators. I say this because the COM interface is scriptable, and VBScript with Windows Script Host (WSH) can take full advantage of it. You'll create two VBScripts here: The first does an inventory of the package, and the second updates the package and modifies it. The complete scripts are in the sample code associated with this chapter, and I'll go through the functionality a snippet at a time. In the interests of readability, not everything is declared explicitly.

The scripting interface into Windows Installer uses a ProgID of "WindowsInstaller.Installer", so first a VBScript creates the interface with code such as this:

```
Dim installer
Set installer = CreateObject("WindowsInstaller.Installer")
```

Note that I'm skipping the error-checking code in these code fragments. With an Installer object, you can now open a database package:

```
Dim database
Const msiOpenDatabaseModeReadOnly  = 0
Set database = installer.OpenDatabase
("trynotepad.msi", msiOpenDatabaseModeReadOnly  )
```

The first parameter to OpenDatabase is simply the path to the package: the actual MSI file. The second parameter says how you plan to use it. In this case, the value zero means that you aren't planning to update the package.

You're going to do an inventory of the files in the package, so you'll be setting up a SQL-like query into the File table that you previously looked at with Orca. This works using the concept of a "view" based on a query. A View object is returned by calling the OpenView method of the Database object, passing the query that returns the data. The returned View object is a collection of records—a dataset if you like.

```
Dim view
Set view = database.OpenView
("SELECT `FileName`,`Version`, `FileSize` FROM `File`")
```

This query should look familiar if you've worked with databases. You're get-ting items from the File table here; those items correspond to the column names in the Orca view of the File table. Incidentally, look carefully at what the column names are surrounded by. Those are grave characters, sometimes known as back quotes or peck marks: `. They are not single quotation marks. It is usually safer to quote the database content items with grave characters to avoid conflicts with reserved words.

The way you iterate through each of the records is to use the Fetch method of the View object:

```
Dim record
Set record = view.Fetch
```

At this point you have a record: a row from the File table. You can retrieve each of the columns with the StringData property of the Record object. You retrieve a single item by indexing StringData with an index that corresponds to its order in the original query, the SELECT statement. The query order was FileName, Version, FileSize, so StringData(1) returns FileName, StringData(2) returns Version, and StringData(3) the FileSize:

```
Dim afile
afile = record.StringData(1)
```

This gives you a string containing the FileName value of the particular row. When all the Record objects in the View have been returned with View.Fetch, the final returned Record object is empty, so the script can check to see if the Record object has the value Nothing to find out whether all the records have been returned. Putting this all together into a code fragment that loops through the File table, you have this code:

```
Set view = database.OpenView
("SELECT `FileName`,`Version`, `FileSize` FROM `File`")
view.Execute
Do
    Set record = view.Fetch
    If record Is Nothing Then Exit Do
    afile = record.StringData(1)
    aversion = record.stringdata (2)
    fsize = record.Stringdata (3)
```

```
        fullmsg = fullmsg & afile & " " & aversion & " " & fsize & vbcrlf
Loop
msgbox fullmsg
```

The principles of updating the package are similar. To make this updating script a bit more interesting, it reads a text file consisting of a series of commands that modify the database. You use FileSystemObject to read the modify.txt file containing the commands:

```
Set fso = CreateObject("Scripting.FileSystemObject")
Set afile = fso.GetFile("modify.txt")
set ts = afile.OpenAsTextStream (1, 0)
```

You create an Installer object and open the database package. However, this time you're updating the package, so you open in transacted mode. This is important when you close the database after your changes:

```
Const msiOpenDatabaseModeTransact = 1
Set database = installer.OpenDatabase
("trynotepad.msi", msiOpenDatabaseModeTransact)
```

Given a command that updates the database package, as in the previous script you use the OpenView method of the Database object, passing the command you expect to run. With this command in a string called "thecommand" that you get by reading the text file, you do the OpenView:

```
Set view = database.OpenView(thecommand)
```

Because you're updating, these commands use verbs such as Update, Insert, and Delete, so you use the Execute method of the View object to cause the change to occur. Put this loop together to read the text file and execute the SQL updates:

```
Dim thecommand, view
Do
    thecommand = ts.readline
    Set view = database.OpenView(thecommand) : CheckError
    view.Execute : CheckError
    if ts.AtEndofStream then exit do
Loop
```

The modify.txt file supplied with the book samples has two updates. The first inserts a new Property into the Notepad installation that you built. The text of this command follows:

```
INSERT INTO Property (Property.Property, Property.Value) VALUES
('ARPHELPLINK', 'http://www.microsoft.com')
```

Note that this is in two general pieces. The first names the table and the columns into which data is being inserted in the form <table>.<column>. The second part lists the values corresponding to those columns. In this example, ARPHELPLINK is a standard Windows Installer property that is displayed in the Add/Remove Programs applet as a "Click here for support information" link. VS's installer doesn't let you specify one, so this example shows the way you add one to point to Microsoft's Web site.

If you refer to Figure 2-9, you see an existing value for the property FolderForm_AllUsers with a value of ME. Your second update changes the value of that existing property in the property table from its previous ME to now say ALL.

```
UPDATE Property SET Property.Value = 'ALL' WHERE Property.Property =
     'FolderForm_AllUsers'
```

When you opened the database, you opened it in transaction mode. This means that none of the changes you've made are in the database package yet. To save the updates, you must commit the changes with the Commit method of the Database object:

```
database.Commit
```

Now that you've been introduced to an example of how to alter the content of an installation package outside the VS environment, you may wonder about the effect on the installation of changing this particular FolderForm_AllUsers property. VS.NET generates this property—it's not a standard Windows Installer one. What happens here is that the value of the FolderForm_AllUsers property drives the state of the Everyone or Just me choice in the installation dialog shown in Figure 2-3. After you change the property value from ME to ALL with that Update statement, when you install the new package you'll note that the radio button now defaults to Everyone. How did I know that ALL is a legal value for the property value? You might have noticed that Orca has a Find choice under the Edit menu. If you do this Find and put FolderForm_AllUsers in the "Find what" text box, the search eventually shows you a ControlEvent table that has an entry with a condition FolderForm_AllUsers="ALL" (see Figure 2-11). I won't go into the deep details of dialog behavior here, but the FolderForm user dialog (the one with those Everyone/Just me radio buttons) has a ControlEvent that is triggered off the Next button of the dialog. This event occurs when the user chooses the Next button, and the event sets the value of the ALLUSERS property to 2 if FolderForm_AllUsers="ALL". It's this value of the ALLUSERS property that determines whether the installation is for the current user or for the system as a whole (meaning that the product is installed for all users of the system).

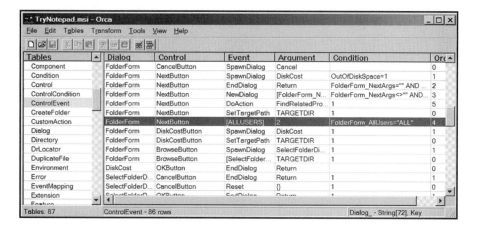

Figure 2-11. ALLUSERS in the ControlEvent table

The ALLUSERS property is a Windows Installer property that you can set to three states:

1. Unspecified (NULL is how the SDK documentation describes this). The installation defaults to a per-user installation.

2. A value of 1. This means a per-system installation, with the caveat that the installation will fail if the user does not have administrative privileges.

3. A value of 2. This causes a per-system installation if the user has administrative privileges, and a per-user installation if the user does not have administrative privileges.

For now, I'll point out that the nondeterministic value of 2 is likely to be unwelcome in some environments. In particular, it's unusual for applications to be installed on servers for the installing user—it's much more likely that the product is being installed for all users of the server. Having it accidentally installed for the current user could be a disaster, so in the cases where you know how the product is intended to be installed and used, force the issue by setting the ALLUSERS property accordingly. You can do that in the ControlEvent table in Figure 2-11 by changing the Argument value to 1 using Orca.

Summary

You've looked at building a basic installation package and seen some of the contents of the underlying database tables that are used during the installation. You've had a brief look at Windows Installer properties and the APIs that you can use to access database packages. One of the key points to take away from this chapter is that a Windows Installer Component is the basic unit of an installation, and you'll come back to this idea many more times.

CHAPTER 3

COM in the Windows Installer World

IN THIS CHAPTER, you'll build a package to install a COM server, but first some background and history.

Let's All Share

You probably know that a COM object is created by a COM server in response to—and on behalf of—a client request for a unique Classid and Interface ID. Look at the specific case of a COM server implemented as a DLL. When installed, this COM server has a Registry entry in HKCR\CLSID\{Classid Guid}\InprocServer32 that usually contains the path to the server. (I say usually because you'll see cases later in the book where InprocServer32 isn't the full path to the DLL.) Consequently, every client that asks for this class causes Windows to go to this unique Registry entry to find the path to load the server. The process whereby these Registry entries are created initially is called self-registration, "self" because the server itself contains the code to write these Registry entries using an exported function called DllRegisterServer. Installation has historically meant that the DLL first is copied to the system, and then its DllRegisterServer entrypoint is called. This is how Regsvr32.exe registers a server, although installation programs generated by proprietary software tools don't usually run Regsvr32.exe—they typically just load the DLL, then use the GetProcAddress Win32 API call to find the location of DllRegisterServer and call it. (You can also have out-of-process COM servers implemented as executables—EXE files—that have a different installation scheme because they don't export a DllRegisterServer function, but the general principle here is the same in both cases.)

What happens if multiple products want to use the same COM server? Clearly this is desirable because a COM component is most often used as a shared component. If a product P1 installs the DLL to location A, and another product P2 installs it later to location B, the DllRegisterServer for the later product will clearly result in the InprocServer32 path now pointing to location B. Three things are wrong with this scenario:

1. The product P2 might have installed an older version of the DLL to location B. Product P1 now fails if it requires new interfaces implemented in the DLL that the registration entries no longer refer to.

2. If product P1 is uninstalled, it has no clue that someone else is using the COM server, so it happily deletes the registration entries and breaks product P2.

3. If product P2 is uninstalled, it uninstalls its Registry entries, and the COM server and product P1 are broken.

The way out of these dilemmas consists for the most part in making sure that every client that uses the COM server arranges to install it to a specific unique location on the system. Windows provides some help and a convention by encouraging use of the Registry to count the references to shared DLLs. What you'll examine here is the reference counting scheme that has historically been used to manage the sharing of common files. I'll use it to show how sharing schemes need to work.

When an installation program copies a DLL to the system, it looks in HKLM\Software\Microsoft\Windows\CurrentVersion\SharedDLLs for the path where the DLL is going to be installed. If the DLL's install path is in this Registry location, the counter for that path is incremented. If it isn't there already, there is usually an option in the installation development tool that causes the path to be entered there with an initial count of one. When the product is uninstalled, the reference count is decremented. When the count becomes zero, this means that the DLL is no longer being used and it can be removed from the system. The behavior you see at this point depends on the uninstall program. Some might ask for confirmation that it's acceptable to remove the shared DLL that's no longer in use. The key point is that removal of the actual DLL is also the trigger that causes the registration entries to be removed as well. I should stress that this SharedDLLs scheme is not the primary mechanism that Windows Installer uses to count references to installer components, although it supports the SharedDLLs mechanism.

Note that this reference counting scheme is based on the path to the DLL. If a COM DLL is installed to the wrong location, the reference counting breaks. It does no good to have the COM DLL with a reference count of one in two separate paths in the SharedDLLs entries. Using the preceding example, you're still in trouble if product P1 has reference counted the DLL's path in one location and product P2 in another because each believes it's the only remaining user of the DLL and removes the Registry entries.

It's worth noting here that you can use this reference counting in any case where a shared file is installed to a common location, not just COM server DLLs.

It isn't unusual for a company's shared DLLs to be installed in a common location and reference counted using SharedDLLs so that the last product to be uninstalled can remove the DLL.

The required convention for a shared COM server is that every product agrees on the common installation location for the file. Each product installs the file to that location, incrementing the reference count in the SharedDLLs Registry entry at install time and decrementing at uninstall time. The critical point here is that by counting the references to the file, you're effectively also counting the references to the registration entries for the server so that the registration entries are not removed until the DLL is removed.

Finally, there is a standard installation convention that a newer version of a versioned file replaces an older version of the same file. This is normal practice for installing versioned files, and it is Windows Installer's default behavior. The result of putting all these together is that references to the COM server and its Registry entries are counted, and that existing client programs depend on new versions of the COM component installed from other products being a superset of the previous versions.

Anyone that has done COM development should be aware of the concept of the COM contract between client and server, whereby the server promises to preserve a particular interface on a class for all time. The contract states that if the server needs to provide new functionality, a new interface is added to an existing class, and this new interface extends the old interface. New clients ask for the new interface to get the new functionality. Old clients continue to ask for the older interface, which provides their required functionality. If you think about this, the COM contract must behave this way because of the installation constraints on sharing that I just discussed. In other words, a substantial part of the COM programming paradigm is driven by installation requirements. If you thought that installation did not have much impact on software architecture, you should take note of its impact on the COM programming model.

Installing a COM Server

In Chapter 1 I talked about the transactional nature of an installation and minimizing the code that runs during an installation. If the registration of a COM server isn't going to call DllRegisterServer, how does the registration code get written to the Registry? A Windows Installer package does contain tables pertaining to COM registration, the contents of which get written to the Registry at install time. That begs the question of how you get the data into the tables in the first place. The answer to that depends on what tool you use to build your installation package. Some tools can spy on the progress of DllRegisterServer and populate the tables for you. If your tool doesn't, a helper program is supplied with the book to let you see the Registry entries.

In this case, you're using VS, and you'll install a COM DLL that's supplied with the book. Use VS to start a new Setup and Deployment project, as with the Notepad installation in Chapter 2. This time the only file you'll be adding to the Application folder is the COM DLL from the COMServer project sample. This COMServer project has been altered so it does *not* do automatic self-registration of the DLL when it compiles. By default the VS development environment for a COM server generates a call to REGSVR32.EXE to register the server, but this postbuild step has been removed from the project to keep registration data off the system until installation time.

As in Chapter 2's Notepad installation, you can create a new Setup and Deployment project and get to the point where you're adding files to the target system. If you add COMServer.dll and look at its properties, you'll see the screen in Figure 3-1.

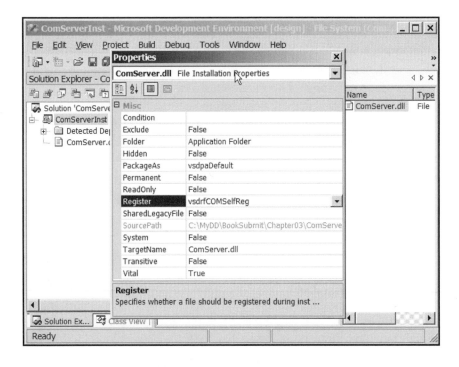

Figure 3-1. COM server properties

Under the Register property, VS has set the default to vsdrfCOMSelfReg, the setting to self-register the DLL by calling DllRegisterServer. Aside from wondering why this should be the default for a Windows Installer project, how did it know this is a COM server? VS looked at the version resources for the DLL and found an OLESelfRegister setting. This is a standard marker for self-registering servers. But in the choices for the Register property, there is another choice: the vsdrfCOM value. Selecting this causes VS to extract the COM registration entries when you build the setup project, and it populates the appropriate tables. After building the package, run Orca on it and look at the Class table that contains the COM class information (see Figure 3-2).

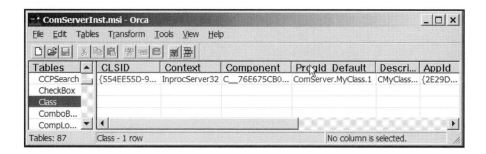

Figure 3-2. The Class table

As you can see, a CLSID column contains a CLSID that the COM server supplies. The Context column shows it to be an InprocServer32 COM server (as opposed to LocalServer32 for an out-of-process server). The default ProgId for the class is there, and so is the Windows Installer component that this COM server is associated with. (At the risk of stating the obvious, this extraction process that VS performed still uses the DllRegisterServer call and monitors what happens. This means that the DLL itself requires its dependent DLLs to load when you build the Setup project, so they need to be present on the development machine. You can verify this behavior by putting a MessageBox call in the DllRegisterServer code. You'll see that it gets called during VS's build process.)

Note the SharedLegacyFile property that appers in Figure 3-1. This setting maps to the SharedDLLs reference counting in the Registry through the msidbComponentAttributesSharedDllRefCount in the Component table of the package. Setting this bit forces creation of a SharedDLLs entry in the Registry, but if you don't set it and Windows Installer finds an existing entry, Windows Installer increments the existing count for the SharedDLLs entry. You can always set this property to True for an installation. It does no harm, and the file won't get removed accidentally if some other non-Windows Installer setup installs the file to the same location and uses the SharedDLLs references.

Although this Orca view in Figure 3-2 is truncated, there is in fact no direct reference to the DLL you're installing—this linkage is indirect, through the Component entry in the Class table. The Component table for this component has a KeyPath entry, and this KeyPath entry is in turn a key that refers to the File table entry for the server. This is another example of the Windows Installer design principle described in Chapter 2, where the Shortcut table has a Component entry with a KeyPath entry referring to a target file.

There is more to COM registration than just the CLSID entries. Figure 3-3 shows the entries for the COM ProgID, showing the version-independent ProgID and the specific versioned ProgID. The version-independent one has a parent linkage to the versioned entry.

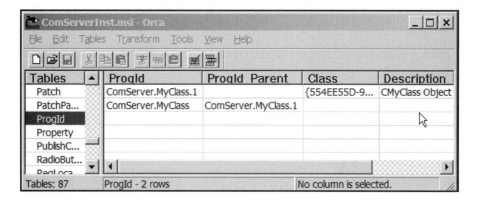

Figure 3-3. The ProgId table

There is also a TypeLib table, which contains the basic type library entry. Again, the Component_ column is a key to the Component table, where the KeyPath column refers to the File table entry for the type library. At install time, Windows Installer registers the type library (the same functionality as the Win32 RegisterTypeLib API). Remember that in this case the type library is embedded in the resources section of the code file.

Type Libraries

In the context of type libraries, it's interesting to take a look at the Registry table with Orca (see Figure 3-4).

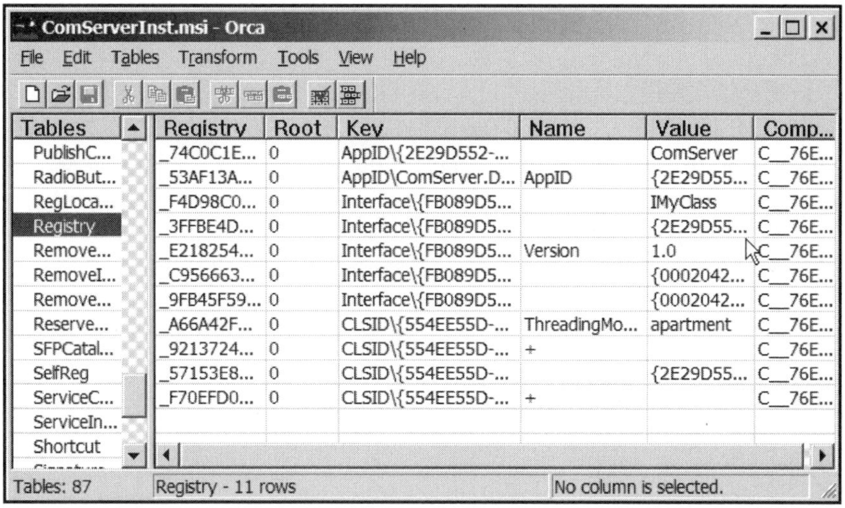

Figure 3-4. The Registry table

The table itself is straightforward: Each entry has a Root to identify the Registry hive, the name of a Registry key, then Name and Value pairs for the contents of the key. The Name column has some values that determine how to create the data (such as +, meaning create the key if it's absent), as well as actual data names. Notice that this table contains some of the COM registration entries that don't have entries in the Class, TypeLib, or ProgId tables. For example, the COM ThreadingModel value is stored in this table. Now if you're familiar with COM registration entries, you probably know that type library registration creates Interface entries in the Registry, so you might wonder why there are entries for COM interfaces here in the Registry table when the type library registration will create them. In fact, you can delete these Interface entries from the Registry table using Orca and install the edited package, and those HKCR\Interface entries are indeed still created. The probable explanation is that this is simply a consequence of a VS mechanism that collects all the registration entries without any attempt to filter them, and any that don't fit into the COM tables are put in the Registry table. There is no harm in having the explicit Interface entries installed from the Registry table as well as through type library registration from the TypeLib table.

If you have a stand-alone type library as a TLB file that you want to install and register, VS will do that for you. If you add the file to the project, you'll see that VS automatically sets the Register property of the file to vsdrfCOM. If you build the package and look at the Registry table with Orca you'll see that all the appropriate Interface entries have been extracted.

InprocServer32 Entries and Repair

After you install this COM server, if you run a Registry editor and take a look at the CLSID entries you might be somewhat alarmed. In the InprocServer32 key entry there is an InprocServer32 data item, a REG_MULTI_SZ apparently consisting of garbage (see Figure 3-5).

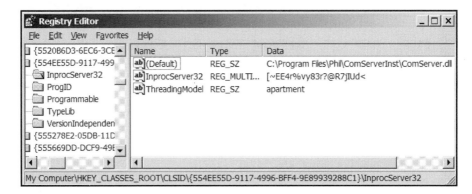

Figure 3-5. The repair descriptor

Occasionally people see this and worry that the installation has corrupted the Registry, but in fact this data—this descriptor—is related to repair. More on this later.

COM Server Dependencies

A COM server might have dependencies on other COM servers or DLLs, so clearly you need to install them somewhere that the COM server can find them. They should be installed in the same folder as the COM server. You might find documentation or advice that refers to installing dependent DLLs into the application folder. This usually means the folder where the client program is installed, but in this context "application folder" means the COM server's folder. This makes a lot of sense. In an object-oriented component world, client programs should be oblivious to the implementation details of the server components, and no client program wants to be in the business of installing a COM server's dependencies in its application folder.

Windows Installer Sharing

I started this chapter by describing the original Windows sharing scheme based on the SharedDLLs Registry data. Windows Installer sometimes uses this mechanism because it must handle the cases where a shared DLL has already been installed (or will be installed later) by some non-Windows Installer method. By default, Windows Installer increments the SharedDLLs reference count for a path if there is an existing entry for it in the Registry. If your product installation requires the Installer to create a new SharedDLLs entry, the msidbComponentAttributesSharedDllRefCount bit must be set in the Attributes data in the Component table. To reiterate: not the File table, the Component table, and as you've seen before, this SharedDLLs setting applies to the KeyPath of the component.

The Windows Installer sharing mechanism works at the component level. Each component has a GUID, and Windows Installer counts the uses of this GUID. However, just like the SharedDLLs mechanism, this reference counting is meaningful only when it counts multiple references to a single location. If product P1 installs a component to its own private application folder, and then product P2 installs the same component GUID to a different private application folder, no sharing is effectively going on. Product P1 reference counts the component to its private folder and product P2 does the same. The key point here is that reference counting has no practical effect unless the same physical location of an installer component is shared by multiple separate products. In other words, the behavior of the installer's sharing mechanism is essentially the same as the SharedDLLs mechanism discussed earlier. Instead of a Registry mechanism where each product install increments a count on a path to a file, the installer uses a GUID to reference count each use of the component. However, it is meaningful for sharing only when the component is installed to the same location by different products.

There's some simplification in that description, because the key path of a component doesn't have to be a file—it can be Registry data.

Merge Modules and Sharing

Although I've mentioned Windows Installer components a lot, VS's IDE doesn't expose the idea of components. When you build a package it creates a component for each file, but you don't get a component view into the package being built. However, because sharing is something that happens at the component level, developers need some way to build shareable components instead of simply replicating all the settings for a shared component over and over again into a collection of packages. The package of reusable components that is designed to be shared by multiple products is called a Merge Module. A Merge Module is practically identical to an MSI package, and you can open Merge Modules and edit them with Orca. However, they have an MSM file extension and usually contain just installer components—they have no user interface if they are designed to contain only shared files. A Merge Module is designed to be merged into an installer package at build time as a subpackage of predefined installation components, and once a Merge Module has been merged into an actual installation database package it loses its separate identity. The contents of the module's database tables, such as the File table, Class table, ProgId table, and so on are merged so that the resulting package has single copies of all the tables.

You just built an installer package to install a COM server, but the proper way to install the COM server so it can be shared properly would be to create a Merge Module and then add it into any other product installation packages that require it.

Building a Merge Module

When you start VS's New Project wizard and choose Setup and Deployment Projects, one of the choices there is for a Merge Module project. If you create a Merge Module project for the COM server using the New Project wizard, you'll find that the process of creating a Merge Module is nearly identical to the way in which you created the setup project earlier on. If you look at Figure 3-6 you'll see that the DLL is being installed into the Common Files folder under a specific folder. This makes sure that all users of this COM server install it to a specific location where they can share it.

Figure 3-6. Merge Module destination

You're also choosing that location because it becomes the standard installation folder for all client setups that include this Merge Module. The other choice of Module Retargetable Folder, as its name implies, is a means whereby client setups get to choose the installation folder for the Merge Module files. You don't want that choice for your sharable COM server. If you build this project and then look at the File, Component, Class, ProgId, and Registry tables you'll see that they contain the same registration information as the package you built before.

A Merge Module is of no use unless you can merge it into an installation. If you open up that Notepad installation project, you can incorporate a Merge Module in a couple of ways. If you select the Project name in the Solution Explorer, the right-click menu has an Add choice that goes on to offer a Merge Module choice. Alternatively, the Project menu also offers an Add to allow a Merge Module to be selected. Once you add it, it shows up in the Solution Explorer with the other files. After you've built the new Notepad installation package that now incorporates the Merge Module for the COM server, you can open it with Orca and find little trace of the original Merge Module. For example, the Orca view of the File table now contains the DLL from the Merge Module (see Figure 3-7).

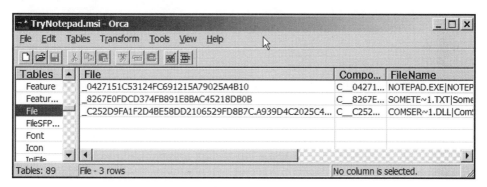

Figure 3-7. File table with COM server

Note that the File column entry for the COM server is different from the other files; the File column for COMServer.dll has a two-part name, where the second part after the period does not exist for the files that were not in a Merge Module. The issue here is that the item in the File column must be unique to the File table. A tool that generates the File table directly, such as VS, can guarantee that each entry it generates is unique to that package. However, when a File table is being merged from an external Merge Module there is no such guarantee of unique File column names. To make them unique, VS appends the package code GUID of the Merge Module that is the source of this File table entry.

Because a Merge Module is literally merged into a containing database package, it's important to realize that there is no sense in which the Merge Module contents are separately installed. The contents of the Merge Module—one or more Windows Installer components—become an integral part of the final package and are installed on the target system in the same way as other components that were created directly in the package.

Relative Paths and Side-by-Side COM Components

Side-by-side COM components are COM components that are installed without an absolute path to the server. You might have noticed that there was a vsdrfCOMRelativePath choice in the VS Register options for COMServer.dll. Perhaps you're thinking that this is the way to install a side-by-side COM server, because a relative path is one of the requirements for a side-by-side installation. However, there is a bit more than that going on here. If you were to use this choice, install the resulting package, and look at the registration entries, you'd see that the InprocServer32 key doesn't contain the absolute path to the server. It does indeed have just the name of the DLL: COMServer.dll. Here's an interesting test to try: In the COMServerInst project, a test VB script (CALLCOM.VBS) displays a property from the COM object with a couple of lines of code:

```
set obj = CreateObject ("COMServer.MyClass")
msgbox (obj.SomeString(1) )
```

If you install the COM server using that vsdrfCOMRelativePath property, it doesn't matter what folder you run this script from. You should find that it works every time, despite the thought that this simply shouldn't be working because the InprocServer32 key entry points only to a relative path, not the complete path to the DLL. What's happening here is that Windows Installer is getting involved at the point that the DLL needs locating. I've mentioned that Windows Installer keeps track of each installer component that gets installed on the system. A component has a KeyPath, located in the Component table in the package, so Windows Installer knows the installed location of every component on the system. This means Windows Installer can locate the complete path to the COM server. Knowing the product code GUID and the installer component GUID for the COM server, Windows Installer can locate the file by locating the component's KeyPath. But how does it know these installer GUIDs? They're encoded into that InprocServer32 data item, the descriptor that looks like a corrupted entry. You can show that this is the case by deleting that InprocServer32 descriptor entry from the Registry, after which the preceding script no longer works. Right-clicking the package, the MSI file, and choosing Repair restores the missing entry, which causes the script to start working again.

A Detour: Locating Components

In Chapter 2 you built a VBScript that listed all the files in an installer package. You can extend this script to do what Windows Installer just did: Locate the component on the system by getting the component's KeyPath. This is part of the listcomponents.vbs file supplied with the COMServerInst project. Error-handling code and opening the database package are removed from these fragments:

```
Sub ListComponents
Dim view, record, componid, componpath, componversion, fullmsg
fullmsg = "Product " & ProductGuid & vbcrlf
Set view = database.OpenView("SELECT `ComponentId` FROM `Component`")
view.Execute : CheckError
Do
    Set record = view.Fetch : CheckError
    If record Is Nothing Then Exit Do
    componid = record.StringData(1)
    componpath=""
    componpath = installer.ComponentPath (ProductGuid, componid)
    if componpath <> "" then
        componversion = installer.fileversion (componpath, false)
        fullmsg = fullmsg & componpath & " " & componversion & vbcrlf
    end if
Loop
msgbox fullmsg
End Sub
```

The beginning of the preceding code should look familiar from Chapter 2. This is a SQL-type query on the Component table to return ComponentID, which is the actual GUID for this installer component. Given the ProductCode GUID and the component GUID, the ComponentPath property of the installer object returns the absolute path to the component's KeyPath. The ComponentPath property requires the ProductCode GUID as well as the component's GUID. That's because the same component might have been installed to any number of different locations by different products, so the owning product needs to be specified. Note that the installer object also has a FileVersion property that retrieves the version from the path to the file. If you wanted to find out the installation location of each component of an installation package, this is the general way to do so. Beware that a KeyPath can also be a Registry key, and write your code accordingly; in these cases the ComponentPath returned starts with a numeric representation of the Registry hive (such as "02" for HKLM).

The point of this exploration of relative paths was to show that Windows Installer is integrated into COM in a rather interesting way. However, to use actual side-by-side COM components you need to go a bit further.

Back to Side by Side

The idea of side-by-side COM is simply that each client installs its own private copy of a COM server in its own application folder with two requirements in the DLL case that

1. The InProcserver32 path to the COM server is a relative one.

2. The application folder contains a clue that the client program requires side-by-side sharing. This clue is in the form of a file with .LOCAL appended to the name of the client program executable.

To implement side-by-side COM with an installer package, you need to look at the IsolatedComponent table. The table itself is uncomplicated; a column called Component_Shared requires the installer Component table row that identifies the COM DLL, and a column called Component_Application that contains the Component table row that identifies the client program executable. In both cases, the KeyPath entry of the component identifies the file. However, there's more to it than just setting these tables in the installation packages:

1. There is clearly no sharing in the side-by-side scenario, so each installation uses its own private copy of the COM server and shouldn't use a common Merge Module. It's not that you cannot use a common shared Merge Module here, but if you do, the COM server will have the same installer component GUID associated with multiple products. So if the idea is truly to keep each COM server separate, then keep them separated in every way, including not sharing the same installer component GUID.

2. The sharing schemes described earlier (the installer scheme and the SharedDLLs scheme) both have the notion that reference counts to an installation path protect the registration information for the COM server. When an uninstall occurs, these reference counts are decremented, and the last product using the COM server removes the registration entry. There is no such sharing scheme in a side-by-side installation, so an uninstall of a product using side-by-side sharing will potentially remove the COM registration entries unless some other mechanism is used to count the number of products using the COM server. The

MSDN article "Implementing Side-by-Side Component Sharing in Applications" (in the Setup section) recommends a Registry item under the InprocServer32 key that is a reference count, incremented at install time and decremented at uninstall time, such that when decremented to zero the registration entries are removed.

3. Everyone must agree to the sharing scheme. For example, if the COM server is already installed on the system and the installation program adds an absolute path to the server, you can't install your copy of the COM server in a side-by-side way.

With these caveats in mind, if you're going to implement your own side-by-side installation, take a look at the IsolatedComponent table and use it to install the COM server in a side-by-side configuration. You can use the sample projects associated with this chapter. As well as the COMServer project that builds this COM server, a COMClient project builds a C++ executable that calls a method in the COM server. To perform side-by-side installations, you need two setup projects that each install the COMClient program and the COMServer DLL to their own private application folders. These two sample setup projects are named COMClientServerInst and COMClientServerInstAgain. Both were built from scratch and have the same general idea (see Figure 3-8).

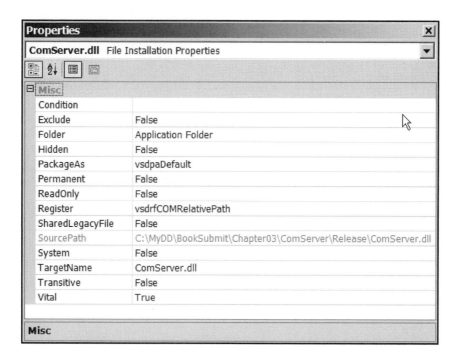

Figure 3-8. COM server with relative path

The client executable and the COM DLL are both being installed to the Application Folder, and the COM DLL is using the vsdrfCOMRelativePath choice for Register. VS has no explicit support for side-by-side COM components, which means you need to edit the IsolatedComponent table with Orca. Although the IsolatedComponent table requires Component values, it's easiest to get those from the File table.

In Figure 3-9 the installer component for the COM DLL and the component for the client executable are in the Component_ column. The Component_ value for the server needs copying to the Component_Shared column of the IsolatedComponent table, and the Component_ value for the client needs copying to the Component_Application column, so you end up with something like Figure 3-10. Follow this process of modifying the IsolatedComponent table with Orca wherever you are using side-by-side installation for a COM server. In the sample code with this chapter, this means modifying the COMServerInst and the COMServerInstAgain package files.

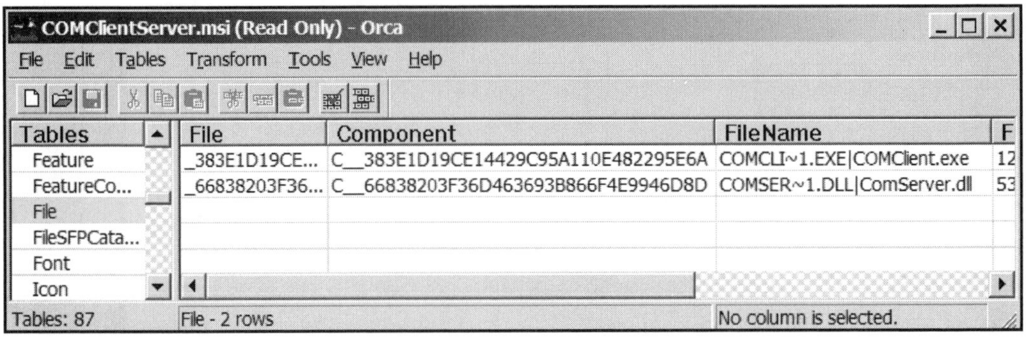

Figure 3-9. The File table with COM client and server

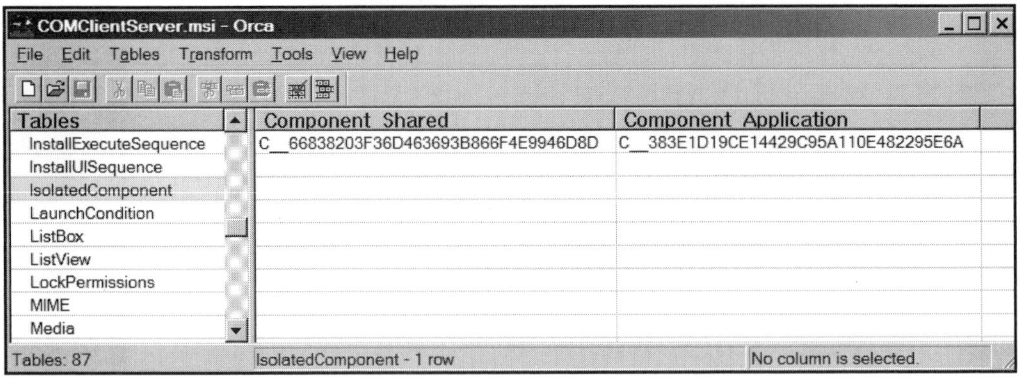

Figure 3-10. The IsolatedComponent table

If you install one of these packages, you'll see that Windows Installer has helped out by creating the required .LOCAL file in each application folder, and the Registry entry for the class has the relative path that you'd expect from using the vsdrfCOMRelativePath choice. Installing both of the packages—COMClientServerInst and COMClientServerInstAgain—also installs shortcuts to their respective client programs. If you use both of the shortcuts, the client programs each display a MessageBox. You can now use a diagnostic program to see what DLLs are loaded into each COMClient.exe (I used the Process Explorer from the Sysinternals Web site at http://www.sysinternals.com). You should see that each separate COMClient.exe is indeed using the COMServer.dll file from its application folder.

Now here's something cool. If you install a single COM server that has the vsdrfCOMRelativePath option for registration and then uninstall it, you can go to the Registry and notice that the uninstall doesn't delete all the registration entries for HKCR\CLSID\{Class GUID}. It leaves some of the entries behind, including the relative path in the InprocServer32 key. Normally you'd consider that to be a bug, but think about the result. If you install both of the sample side-by-side setups and then uninstall one of them, that uninstall should delete all the registration info because that's what you'd expect from an uninstall. But it doesn't. What Windows Installer does at install and uninstall is just alter the contents of the InprocServer32 data descriptor that contains an encoding for installer product and component GUIDs. Windows Installer is effectively making side-by-side COM work by keeping those Registry entries present, and altering the content of the InprocServer32 descriptor as other products use the same COM class registration. The cool part about this behavior is the effect it has on other COM clients—those that don't have their own side-by-side installation. If you run the Callcom.vbs script, the script continues to work when two products are installed, each with its own private side-by-side copy of the COM server. If you uninstall one of these products, that script still continues to work. That's because, as you saw before when you ran this script, Windows Installer uses the InprocServer32 descriptor to get the installer component's KeyPath and find the absolute path to the COM server.

In effect Windows Installer can give you all the available options for sharing side-by-side COM servers without having to write any code to do reference counting on the HKCR\CLSID\{Class GUID} key (as in point 2 in the preceding numbered list), which you'd need to do if you didn't use Windows Installer. You get side-by-side sharing, you don't need to build your own reference counting, and Windows Installer finds the latest version of the COM server for other non-side-by-side clients. It does this by finding the path to the server from the Inprocserver32 descriptor and the component KeyPath. When you uninstall the final side-by-side product, the InprocServer32 descriptor disappears as well, so there is no longer any path information anywhere.

Summary

You've looked at sharing, specifically in the COM context, and drilled down into some of the Installer's interesting behavior. You saw that Windows Installer uses the descriptor associated with a COM server to locate the actual file, and you used a VBScript to locate an installed file in the same way. Because that descriptor can locate Installer components, it is the mechanism that Windows Installer uses to determine the health of the component and whether it needs repair. As you might guess, the repair that occurs when the target file of a shortcut is missing (see Chapter 2) is triggered by a similar descriptor associated with an advertised shortcut.

CHAPTER 4

Searches and Conditions

YOU'VE HAD A look at some of the properties that are standard to Windows Installer, such as ALLUSERS and VersionNT. You'll take a closer look at them here in the context of conditions for the entire installation, called Launch Conditions, and for transitive components, which are components of the installation that get installed based on the values of properties.

Searches and Launch Conditions

One of the most straightforward conditions to use is a Launch Condition, especially when it's based on a standard Windows Installer property that tells you something about the target system. VersionNT is a good example, because a product that should only be installed on the NT series (NT/Windows 2000/XP/Server 2003) can have a Launch Condition of VersionNT. Remember that you can also treat properties as Boolean values if you specify them without comparison to any particular value, so VersionNT by itself is valid as a Launch Condition even though it has a value denoting the version of the operating system.

Figure 4-1 shows a slightly more interesting condition. This one has a condition of VersionNT>=501, requiring that the target system be at the Windows XP level or later.

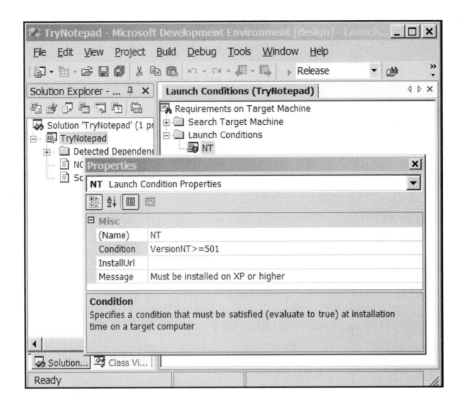

Figure 4-1. Launch Condition for Windows XP

You're not restricted to only one condition, by the way. You can add more Launch Conditions for the specific property values you're checking. Apart from the ability to use a number of simple conditions instead of a single complicated one, this also lets you specify the message that applies to each separate condition. For example, you could have a Launch Condition of "VersionNT and MsiNetAssemblySupport," meaning that you will install only on the NT series that also have the .NET Framework runtime installed. You could show a message saying that the system should be the NT series or that you haven't installed the .NET Framework runtime. However, it's much more useful to split the Launch Condition into two conditions, the first on VersionNT with its own message and the second on MsiNetAssemblySupport with a message saying that the .NET Framework needs installing. Note that multiple LaunchCondition entries are evaluated in nondeterministic order—you cannot know the order in which they'll be checked. If you do care about this ordering, you can use Type 19 custom actions, discussed in Chapter 5.

If the installation requires a minimum version of the .NET Framework, you can use the value of MsiNetAssemblySupport in a comparison, as in Figure 4-2.

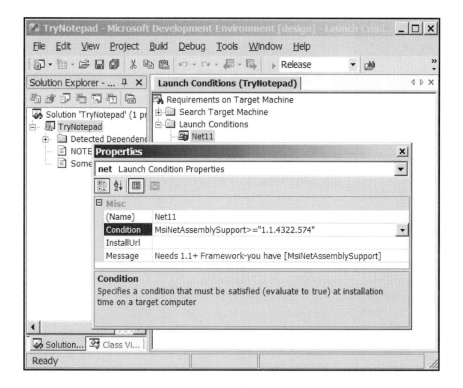

Figure 4-2. Launch Condition on .NET runtime

Let's note a few details here. First, the comparison is a string comparison with the required version of the runtime in quotes: "1.1.4322.574". This version is nonexistent at the time of this writing (the actual value of MsiNetAssemblySupport with the 1.1 Framework installed is 1.1.4322.573), but I use it here for demonstration purposes. This comparison is in string format because the version can't be conveniently represented as a number like VersionNT could; VersionNT is a version such as 5.01 multiplied by 100. The second thing to notice is in the error message where MsiNetAssemblySupport appears in brackets in the message. As in many other places, this property name in brackets is resolved to the actual value at install time, so running the installation puts out a message telling the users exactly what version is on their system.

The mapping from what you see in VS to the contents of the package is direct (see Figure 4-3). The LaunchCondition table consists of exactly what was specified in the VS IDE: a Condition and a Description message to be displayed if the condition evaluates to false.

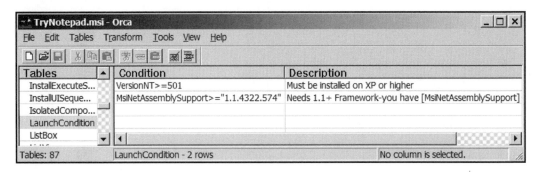

Figure 4-3. The LaunchCondition table

Keep in mind that Launch Conditions don't apply only to the installation of a product—they apply to maintenance and uninstall as well. For example, you need to be careful that you don't provide a Launch Condition that prevents the product from being uninstalled.

So far what you're doing is straightforward because the conditions are using standard properties that are static for the most part. But what do you do if you need to base a Launch Condition on something that might or might not be on the client system? That's where the Search Target Machine option fits in. You can perform several types of search, and you'll examine each of them using the Notepad installation project from Chapter 2. All these searches have some common attributes:

1. They use the installer's AppSearch and Signature tables. Together these define the target of the search.

2. They create a user-defined property if the search is successful. You can use this property as a Launch Condition, as you might expect from the fact that Search Target Machine and Launch Conditions are together in the IDE. However, a public property (an uppercase identifier) created as the result of a search is also available throughout the installation process and you can use it as a condition on other actions, as you'll see in Chapter 5.

File Search

Right-clicking Search Target Machine allows an Add File Search choice.

In Figure 4-4 you see that the search is looking for NOTEPAD.EXE in the target system's [SystemFolder], which is resolved at run time to the actual Windows system folder. The file search depth is five (go five folders deep during the search). There are options for the range of versions that will result in the search being successful, and this example ignores any search constraints based on creation dates. The name GOTNOTEPAD is the user-defined property that's created if the search is successful. The user-defined property is in uppercase because that makes it a public property, visible throughout most of the installation process. What this means is that you can now use this condition as a Launch Condition. You could go to the Launch Conditions item and add a condition with a value of "Not GOTNOTEPAD" (without the quotes) with a message such as "You've already got Notepad" (again without the quotes). The installation wouldn't proceed if it found a version of NOTEPAD.EXE in the specified version range. If you didn't care what version of NOTEPAD.EXE might be present on the system, you could just leave the version choices blank.

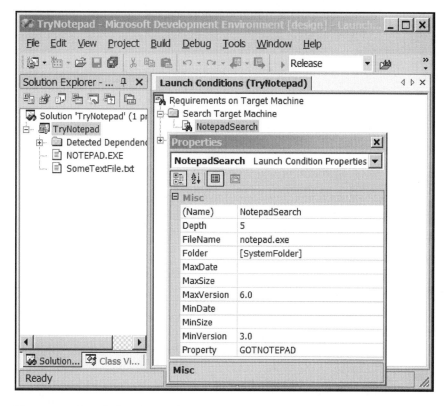

Figure 4-4. Search for Notepad

Note that this artificial situation is intended only to illustrate the principle of searching for the presence of a file in a directory on the target system, and then relating that search to a LaunchCondition table entry. In practice it's unlikely that you would search for a file that you're about to install. If you're searching for a file that might have been previously installed with a Windows Installer setup, a component search might be more appropriate (discussed later in this chapter).

If you were to look at the actual value of the GOTNOTEPAD property you'd see that it contains the path to NOTEPAD.EXE on the target system, such as C:\WinNT\System32\Notepad.exe. The file search doesn't return all the versions of NOTEPAD.EXE if you have multiple copies in that folder and its sub-folders; it just returns when it finds one that fits the search criteria. For example, in this specific search it returns NOTEPAD.EXE from the System folder and it doesn't carry on to find the one in the dllcache subfolder.

If you look at the generated package with Orca you see an AppSearch table (see Figure 4-5).

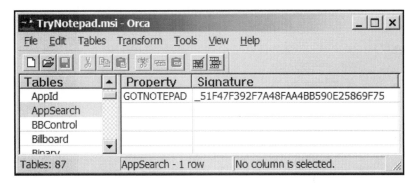

Figure 4-5. The AppSearch table

The Property column contains the name of the property to be created if the search defined by the content of the Signature column is successful. The Signature table contains the definition of the file being searched for and matches what you entered into the VS IDE (see Figure 4-6).

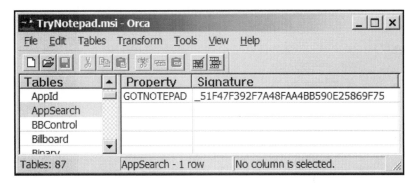

Figure 4-6. The Signature table

The FileName column contains the file name in the same format that you saw in the File table: short and long names separated by a vertical bar. The sharp-eyed will notice that there is no specification of the depth of the search in the Signature table or the path (the [SystemFolder] value). This is in the DrLocator table, which contains the Signature value from the AppSearch table together with the path and the depth (see Figure 4-7). You can leave the folder being searched (Path in the Orca view) unspecified to cause all the fixed drives on the system to be searched.

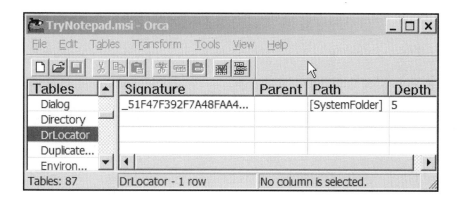

Figure 4-7. The DrLocator table

There's a bit of a problem with the short and long file names in the FileName column of the Signature table. If you specify a long file name (longer than the 8.3 format) in VS, you'll get a short/long pair of file names in the FileName column of the Signature table, and you'll find that the file search uses the short name to search for the file. Because short file names aren't unique, you might well find that you get a false positive from the search because it found a file with a short name that matches the short name in the Signature table. The FileName column here isn't required to be a short name/long name pair, so you can edit this to have only the long file name detour this behavior.

Registry Search

Figure 4-8 shows Registry search settings, created by right-clicking Search Target Machine and choosing Add Registry Search.

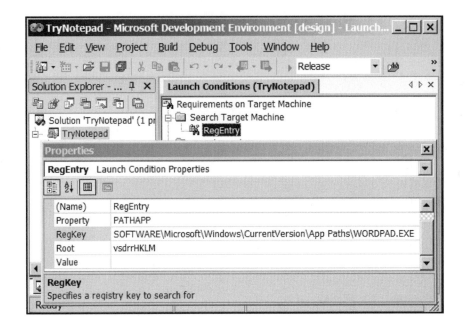

Figure 4-8. VS's Registry search

This search creates a property called PATHAPP if the search succeeds. A Registry search in general looks for the presence of a named item (specified in the Value property) in a specified key. This search is looking in the App Paths Registry location named in the key, but note that the Value has been left empty. This causes the search to find the contents of the default item, usually shown as "(Default)" in the Registry editor. If the default item is found, the value of the named property (PATHAPP in this case) is set to the default item. One of the interesting features of this search is that this value is usually stored in the Registry as something like "%ProgramFiles%\Windows NT\Accessories\ WORDPAD.EXE," but when you get the value of this string into the property it's resolved to an actual path name such as "C:\Program Files\Windows NT\ Accessories\WORDPAD.EXE."

Figure 4-9 shows a search for a specific item. In this case, the search retrieves the value of the Version item from the DataAccess Registry key, the contents of which are the version of Microsoft Data Access Components (MDAC) installed on the system, returned as a string such as 2.71.9030.0.

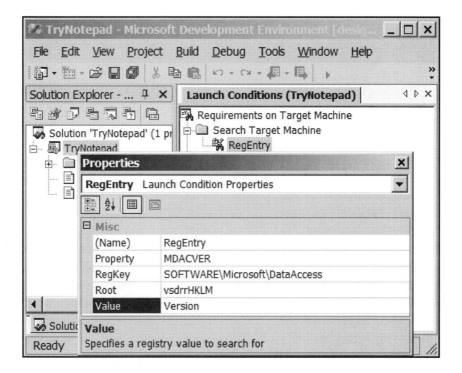

Figure 4-9. Search for MDAC version

A Registry search in Orca is slightly different from a file search. An entry is still in the AppSearch table, but no entry is in the Signature table. Instead, the signature named in the AppSearch table is a key into the RegLocator table, where you'll see something like Figure 4-10.

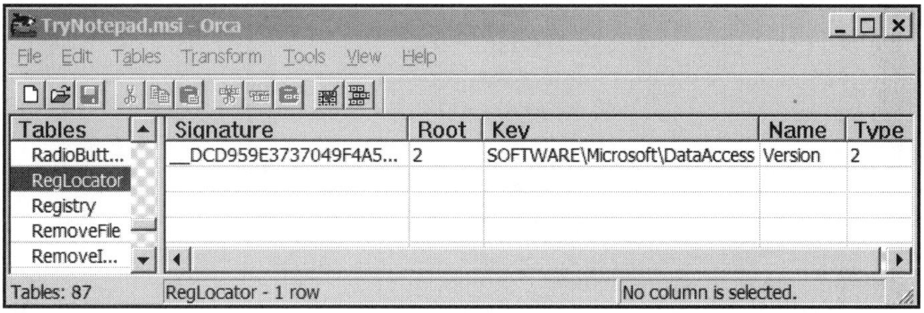

Figure 4-10. The RegLocator table

This isn't very complicated; the Signature_ column contains the Signature_ value from the AppSearch table, the Root column contains a value denoting the target Registry hive, and the Key and the Name columns are the actual Registry key and item being searched for. The Type column has a value of 2 (msidbLocatorTypeRawValue in the documentation), meaning that the item being searched for is a Registry value. It seems self-evident that you're looking for a Registry item here—after all, this is the RegLocator table.

The Registry data examples you just looked at were searches for string data—REG_SZ—which is returned in the named property as the actual string value. The value returned is prefixed with a special character if it's in other formats. For example, if you retrieve a value that is a REG_DWORD, the value is preceded with a # character. Refer to the SDK documentation for the prefixes used for other Registry data types.

Component Search

The final choice for adding a search is an "Add Windows Installer" search, which in fact is a search for a specific Windows Installer component, named with a GUID in Registry format. Figure 4-11 shows a search for an installer component; this one is the component GUID for EXCEL.EXE, a part of Microsoft Office 2003.

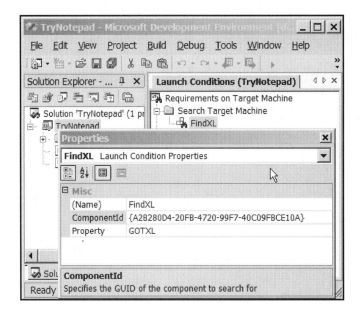

Figure 4-11. VS component search

If this search succeeds, the property is given the name of the path to that component, excluding the actual file name. You see something like "C:\Program Files\Office\Office11\" as the property value. The generated installation package again contains an AppSearch entry with a property name and a signature, except that now the signature is a reference to an entry in the CompLocator table, where the row contains that signature and a ComponentID column contains the GUID.

Note that this component search returns a property that's a folder path. If you ever need to install your application in the same location as a previously installed product, this technique is a potential starting point because you might be able to retrieve its path through one of that product's installed components. You need to choose the component carefully if you're using it to detect a previously installed product, because the component must be unique to that product, not shared with any other products. If you're looking for the main application folder of a previously installed product, it's also true that the component you choose might not have been authored to install into the main application folder. Nevertheless, being able to detect the location of a Windows Installer component is a useful approach to be familiar with as an alternative to searching the file system.

More Uses for Conditions

You can use standard Windows Installer properties as Launch Conditions for the installation, and you can use the AppSearch installer table to create user-defined properties that you can also use as Launch Conditions. You can use conditions based on properties in other useful places; one of them is at the installer component level, as you'll see now.

When VS adds a file to the install, it lets you specify a condition. See Figure 4-12 for the Properties display for a file.

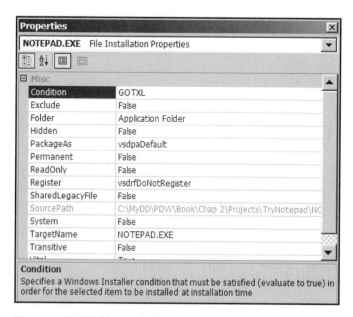

Figure 4-12. VS file condition

The condition isn't really on the file, because Windows Installer doesn't have conditions on individual files. This condition is a component condition. VS creates an installer component for each file and this condition is on that component. However, this can be confusing in the cases where VS associates other parts of the installation with that component. Shortcuts are one of these cases; in your Notepad installation the shortcut to NOTEPAD.EXE is in the same component as the file NOTEPAD.EXE. This makes perfect sense (recall Chapter 2's description of shortcuts), because the shortcut is bound to its target via Windows Installer's repair mechanism using a descriptor that checks the health of the target file's component. Consequently, it's difficult to install a shortcut separately from the file it's pointing to, because a component condition affects both the target file and the shortcut. This is VS's design choice, not a Windows Installer limitation; you can author a shortcut in a separate component using other authoring tools.

As well using standard built-in properties as Launch Conditions, you can also use them to condition the installation of a component. So, you can use properties such as VersionNT to decide whether to install the Windows NT or Windows 9x version of a file. You can also use the properties created by a Search Target Machine—an AppSearch table entry—as a powerful method of basing what you install on searches of the target system.

There's another use for conditions and properties that isn't really useful with VS setup projects, and that's to control the installation of the separate features of a product. VS setup projects build a package containing a single feature, but other authoring tools allow a product to be designed as a collection of features. When this is the case, you can use the Condition table to control which features are to be installed. This is often convenient because instead of specifying conditions on each component, you can specify the condition once at the feature level in the Condition table.

Conditions and Transitive Components

The default behavior of a component condition is that it's evaluated only once when the product and its components are installed. There's a choice in the properties for a file to set the Transitive property, which becomes the msidbComponentAttributesTransitive bit in the Attributes column of the package's Component table. This value causes the condition to be reevaluated on every reinstall instead of just once at product installation time. I can illustrate this with the Notepad installation project.

Figure 4-13 shows a search in the Windows folder for a file called MyFile.txt, and Figure 4-14 shows the Properties pane to condition the installation of NOTEPAD.EXE on the property GOTMYFILE created by the file search.

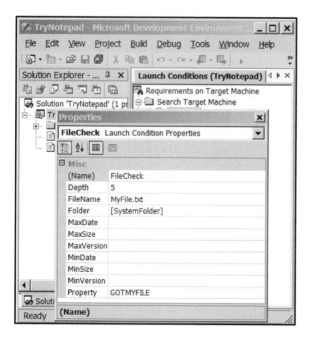

Figure 4-13. VS file search

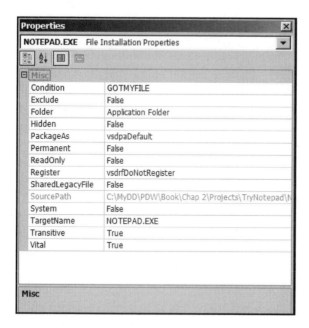

Figure 4-14. Transitive file

When this product is installed, it installs NOTEPAD.EXE if the GOTMYFILE property is set. So far this is no different from a nontransitive condition. Remove MyFile.txt from the Windows folder and then repair the installation (either by right-clicking the MSI package and using Repair, or through Add/Remove Programs ➤ Change) and you'll see that NOTEPAD.EXE and the shortcut from the Start Programs menu disappears. If you restore MyFile.txt and repair again, NOTEPAD.EXE and its shortcut are reinstalled. Whether NOTEPAD.EXE is installed or not, even during a repair, depends on the GOTMYFILE property.

Microsoft's example of transitive components talks about upgrading from one type of operating system to another. If clients are upgrading from a Windows 9x version to a Windows NT series, the installation can be designed with both 9x and NT components, and after the upgrade the user can repair the installation to add or remove the appropriate components. This isn't automatic by any means—the author of the setup has to provide the means and the instruction about how to do this—but nevertheless the idea that the installed components can be conditioned on properties is flexible and powerful. But beware of a few pitfalls. One of these pitfalls is that properties can get created in a number of ways, not just by using the AppSearch method. Windows Installer doesn't preserve or persist the values of user-created properties after the installation, which means that you sometimes need to persist them yourself. For example, one of the ways you can specify the values of public properties is by specifying them in a command-line install using the Msiexec.exe program (I'll cover this in more detail later). You can specify public properties (all uppercase identifiers) like this:

```
Msiexec /i  <path to the installation package> SOMEPROPERTY=Marketing
```

It's not unusual for installations to be done like this if you're tailoring them for different environments. If you perform the initial installation like this and you use SOMEPROPERTY as a transitive condition on a component, this property value won't exist during a repair. To preserve the components on the system, you also need to preserve this property value in case the user does a repair. This is easy to illustrate by changing the transitive condition on NOTEPAD.EXE to SOMEPROPERTY and starting the installation with the preceding command line, which installs NOTEPAD.EXE. But NOTEPAD.EXE is removed if you repair the installation because you haven't reinitialized SOMEPROPERTY for the repair.

Whether you need to persist properties depends on what you use them for and how they are initialized. In the preceding case, the installation of a transitive component is based on a property that was supplied from the command line, and that therefore needs persisting (and restoring) to preserve the installed state of that component. If the property is always initialized dynamically (such as with AppSearch, or is system-provided or created by code in a custom action), there is no need to persist its value.

Persisting Properties

Property persistence is much more than just keeping transitive components installed. Windows Installer doesn't preserve properties that you create during the installation, either on the command line or by any other way. Even the main installation folder, TARGETDIR, isn't preserved anywhere unless you explicitly save it, and this can often cause problems later when you need to locate where your product was installed. In the "Component Search" section of this chapter there's a discussion about the potential use of AppSearch and the CompLocator table to locate the path to a component on the target system. Perhaps you could use that technique to find the location of the main application folder, but it's often better to preserve TARGETDIR explicitly for later use.

One of the ways to preserve properties is to write them into the Registry. Figure 4-15 shows the VS Registry view where the Registry keys are specified as the product's Manufacturer and ProductName properties, and the contents of the SomePropValue Registry item are set to the value of the SOMEPROPERTY property; the square brackets cause runtime evaluation of the property. Looking at Figure 4-16, the values in the Registry table of the package should be no surprise.

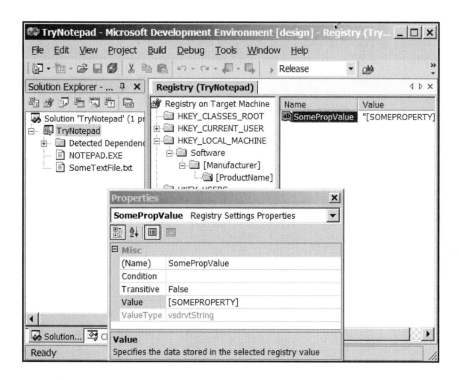

Figure 4-15. Putting a property value in the Registry

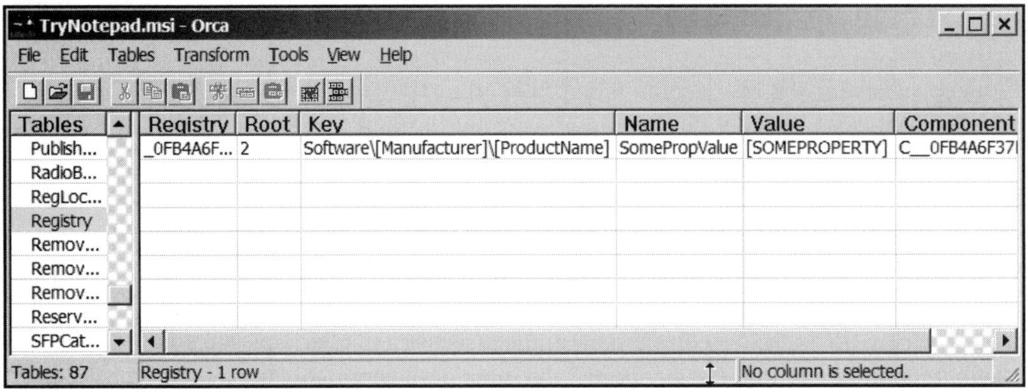

Figure 4-16. Registry table storing property values

If you're wondering which installer component is associated with this Registry entry, VS made a new component for this Registry entry, and the KeyPath of the component is now the Registry item named SomePropValue. So you can store a property you initialized into the Registry and retrieve and reinitialize it in an AppSearch for subsequent installations and repairs. *Beware of one situation*—if you remove the Registry entry where you saved SOMEPROPERTY, you cannot repair it because the source of that property value is the Registry data itself. So, at this point, you have no solution if someone removes that Registry data and then repairs the product, because the repair of the product needs to get the value of SOMEPROPERTY from somewhere, and it can clearly no longer get it from the Registry. All things being equal, you could argue that there's not much you can do if a client removes data from the Registry (or indeed removes any saved data, such as a file).

To wrap up the transitive component condition problem, you started with NOTEPAD.EXE being a transitive component that required the presence of the SOMEPROPERTY value for it to remain installed. For the initial installation, you specified SOMEPROPERTY on the command line. This initial value is preserved in the Registry as in Figure 4-15. Now, to make sure that SOMEPROPERTY still gets initialized on subsequent installations or repairs, you add a Search Target Machine to collect its value from the Registry (see Figure 4-17).

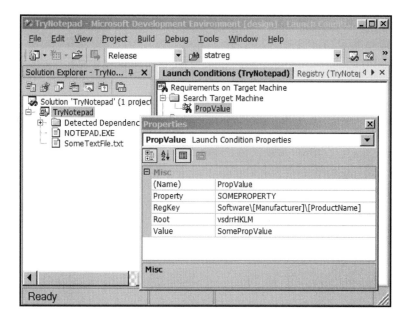

Figure 4-17. Searching for SOMEPROPERTY

You can preserve TARGETDIR in the same general way as shown in Figure 4-17, which is convenient compared with what might be considered the recommended way (see the "Preserving the Installation Location with a Custom Action" section in Chapter 5). You must decide whether you need to preserve TARGETDIR based on what you anticipate your future requirements to be. Remember that Windows Installer keeps track of where each component has been installed on the system (which is why the CompLocator table and APIs such as MsiLocateComponent work), and this means that you can locate installed component paths if you know their component GUIDs.

Summary

The AppSearch mechanism is the main tool supplied by Windows Installer to search the target machine for data. It sets the values of properties that you can then use as conditions for actions later in the install. Windows Installer doesn't persist these properties and others that you create; consequently, you must sometimes preserve them yourself to retrieve them next time you run the install package. This is clearly something that depends on the design of the installation. However, it's worth pointing out, because there's a common misconception that Windows Installer preserves properties specified on the command line or that are otherwise created transiently during the product's initial installation.

CHAPTER 5

Sequences of Events and Custom Actions

IT'S CLEAR FROM WATCHING an installation that it starts with a user interface (UI) sequence in which data is collected and shown to the user, but nothing yet seems to have changed on the target system. This sequence typically concludes by displaying a Next button (maybe an Install button with other packages), after which a progress bar is shown while the installation happens. A Cancel button is on display, and if you click it you'll see that the installation rolls back, undoing whatever the installation had done to the system. This UI viewpoint does reflect the inner workings of the installation process fairly accurately.

The UI Sequence

There are two main sets of sequences during an installation—the UI sequence and the execute sequence—and (no surprises here) these exist as separate tables in the database package, called the InstallUISequence table and the InstallExecuteSequence table. Other sequence tables that have UI and Execute stages are used in other deployment scenarios, such as administrative or advertised installs. Tables such as AdminExecuteSequence and AdvtExecuteSequence are typically subsets of other sequence tables, and aren't covered in this book. Figure 5-1 shows the content of the InstallUISequence table.

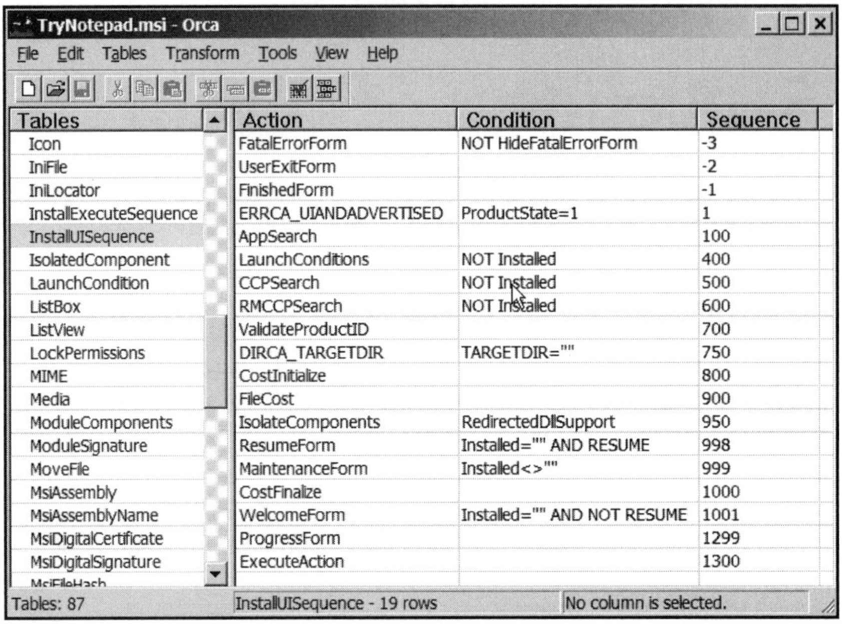

Figure 5-1. Orca view of the InstallUISequence table

This view is sorted on the Sequence column because the value of the Sequence column determines the order in which each of the actions is processed. The Condition column determines whether that particular action will happen. Some of the actions in the Action column are standard Windows Installer actions, documented in the SDK, but some of them are custom actions (CAs) inserted by VS at build time; you'll look at CAs later in this chapter. Some of the Sequence values are less than zero; these are termination actions that the installation will finish with, each indicating some flavor of termination. Examining this table in more detail, some of the actions should be familiar; the following sections describe them.

AppSearch and LaunchConditions Actions

AppSearch is the standard action that causes the AppSearch table to be processed, corresponding to the Search Target Machine option in VS that you used in Chapter 4. AppSearch is followed by the LaunchConditions standard action, which processes the LaunchCondition table to make sure that the conditions are met for starting the installation. This ordering makes perfect sense because AppSearch frequently sets properties that the LaunchConditions action will use. Note that there is a Not Installed condition on the LaunchConditions action. The Installed property is a standard one that tells you whether this product (as defined by the product code GUID) is installed on the system, so that entries in the LaunchCondition table are evaluated only if the product isn't already installed.

IsolateComponents Action

When you installed side-by-side COM servers in Chapter 3 you used the IsolatedComponent table. The IsolateComponents standard action sets up the processing for the contents of the IsolatedComponent table. The action is conditioned on the RedirectedDLLSupport property, a standard property that tells you whether the installing operating system supports isolated components (Windows 2000 and later all do).

The Forms

A large part of the UI sequence is—you guessed it—the actual UI. The actions here that terminate with Form, such as WelcomeForm, are the names of UI forms that are specified in the Dialog table of the package. The Condition column gives you a clue as to what forms get presented when the installation runs. The standard property RESUME is set if the installation is resuming (restarting after a reboot). With that in mind, the WelcomeForm is shown if the Installed property is empty and RESUME is false, in other words, the "normal" case. The MaintenanceForm is shown if the product is already installed, and a ResumeForm is shown to complete the installation following a reboot. (The forms themselves are in the Dialog table of the package.) The negative sequence numbers are special because the installation process invokes the actions with these sequence numbers depending on the installation's outcome: –1 for success, –2 for a user cancellation, –3 for failure, –4 for a suspended installation sequence.

The Execute Sequence

The final standard action in the UI sequence is ExecuteAction. In the default case that you're looking at here, ExecuteAction causes the installation to start the next stage of the process: the InstallExecuteSequence table. You'll look at this in two separate pieces; see Figure 5-2 first.

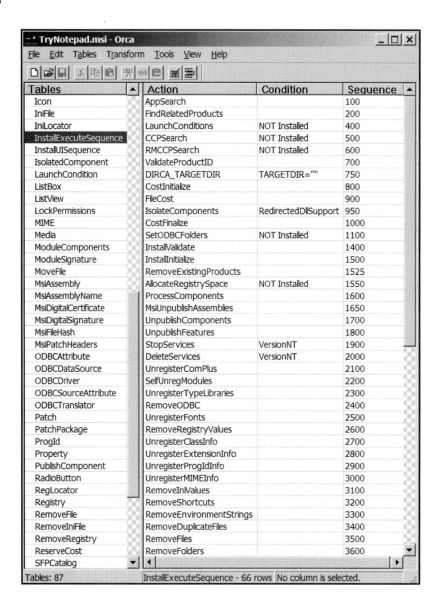

Action	Condition	Sequence
AppSearch		100
FindRelatedProducts		200
LaunchConditions	NOT Installed	400
CCPSearch	NOT Installed	500
RMCCPSearch	NOT Installed	600
ValidateProductID		700
DIRCA_TARGETDIR	TARGETDIR=""	750
CostInitialize		800
FileCost		900
IsolateComponents	RedirectedDllSupport	950
CostFinalize		1000
SetODBCFolders	NOT Installed	1100
InstallValidate		1400
InstallInitialize		1500
RemoveExistingProducts		1525
AllocateRegistrySpace	NOT Installed	1550
ProcessComponents		1600
MsiUnpublishAssemblies		1650
UnpublishComponents		1700
UnpublishFeatures		1800
StopServices	VersionNT	1900
DeleteServices	VersionNT	2000
UnregisterComPlus		2100
SelfUnregModules		2200
UnregisterTypeLibraries		2300
RemoveODBC		2400
UnregisterFonts		2500
RemoveRegistryValues		2600
UnregisterClassInfo		2700
UnregisterExtensionInfo		2800
UnregisterProgIdInfo		2900
UnregisterMIMEInfo		3000
RemoveIniValues		3100
RemoveShortcuts		3200
RemoveEnvironmentStrings		3300
RemoveDuplicateFiles		3400
RemoveFiles		3500
RemoveFolders		3600

Tables in left panel: Icon, IniFile, IniLocator, InstallExecuteSequence, InstallUISequence, IsolatedComponent, LaunchCondition, ListBox, ListView, LockPermissions, MIME, Media, ModuleComponents, ModuleSignature, MoveFile, MsiAssembly, MsiAssemblyName, MsiDigitalCertificate, MsiDigitalSignature, MsiFileHash, MsiPatchHeaders, ODBCAttribute, ODBCDataSource, ODBCDriver, ODBCSourceAttribute, ODBCTranslator, Patch, PatchPackage, ProgId, Property, PublishComponent, RadioButton, RegLocator, Registry, RemoveFile, RemoveIniFile, RemoveRegistry, ReserveCost, SFPCatalog

Tables: 87 | InstallExecuteSequence - 66 rows | No column is selected.

Figure 5-2. Orca view of the first part of InstallExecuteSequence

This table follows the same principle as the UI sequence: The Sequence column determines the order in which things happen. The key points about the execute sequence are as follows:

- Most of the actions here are standard installer actions; note how many of them seem to be about removing something from the system. That's because this isn't just an install sequence, it's also an uninstall sequence. In other words, many of these actions are performed whether the product is being installed or uninstalled. For example, the actions that control Services (start, stop, delete) and the RemoveFiles action are always called. Note that some of the actions have conditions; for example, those actions relating to Services apply only to the NT series of systems. Also recall that in Chapter 4 you looked at transitive components and the way that a repair can cause components to be installed or uninstalled; there is no special table for repair. The InstallExecuteSequence table is also processed during a repair.

- Some of these actions are duplicated here and in the InstallUISequence table. That doesn't necessarily mean they run twice (although some do); it's because the UI sequence can be suppressed. An install can suppress the UI (for example, with a command-line option), but perhaps more importantly, the uninstall and some repair options don't show the UI. If you recall the UI of the uninstall process, all you see is a progress dialog. So there are cases where an action is performed in the UI sequence so that it doesn't need to be run in the execute sequence. However, when the UI sequence is suppressed, the action still runs because it's also in the execute sequence.

- The Windows Installer Service processes the execute sequence. When you start an installation by double-clicking an MSI file, the Msiexec.exe program starts and runs the UI sequence. However, at this stage it's not running as a Service process, so the data-gathering part of the installation typically runs as a normal user process with user account privileges. If you were to use an installer API to start an installation, a similar thing would happen: The UI sequence would run on your process. In other words, the UI sequence is shown from some user process with user account privileges and use of the interactive desktop. When the installation starts on the execute sequence and prepares to update the system, control is transferred to the Windows Installer Service process. This goes with the idea that a user shouldn't need special privileges to install software when only the contents of the package's database tables are being updated onto the system (subject to approval by the administrator).

- The execute sequence order matters, not just in the general sense that the actions that remove things from the system should come before actions that update the system, but also because some standard actions must occur in a particular order. For example, InstallInitialize must occur before any actions that change the system. The Platform SDK documents these requirements.

- Windows Installer treats part of the InstallExecuteSequence differently, the reason being that the changes to the system need to be rolled back if the install fails. It accomplishes this rollback by keeping an audit script of everything that will be done to the system in a form that allows it all to be undone so that the system can be reverted to its former state. The first pass through the InstallExecuteSequence creates the audit script for roll-back, and the second pass runs the script. More specifically, the boundaries for this auditing are InstallInitialize and InstallFinalize. As you can see by looking at the sequences, it is between these two actions that modifications are made to the target system. During the first pass between these two actions, the audit script is written and conditions evaluated to determine which actions will eventually run. At InstallFinalize, the second stage occurs, which is when this script of actions that started at InstallInitialize is executed. As each step is processed during this execution stage, it first produces a rollback operation for its activity before performing the action. In this way, Windows Installer can undo each action if there is an install failure. It can restore the system by processing the rollback operations. The difference between these two stages is very important when you look at CAs and put your own code in these sequences. The first script-writing stage is called the immediate stage, and the processing of the actions between InstallInitialize and InstallFinalize is called the deferred stage.

- There are no dialogs in this sequence. Windows Installer doesn't process forms in this sequence, so you must use different methods to have your own CAs interact with the user. However, an installation shouldn't be interacting with the user here—you should always gather required data during the UI sequence.

- All traces of any specific features, components, and Merge Modules are nowhere to be seen. Whether the files, Services, and COM servers are derived from Merge Modules or reside in multiple features is largely irrelevant here. For example, one InstallServices action installs all the Services in the package. There's no order in which first one feature is installed, then another.

- A system-wide mutex protects the InstallExecuteSequence. The result of this is that only one installation per system can enter the execute sequence. So you cannot launch other installer packages from the execute sequence unless you use one of the supported ways of nesting installations (discussed later in this chapter).

You can see from Figure 5-3 that the guts of the installation process occur in the InstallExecuteSequence, which updates the system with files, Services, and so on.

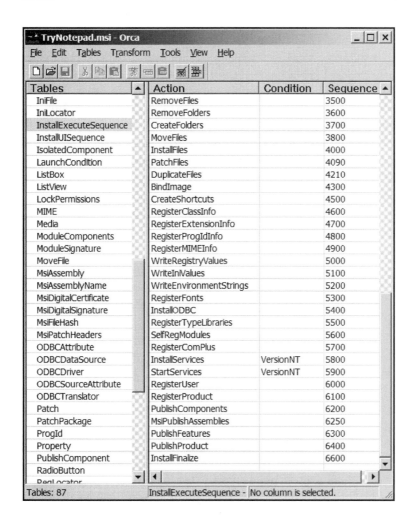

Figure 5-3. Orca view of the second part of InstallExecuteSequence

Most of the actions in Figure 5-3 should be self-explanatory. For example, the CreateShortcuts action processes the contents of the Shortcut table and WriteRegistryValues updates the system with the contents of the Registry table.

Within the sequences the ordering must make sense as well; the StartServices action is after InstallServices, and both are before the StopServices and DeleteServices actions.

The Windows Installer Service

As you've just seen, Windows Installer runs a Service when it's processing the execute sequence and updating the target system. When you first start an install of an MSI file from the command line or by double-clicking an MSI file, a copy of Msiexec.exe runs as a user process, displaying the UI and gathering data before it transfers the processing to the Service process. This is the reason you'll see more than one copy of Msiexec.exe running during an install. In the absence of any activity, the Service process terminates after a few minutes (as of the 2.0 version of the installer). You might see several copies of Msiexec.exe running during an install because of the way CAs are processed. You'll see later in this chapter that CAs called from the execute sequence don't run with a Service account privilege, so sometimes more copies of Msiexec.exe are initiated to host CAs from a non-Service process.

MSI.DLL implements most of the guts of the installer's functionality; the Win32 API calls are implemented here, as well as the COM automation that scripting clients can use.

Using the Windows Installer Log

You can debug installations by using Windows' built-in logging functionality. One way to cause Windows Installer to create this log file is to install the package using a command-line string that specifies the name of the package, the data to be logged, and the name of the log file that will be produced. For example:

```
Msiexec /i trynotepad.msi /l*v trynotepad.log
```

The /l option specifies logging, the asterisk is a wildcard choice that enables most of the choices about what to log, and the "v" causes the output to be verbose. (Some of the log entries you'll see below are split over two lines.)

The InstallUISequence starts with entries such as this, a little way into the log:

```
MSI (c) (E8:64): UI Sequence table 'InstallUISequence' is present and populated.
MSI (c) (E8:64): Running UISequence
MSI (c) (E8:64): Skipping action: ERRCA_UIANDADVERTISED (condition is false)
```

```
MSI (c) (E8:64): Doing action: AppSearch
Action start 15:08:51: AppSearch.
MSI (c) (E8:64): Note: 1: 2262 2: AppSearch 3: -2147287038
Action ended 15:08:51: AppSearch. Return value 1.
MSI (c) (E8:64): Doing action: LaunchConditions
Action start 15:08:51: LaunchConditions.
MSI (c) (E8:64): Note: 1: 2262 2: LaunchCondition 3: -2147287038
Action ended 15:08:51: LaunchConditions. Return value 1.
```

These should be self-explanatory; Windows is starting the UI sequence and executing the actions in the sequence, and you should recognize AppSearch and LaunchConditions that you've looked at before. This package doesn't have any AppSearch or LaunchConditions; you can tell because of the values being displayed. The value 2262 is a Windows Installer error meaning "stream does not exist," and that large negative number is the decimal representation of a COM HRESULT. This one is 0x80030002 in hexadecimal representation, another type of "Could not be found" error. There aren't really two separate errors here, just one meaning "table does not exist" with error results returned from different internal APIs.

There are also entries in this particular log saying the following:

```
MSI (c) (E8:64): Skipping action: ResumeForm (condition is false)
MSI (c) (E8:64): Skipping action: MaintenanceForm (condition is false)
```

When you previously looked at the forms in the execute sequence, you saw that they were conditioned on whether the product was already installed or was resuming, so you'd expect the log to report these conditions as false on the first install of a package.

At the end of the InstallUISequence there are entries:

```
MSI (c) (E8:64): Doing action: ExecuteAction
Action start 15:08:56: ExecuteAction.
MSI (c) (E8:64): Grabbed execution mutex.
MSI (c) (E8:64): Incrementing counter to disable shutdown. Counter after
                increment: 0
MSI (c) (E8:64): Switching to server: TARGETDIR="C:\Program
                Files\Phil\TryNotepad\"
```

As the log says, this is the point at which the installation switches from the UI mode to the Service mode (called server here, denoting a client/server architecture). In this particular log where the install transitions from the UI to the execute sequence, ExecuteAction is the action that makes this switch to the server. Note that line about grabbing an execution mutex. It's a characteristic of

Windows Installer that only one installation is allowed to be in the server mode (running on the Service) at once. As a programmer you're probably aware that a mutex is a mutual exclusion object that blocks subsequent callers after the first one. Another installation that tries to enter server mode won't proceed beyond this point. The next interesting area further down is this:

```
MSI (s) (FC:C4): Doing action: InstallValidate
Action start 16:59:52: InstallValidate.
MSI (s) (FC:C4): Feature: DefaultFeature; Installed: Absent;
                 Request: Local;   Action: Local
MSI (s) (FC:C4): Component: C__0427151C53124FC691215A79025A4B10; Installed:
                 Absent;   Request: Local;   Action: Local
MSI (s) (FC:C4): Component: C__8267E0FDCD374FB891E8BAC45218DB0B; Installed:
                 Absent;   Request: Local;   Action: Local
MSI (s) (FC:C4): Component: C__746C69616E6711D38E0D00C04F6837D0; Installed:
                 Absent;   Request: Local;   Action: Local
```

The InstallValidate action is giving you a status report on what is marked for installation. First it names your only feature, DefaultFeature, and notes that its current Installed state is absent; the request is Local, meaning it's to be installed to run on the machine; and the consequent Action is that it will be installed. The same is reported for your three components.

InstallInitialize, in the following log extract, is where the installation checks whether any of the security policies have been set. You can set the AlwaysInstallElevated policy in the system Registry to enable non-privileged users to install the package with elevated privileges; it has both machine-level and user-level settings. (This policy is discussed in Chapter 13, but I'll mention here that setting it compromises your system security.)

Note that the log indicates that the server is being locked for this ProductCode GUID, presumably to prevent other updates to this product during the installation process.

```
Action start 16:59:52: InstallInitialize.
MSI (s) (FC:C4): Machine policy value 'AlwaysInstallElevated' is 0
MSI (s) (FC:C4): User policy value 'AlwaysInstallElevated' is 0
MSI (s) (FC:C4): BeginTransaction: Locking Server
MSI (s) (FC:C4): Server not locked: locking for product {B3E1B56E-D853-4780-
       BF62-47B95195CD6B}
Action ended 16:59:53: InstallInitialize. Return value 1.
```

Remember that the first phase of the InstallExecuteSequence—the immediate phase—is writing a script of the actions that will be performed. Sure enough, a log entry indicates the script generation is starting, and the actions following it are writing the script, not updating the system yet:

```
Action 16:59:53: GenerateScript. Generating script operations for
                 action: GenerateScript:
Updating component registration
Action ended 16:59:53: ProcessComponents. Return value 1.
MSI (s) (FC:C4): Doing action: MsiUnpublishAssemblies
Action start 16:59:53: MsiUnpublishAssemblies.
Action ended 16:59:53: MsiUnpublishAssemblies. Return value 1.
MSI (s) (FC:C4): Doing action: UnpublishComponents
Action start 16:59:53: UnpublishComponents.
MSI (s) (FC:C4): Note: 1: 2262 2: PublishComponent 3: -2147287038
Action ended 16:59:53: UnpublishComponents. Return value 1.
```

Eventually all the script entries have been written and the sequence arrives at InstallFinalize, after which the log names the script file Windows Installer built and starts processing. Note that the critical scripted (and therefore audited) part of the installation is between InstallInitialize and InstallFinalize.

```
MSI (s) (FC:C4): Doing action: InstallFinalize
Action start 16:59:53: InstallFinalize.
MSI (s) (FC:C4): Running Script: C:\WINNT\Installer\MSI98.tmp
```

The system is updated during the script processing stage, as follows:

```
Action 16:59:53: InstallFiles. Copying new files
MSI (s) (FC:C4): Executing op: ProgressTotal(Total=50960,Type=0,
                 ByteEquivalent=1)
MSI (s) (FC:C4): Executing op: SetTargetFolder(Folder=C:\Program
                 Files\Phil\TryNotepad\)
MSI (s) (FC:C4): Executing op: SetSourceFolder(Folder=1\)
MSI (s) (FC:C4): Executing op: ChangeMedia(,MediaPrompt=Please insert the
                 disk:,MediaCabinet=_3E74C89917B7A86587F44D294F5797D5,
                 BytesPerTick=32768,CopierType=2,
                 ModuleFileName=C:\WINNT\Installer\411e31.msi,,,,,
                 IsFirstPhysicalMedia=1)
MSI (s) (FC:C4): Executing op: FileCopy(SourceName=NOTEPAD.EXE|NOTEPAD.EXE,
                 SourceCabKey=_0427151C53124FC691215A7 9025A4B10,
                 DestName=NOTEPAD.EXE,
                 Attributes=512,FileSize=50960,PerTick=32768,,
                 VerifyMedia=1,,,,,CheckCRC=0,Version=5.0.2140.1,
                 Language=1033,InstallMode=58982400,,,,,,)
MSI (s) (FC:C4): File: C:\Program Files\Phil\TryNotepad\NOTEPAD.EXE;
```

```
                      To be installed;  No patch;  No existing file
MSI (s) (FC:C4): Source for file '_0427151C53124FC691215A79025A4B10' is
                 Compressed InstallFiles: File: NOTEPAD.EXE,
                 Directory: C:\Program Files\Phil\TryNotepad\,  Size: 50960
MSI (s) (FC:C4): Note: 1: 2318 2: C:\Program Files\Phil\TryNotepad\NOTEPAD.EXE
MSI (s) (FC:C4): Note: 1: 2360
```

This section of the log shows the actual installation of the file NOTEPAD.EXE. Most of this log is fairly obvious. It sets up a progress marker based on the size of the file so that a progress bar can be used; it sets the destination (the target folder); it sets the source folder as a location within the Media table in the package; then it decides to install NOTEPAD.EXE because no version of this file already exists at the target folder. Interestingly enough, the log reports error 2318 for the file NOTEPAD.EXE, the Windows Installer error for "File does not exist." The number 2360 is the error code for Progress Tick, so a bit of detective work helps you confirm what's going on here.

One thing you'll see in a couple of places in a verbose log is a listing of all the properties of the installation, both Windows Installer and custom properties. This can be useful in debugging. Here's an example showing values of some of the Windows Installer standard properties reported in the log:

```
Property(S): VersionMsi = 2.00
Property(S): WindowsBuild = 2195
Property(S): ServicePackLevel = 3
Property(S): ServicePackLevelMinor = 0
Property(S): MsiNTProductType = 3
Property(S): MsiNTSuiteEnterprise = 1
Property(S): WindowsFolder = C:\WINNT\
Property(S): WindowsVolume = C:\
Property(S): SystemFolder = C:\WINNT\System32\
Property(S): System16Folder = C:\WINNT\System\
Property(S): TempFolder = C:\DOCUME~1\wilsonpd\LOCALS~1\Temp\
Property(S): ProgramFilesFolder = C:\Program Files\
Property(S): CommonFilesFolder = C:\Program Files\Common Files\
```

You should now have an idea of the sequencing and overall flow of an installation, and understand the idea of the sequences writing the script (called the immediate phase) and the actual process of updating the system (the deferred phase). You need to understand this so you know how and where to add your own code to the installation using CAs.

Custom Actions

You add your own code to the installation using a CA. Windows Installer stores CAs in the CustomAction table in the package, and they occur in the appropriate sequences at the required point. I'll talk about what "appropriate" and "required" mean shortly.

A CA usually has three main attributes:

1. The Type of the CA. You can define a CA to run a program, call a VBScript or a JScript, call into an external DLL, set a property value, and so on. The main variation within this Type is the location of the item. For example, if the CA is running a program, that program can be one that's being installed with the product, it can be part of the package in the Binary table, or it can be named by the value of some property. This general idea is true for other items such as scripts or calling DLLs.

2. The point at which the CA will be processed. Not only is this the location on the sequence tables, but also whether it's called immediately upon being encountered or when the system is being modified. These choices correspond in the InstallExecuteSequence to whether the CA is called during the script generation phase or during script processing and system modification. These choices are described in the documentation as the in-script execution options, and are referred to as immediate (processed when the script is being written) or deferred, meaning that the CA is written to the audit script and is called when the audit script processes it in the deferred sequence. There are variations within this general idea because you can specifically mark CAs to be called during a rollback or when the installation is being committed to the system.

3. The return options. Some CAs can return a value indicating whether the install should proceed further or not. The value returned by a call to a DLL, the exit code from a program, or the return value from a VBScript function can determine whether the install should continue or not. In some cases (such as external executable programs) there is an option to not wait for completion.

Creating a Custom Action

With these attributes in mind you'll look at VS, create a CA, and view the result.

VS has a Custom Actions view that shows four choices: Install, Commit, Rollback, and Uninstall. Choosing Install ➤ Add Custom Action points you at

File System on Target Machine. In other words, at first glance it looks like VS is
letting you call a CA that's a file, one that's being installed with the product. So
using your Notepad installation as a base, add a simple VBScript to the project,
one line that says only

```
msgbox "pausing the installation....."
```

Not very exciting, but it'll do for now. Figure 5-4 shows the VS view of adding
the file to the Application Folder on the target machine and using the Add
Custom Action file browser to select it.

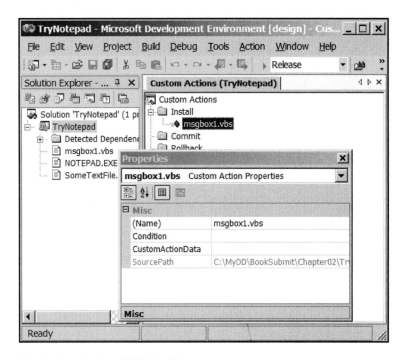

Figure 5-4. An Install CA in VS

Building the project and installing the resulting package shows that message box. However, none of the attributes of a CA that were described previously
are apparent in the VS IDE, and neither did you get a sequencing option, so
examining the actual database package with Orca is required to see the characteristics of this Install CA.

There's no trace of this CA in the InstallUISequence table, but the CA is
in the InstallExecuteSequence, hiding under a manufactured name (see
Figure 5-5). Its sequence isn't very interesting—just after StartServices—but
its Condition value is. This is a component condition. The variable name in
the Condition column is the name of the component; the $ prefix means that
this condition is based on what's happening to this component during the

installation process. The Platform SDK documentation refers to this as the action state of the component. The value 2 is one of the state values that are sometimes referred to by their "C" header file values from MSI.H (as in INSTALLSTATE_LOCAL) and sometimes by their automation interface names (where msiInstallStateDefault is the same as INSTALLSTATE_DEFAULT). The bottom line here is that a value greater than 2 means that the action state of the component is 3, 4, or 5. These numbers correspond to INSTALLSTATE_LOCAL (3), installed on local drive; INSTALLSTATE_SOURCE (4), run from source, CD, or network; or INSTALLSTATE_DEFAULT (5). All of these correspond to some variation of the component being installed on the client system. The point here is that the only thing that makes this an install-time CA is the fact that VS added that condition for you. So, keep in mind that there isn't really an Install CA, just a CA that you can condition on a component being installed. Looking back at Figure 5-4, note that there's room for you to add a condition. If you were to put a condition in there, you'd find that your condition would be ANDed with this install component condition. Note that this component condition is also true when you repair the product, because a repair marks the component for installation whether it ultimately needs to replace or repair any files or not.

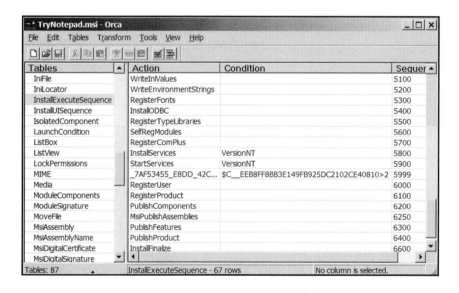

Figure 5-5. The CA in the execute sequence

Looking at the CustomAction table with Orca, Figure 5-6 shows what kind of CA VS created. The value in the Type column contains bits corresponding to the preceding list of three attributes. Breaking apart the bits in a Type 1046 CA (without duplicating the SDK documentation here) gives you 22 + 1024. As you might expect, this means that this is a VBScript CA, Type 22, together with the msidbCustomActionTypeInScript value. This value is a deferred CA because "in script" means that it's written to the script for deferred execution. Before looking at the implications of deferred CAs, you should look at the Source column of that CustomAction table entry. The semantics of a Type 22 CA are that the CA VBScript is being installed with the product, and the Source column is indeed the key into the File table of that VBScript. Remember that this is an Install CA only because VS created an installation component condition. If there were no such component condition, you'd find that Windows Installer would attempt to call the VBScript during the uninstall as well. In this case, it would fail because the CA is sequenced to run after the VBScript file has been removed. The Target column in this type of CA can be the name of a function to be called in the script. VS doesn't offer a way to name a script function; you must use Orca to name a function in the script file.

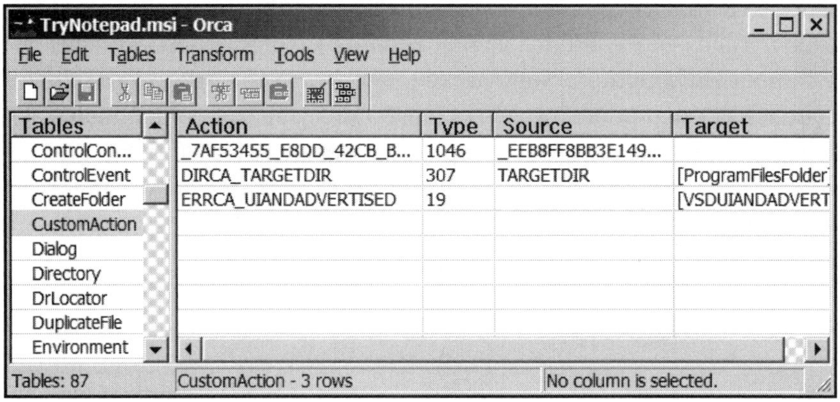

Figure 5-6. CA definition

Although there are many types of CAs, it's plain from the VS dialogs that the choice is primarily restricted to files that are part of your installation package. Other products offer much more access to the full range of CAs available in Windows Installer, so you'll be using Orca to add the ones that VS doesn't give you. But VS offers a variation here, which is that you're not required to install the CA file on the target system. You can set the Exclude value to True or False in the properties of the file. When the file is excluded, it won't be installed on the target system, so for these cases VS stores the CA file in the Binary table of the package. You'll see more of this shortly.

The VBScript Install CA that you added is a deferred CA. In the context of the execute sequence described earlier in the chapter, this means that the installer calls the CA while updating the system. You'd expect this anyway, because the file clearly needs to be on the target system before Windows Installer can run it from that location as a CA. The other type of CA is immediate, meaning that the installer will call it when it encounters the CA during the first phase of the execute sequence when the audit script is being written.

There's a critical difference between immediate and deferred CAs: Immediate CAs have full access to the properties of the current installation and deferred CAs do not. In fact, deferred CAs can see a small set of the installation's standard properties: ProductCode, UserSID, and CustomActionData. You use this last property—CustomActionData—to pass information to deferred CAs. Because a deferred CA cannot see properties, you can pass these property values using this CustomActionData property.

Deferred CAs also don't have access to other state information about the install. For example, they cannot evaluate whether a component or a feature is to be installed using a component condition expression such as the one in Figure 5-5. This seems to be a contradiction of the fact that the CA shown in Figure 5-5 is deferred and is using a component condition that I just said wasn't available to a deferred CA! However, VS sequenced the deferred CA between InstallInitialize and InstallFinalize, which is the range of actions where a script is written and then processed later. What's happening here is that the installer evaluates the component condition during the script-writing phase when properties and conditions are available. The installer doesn't use the condition during the deferred phase because the CA condition was already evaluated during the script-writing phase. The notion that you can pass the values of properties and states from the script-writing phase to the deferred phase is an important one, as you'll see later in the chapter when you look at the CustomActionData property.

So there's a bit of a quandary here. To run a program or script that's being installed you need a deferred CA (because that's when the program has been installed onto the system), but these CAs can't see properties. An immediate CA can see the full set of installer properties but cannot refer to a file being installed, because that file isn't installed yet. There are a number of ways around this quandary. I've hinted at one solution, use of the CustomActionData property. Another solution uses the fact that Windows Installer allows a CA's code file to be in the Binary table (as you saw with the VS case of the "Excluded" file), or even to have the code in the CA table itself. In other words, you don't need to install code onto the target system to call it through a CA. You'll examine how to do this with an immediate CA written with VBScript.

The way a CA VBScript accesses installer properties is by using the term "Property," passing the name of the property quoted in parentheses. To display the "Installed" and "ComputerName" standard properties, here's what the script fragment would be:

```
msgbox "Installed = " & Property("Installed") &
    " ComputerName = " & Property("ComputerName")
```

Strictly speaking, the property is being retrieved from the Property property of the Session object, so the call should really be this, using "Installed" as the example:

```
Session.Property("Installed")
```

However, the default object in the object model that Windows Installer provides for VBScript CAs is the Session object, so you can use Property() by itself.

Because you can't implement this VBScript as an immediate CA in VS using its development environment, you must add it using Orca.

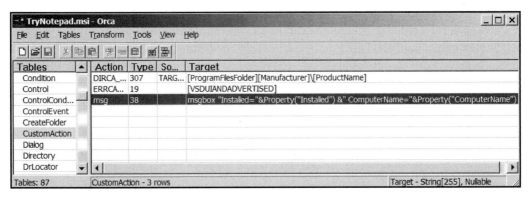

Figure 5-7. Type 38 CA manually defined in Orca

A Type 38 VBScript CA stores the text of the script with the CA itself, shown in Figure 5-7.

After defining the CA here, you can add it to the InstallExecuteSequence table as shown in Figure 5-8, with a Condition value of 1 (or no condition at all) so that it runs during the install and uninstall of the product. The Type 38 CA defined here has no other options set, which means that it's an immediate CA, running when the execute sequence is creating the audit script.

When this install runs, it shows the value of the standard installer property ComputerName, which, to state the obvious, is the name of the computer. However, the Installed property value isn't shown (leaving aside its value for now). This is what you'd expect—the Installed property reports whether the product is installed or not, and at this stage of the installation the product isn't yet marked as installed. Uninstalling the product is a different matter. The message box shows the value of the Installed property as a string containing the date and time that the product was installed (YYYY/MM/DD HH:MM:SS on US English systems; for example 2003/05/05 11:19:55). The fact that the Installed property is a string is the reason you see a comparison to a string in Figure 5-1.

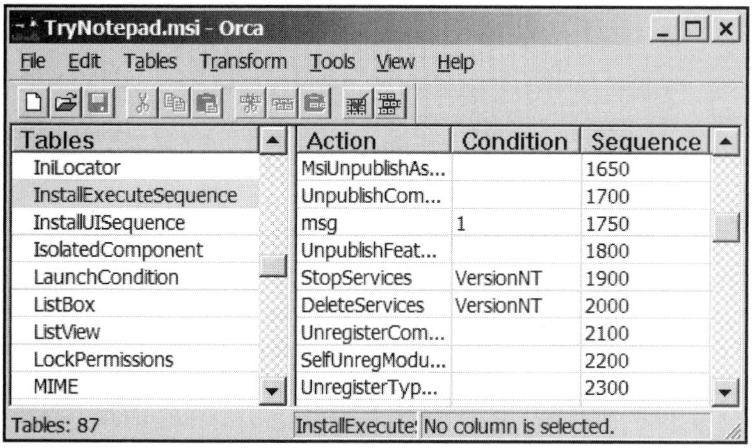

```
TryNotepad.msi - Orca                                    _ □ ×
 File   Edit   Tables   Transform   Tools   View   Help

 D ⌐ ⊟  % ⓑ ⓑ   ╬ ⓑ ⓑ   ▦ ▦
 Tables                    ▲    Action          Condition   Sequence   ▲
  IniLocator                    MsiUnpublishAs...            1650
  InstallExecuteSequence        UnpublishCom...             1700
  InstallUISequence             msg              1          1750
  IsolatedComponent             UnpublishFeat...            1800
  LaunchCondition          —    StopServices     VersionNT  1900
  ListBox                       DeleteServices   VersionNT  2000
  ListView                      UnregisterCom...            2100
  LockPermissions               SelfUnregModu...            2200
  MIME                     ▼    UnregisterTyp...            2300     ▼
 Tables: 87                     InstallExecute No column is selected.
```

Figure 5-8. Type 38 in the execute sequence

In practice, this type of CA is limited to the size of the Target column in the CustomAction table, so you need to store larger chunks of CA code in the Binary table. If you open a package with Orca and go to the Binary table, it consists of rows containing a Name to identify the item and a column shown as [Binary Data] that contains the actual file. You can use Orca to add a row to this table using a Name of your choice (I used myvb), and then use Orca's Browse button to stream the file into the Target column of the table. The next steps are to add the CA to the CustomAction table in much the same way as before, except that this time the CA is Type 6 (VBScript in the Binary table, an immediate CA) and the Source column is the Binary table entry you created: myvb. This works in the same general way as your earlier VBScript except that Windows streams the file out of the Binary table to run it.

So, you can add a CA to call this VBScript, using Orca to store the VBScript into the Binary table, create a Type 6 CA, and put it in sequence. If you want to be a bit lazier when creating immediate Install or Uninstall CAs, here's a tip. Using your VBScript again as an example, you could add these CAs using VS and browsing to the file, but (and here's the nugget) you set Exclude to be True in the properties for the file. This causes VS to put the file in the Binary table, and now you only have to change the Type of the CA in the CustomAction table. If it's a VBScript such as the preceding one, VS makes it a Type 1030, 6 + 1024, a deferred CA—a VBScript stored in the Binary table—so just make the CA a Type 6 and you've achieved a Type 6 somewhat more easily than the way you added it using Orca.

Calling a Custom Action DLL

One of the most flexible types of CA is a Type 1 CA with the DLL stored in the Binary table, which gives you the ability to call a function in a custom DLL. You use this prototype for the function call:

```
UINT __stdcall SomeCA (MSIHANDLE hInstall)
```

You must export the function name, and to avoid issues with decorated names (sometimes known as name mangling), it's probably easiest to do this export with a DEF file. The MSIHANDLE passed as a parameter is a handle to the current installation process. You can use it for a number of things, particularly setting and getting property values and accessing the running package file. By the way, your code doesn't own this handle, so your CA code must not close it.

The following UpgradeList function is a complete CA function; you'll go through it looking at some of the important points.

```
UINT __stdcall UpgradeList (MSIHANDLE hInstall)
{
TCHAR msg[255] = {0};
UINT nResult = 0;
TCHAR Qry [ ] = {TEXT("SELECT `UpgradeCode`, `VersionMax`
    FROM `Upgrade`") };
PMSIHANDLE hView = 0;     // Class wrapper for MSIHANDLE
PMSIHANDLE hDatabase = 0;
//get the handle to the package
hDatabase = MsiGetActiveDatabase(hInstall);
//open it
nResult = MsiDatabaseOpenView(hDatabase, Qry, &hView);
if (ERROR_SUCCESS !=nResult )
    {
    StringCchPrintf (msg, sizeof(msg)/sizeof(TCHAR),
      TEXT("UpgradeList:    MsiDatabaseOpenView returned error %d "), nResult);
    LogMessage (hInstall, msg);
    return 0;
}
nResult = MsiViewExecute(hView, NULL);
if (ERROR_SUCCESS !=nResult )
    {
    StringCchPrintf (msg,sizeof(msg)/sizeof(TCHAR),TEXT("UpgradeList:
        MsiViewExecute returned error %d "), nResult);
    LogMessage (hInstall, msg);
    return 0;
}
```

```
PMSIHANDLE hRec = 0;
//retrieves records from the database
while (ERROR_SUCCESS == (nResult = MsiViewFetch(hView, &hRec) ) )
{
    TCHAR szCode [100] = {0};
    DWORD codelen = sizeof(szCode)/sizeof(TCHAR);
    UINT getRecord = MsiRecordGetString(hRec, 1, szCode, &codelen); //
UpgradeCode
    if (getRecord != ERROR_SUCCESS)
    {
    StringCchPrintf (msg,sizeof(msg)/sizeof(TCHAR),TEXT("UpgradeList:
        MsiRecordGetString (1) returned error %d "), getRecord);
    LogMessage (hInstall, msg);
    return 0;
    }
    TCHAR VMinBuff [100] = {0};
    DWORD vminbufflen = sizeof (VMinBuff)/sizeof(TCHAR);
    getRecord = MsiRecordGetString(hRec, 2, VMinBuff, &vminbufflen);
    if (getRecord != ERROR_SUCCESS)
    {
    StringCchPrintf (msg,sizeof(msg)/sizeof(TCHAR),TEXT("UpgradeList:
        MsiRecordGetString (2) returned error %d "), getRecord);
    LogMessage (hInstall, msg);
    return 0;
    }
    TCHAR VMaxBuff [100] = {0};
    DWORD vmaxbufflen = sizeof (VMaxBuff)/sizeof(TCHAR);
    getRecord = MsiRecordGetString(hRec, 3, VMaxBuff, &vmaxbufflen);
    if (getRecord != ERROR_SUCCESS)
    {
    StringCchPrintf (msg,sizeof(msg)/sizeof(TCHAR),TEXT("UpgradeList:
        MsiRecordGetString (3) returned error %d "), getRecord);
    LogMessage (hInstall, msg);
    return 0;
    }
    StringCchPrintf (msg, sizeof(msg)/sizeof(TCHAR), TEXT("Upgrade:  Code %s
        VersionMin %s VersionMax %s "),szCode, VMinBuff, VMaxBuff);
    LogMessage (hInstall, msg);
    }
return 0;
}
```

This code is similar to the VBScript that you used in Chapter 2. That script opened a package and queried the File table, returning a list of the files. This CA function queries the running installation's Upgrade table and returns the results.

You're using the Win32 API calls into Windows Installer and not the automation interface. So, plunging straight into the code, the SQL-type query you're using selects the UpgradeCode, VersionMin, and VersionMax from the Upgrade table.

You'll use PMSIHANDLE declarations as handles to various pieces of your query. Despite some naming conventions you might have come across, this isn't a pointer to an MSIHANDLE. In fact, it's a class defined in MSI.H that wraps an MSIHANDLE, and has the advantage that the class destructor properly releases the contained MSIHANDLE to avoid handle leaks. This is a good time to point out that compiling this code requires a library reference to MSI.LIB. Although MSI.H needs to be #included in the project, you'll find it more convenient to include just MSIQUERY.H for the extra definitions there; it includes MSI.H anyway.

MsiGetActiveDatabase returns a database handle that has the same general use of opening the database as a file as you did in Chapter 2 with Installer.OpenDatabase, except that this handle refers to the package for the currently running installation, not the static copy of the package on a disk somewhere. MsiDatabaseOpenView returns a handle to the database view associated with the query, and MsiViewExecute processes the query. You'll look at what those LogMessage calls do shortly. If these calls are successful, the code loops through the list of returned records using MsiViewFetch. You separate each returned record out into the individual items (UpgradeCode, VersionMin, and VersionMax) by using MsiRecordGetString, passing in the handle to the record, the item number you want, and a specification of buffer and buffer length parameters to store the returned data. The item number, that second parameter, corresponds to the order in which the items were specified in the query, so asking for item 1 returns the UpgradeCode, 2 returns VersionMin, and 3 returns VersionMax. Note that this ordering isn't a zero-based index into a structure; it's the order in which the items appear in the list, starting at 1. Finally, if the code successfully returns this data, it calls the LogMessage function for each entry in the Upgrade table.

The code for LogMessage is deceptively simple and yet can be incredibly useful:

```
UINT LogMessage (MSIHANDLE hInstall, LPCTSTR szMsg)
{
PMSIHANDLE hRecord = MsiCreateRecord(1);
MsiRecordSetString(hRecord, 0, szMsg);
MsiProcessMessage(hInstall, INSTALLMESSAGE(INSTALLMESSAGE_INFO), hRecord);
return ERROR_SUCCESS;
}
```

MsiCreateRecord creates a database record object, where the parameter 1 means that there will be one field in the record, and returns a handle to the created record. MsiRecordSetString adds the string parameter to the record.

You're using zero as the second parameter, which means that the string is going into field zero of the record. Note that messages have format templates in field zero—see the MsiFormatRecord API documentation. That's why field zero isn't used in some types of messages. In this case, there are no values to substitute in the template because you're passing only a string. Calling MsiProcessMessage with that particular INSTALLMESSAGE passes the record to the installation process such that it's written to the installation log if one is being created. So if you want to integrate your CA diagnostics or tracing into the installation process (and you should), this is the way to do it. When you install this package and create a log, this is what this code results in:

```
MSI (s) (84:94): Doing action: Upgrades
Action start 15:47:39: Upgrades.
MSI (s) (84:94): Creating MSIHANDLE (12) of type 790542 for thread 660
Upgrade:  Code {A0E3FD00-4838-4A98-8F60-0F7E96A28294} VersionMin 1.1 VersionMax
Upgrade:  Code {A0E3FD00-4838-4A98-8F60-0F7E96A28294} VersionMin 1.0.0.0
VersionMax 1.1
Action ended 15:47:40: Upgrades. Return value 1.
```

"Upgrades" is the name of the CA, the log notes that it's creating an MSIHANDLE to pass to your function, and the two lines beginning with "Upgrade" are the data that the CA code logged.

You'll now set about adding this CA call to the Notepad installation project. I'll say up front that this CA won't work after you're done; you'll examine why, and fix it.

Adding an Install CA using VS, as before, you can browse to a list of the files in the project. The sample code supplied with the book has a CA DLL named CaDll.dll that you can add to the Application Folder first, so go ahead and add the DLL. In the Properties window for this DLL, set the Exclude property to True so that the DLL is stored in the Binary table of the package. The resulting Properties window for the CA call into this DLL is shown in Figure 5-9. The interesting item for now is EntryPoint; this is where you name the function in the DLL, which is UpgradeList from your code. Leaving InstallerClass set to False, you can now build the project. However, if you run this install, it fails; the log shows the error "UpgradeList: MsiDatabaseOpenView returned error 6" from the error handling code in the function. The reason it fails is that this CA, like all CAs generated by VS, is a deferred one: Type 1025 (visible as usual in the CustomAction table). This Type decodes as 1024 (a deferred CA) + 1 (a call to a function in a DLL stored in the Binary table). Deferred CAs don't have access to much of the state of the running installation. Error 6 means that a handle is invalid; in other words, the MSIHANDLE parameter that Windows Installer passed to UpgradeList was invalid for this particular use. Saying that a deferred CA can't access installation state, or that the handle passed to your CA is invalid, are two ways of saying the same thing. If you change the CA Type to 1, making it immediate (using your friend Orca again), it will work properly, writing the contents of the Upgrade table to the log file.

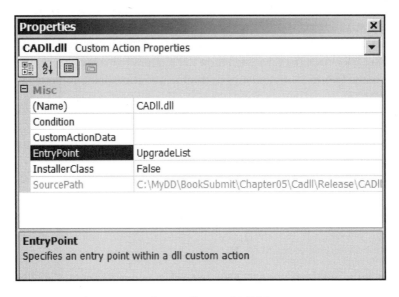

Figure 5-9. VS properties for a call on a CA DLL

Passing Data to a Deferred Custom Action

The code in the UpgradeList function in that CA DLL uses the MSIHANDLE input parameter to open the current installing database package and list the contents of the Upgrade table. It's a somewhat artificial scenario to illustrate CAs. The most useful thing CAs usually do is get or set the properties of the running installation. The Windows API call that gets a property from the running installation has this prototype:

```
MsiGetProperty (MSIHANDLE hInstall, LPCTSTR szName, LPTSTR szValueBuf, DWORD*
    pchValueBuf);
```

That first parameter is the handle to the installation passed in to the CA function; szName is the text name of the property; szValueBuf is where the value of the property will be returned into; and pchValueBuf is an [in, out] parameter that's the buffer length in characters on input, and the length of the property string in characters (excluding the terminating \0) after the call returns. In the same general way as your call on MsiDatabaseOpenView in the previous CA function, this handle is invalid if you pass it to MsiGetProperty in a deferred CA and try to get a property that cannot be accessed from a deferred

CA. So you're back to a key concern: How do you pass data in the properties of the installation into a deferred CA? If you refer back to Figure 5-9, the answer is in that CustomActionData property. I'll illustrate its use in VS together with another CA function that retrieves it. The main point to understand is that CustomActionData is a standard Windows Installer property that is an indirect way of passing properties from the installation into a deferred CA.

In VS, you can show passing properties by putting the value of a property into that CustomActionData property. Figure 5-10 shows [TARGETDIR] there, together with the following new CA function:

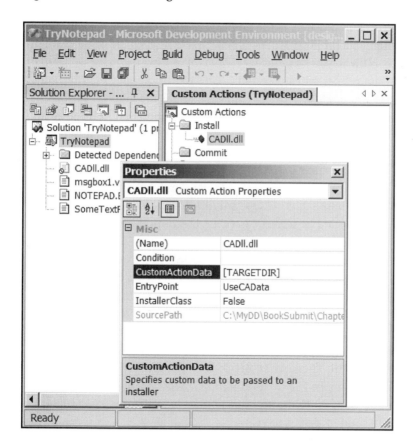

Figure 5-10. Installer properties passed via CustomActionData

```
UINT __stdcall UseCAData (MSIHANDLE hInstall)
{
    TCHAR vbuff [500] = {0};
    DWORD vlen = sizeof(vbuff)/sizeof(TCHAR);
    UINT gp = MsiGetProperty(hInstall, TEXT("CustomActionData"), vbuff, &vlen);
    TCHAR msg [500] = {0};
    StringCchPrintf (msg, sizeof(msg)/sizeof(TCHAR),TEXT("gp = %d vlen = %d
```

```
        vbuff = %s"), gp, vlen, vbuff );
    MessageBox (NULL, msg, TEXT("Result"), MB_OK);
    return 0;
}
```

This function uses MsiGetProperty to return the value of the CustomActionData property, and then displays a message box of its contents. Running the resulting installation package shows you a message box containing something like C:\Program Files\Company Name\Product Name (as well as success/failure indication and the property length shown in the preceding code). The TARGETDIR property is the destination folder for the installation, so the CustomActionData property works as advertised: It saves the value of the property TARGETDIR so you can retrieve it later, by getting the value of the CustomActionData property in a deferred CA. It's more complicated internally, as you'll see by examining the package with Orca. If this mechanism simply saved the value of a property in the CustomActionData property you'd only be able to use the CustomActionData property once, but there's no such restriction; you can use it multiple times.

You can see the way that CustomActionData works internally in Figures 5-11 and 5-12. The CA, Type 1025, has that long manufactured name, the Target is the function name UseCAData, and the Source is a key into the Binary table where the DLL is stored. However, there's another CA, a Type 51 with a ".SetProperty" suffix. It has a Target containing the [TARGETDIR] value you named in CustomActionData in VS, and a Source that's exactly the same as the name of the CA itself. A Type 51 CA sets a property (in Source) from a value in Target. So the way that you pass data via the CustomActionData property to a deferred CA is to set the value into a property with the same name as the CA. If you want to pass the value of the TARGETDIR property into a CA called Fred, you use a Type 51 that creates a property called Fred containing the value of TARGETDIR. Then, when the code in the CA Fred requires the value of TARGETDIR, it gets the CustomActionData property instead. I use TARGETDIR here just as an example—this applies to any property or install state you want to send to a deferred CA.

Some points to note here: Although VS inserts the Type 51 CA just before the call to the deferred CA, the Type 51 is immediate; it must be in order for it to see the installation's properties. During the script generation immediate phase, the Type 51 generates a script entry passing the current value of TARGETDIR, then Windows Installer creates a script entry to call the deferred CA later. The value of TARGETDIR has been saved in the generated script such that you can retrieve it using CustomActionData.

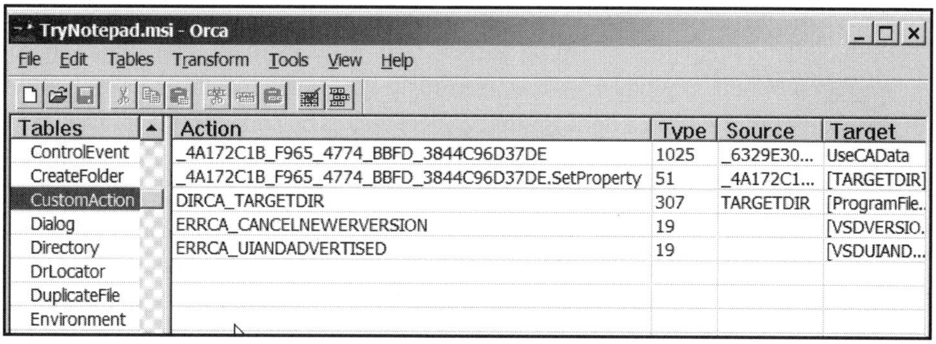

Figure 5-11. CAs for deferred use with CustomActionData

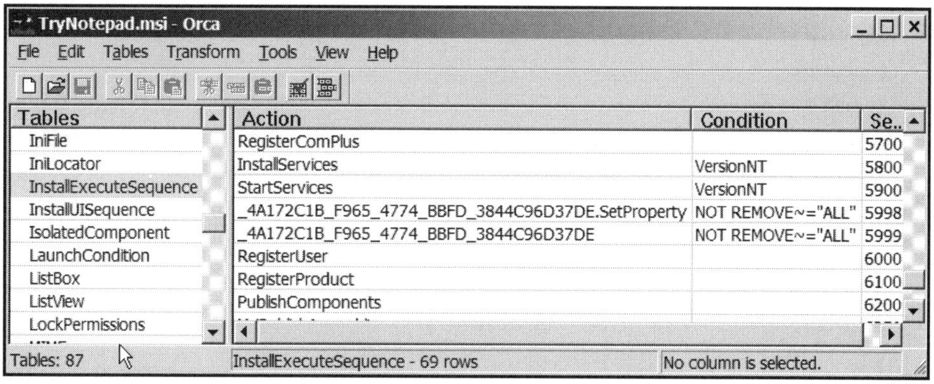

Figure 5-12. Setting CustomActionData in the ExecuteSequence

Occasionally the use of the CustomActionData property is misunderstood to mean that you can only use it once, but you can really use it once per CA, because each use is linked to the name of the CA.

You can also use the same general scheme if you need to pass several properties to a deferred CA. For example, say you set VS's CustomActionData property to this:

```
<[TARGETDIR]><[OriginalDatabase]>
```

When you retrieve the value of the CustomActionData in your CA, you'll see both of the resolved values delimited by those angle brackets.

Note also the Condition column entries for these CAs: NOT REMOVE~="ALL". That tilde ~ makes the comparison case-insensitive, and the REMOVE property is a standard property that returns a list of features that are being uninstalled. A condition of REMOVE="ALL" is true when the product is being uninstalled, so the condition here effectively means that the CA will be called in all cases when the product isn't being uninstalled. Although this condition clearly means that the CA will be called when the product is being installed, it also has the same characteristic that you saw before, namely that this CA will be called when there is a repair. When you looked at CAs previously, you saw a condition based on the installation of the component, so that the CA would be called if the component was being installed ($ComponentName>2). But if the install isn't installing the file that contains the CA code (because the file is in the Binary table), it can't set a condition based on the file's component action state. So, the install condition is component-based if the CA file is being installed to the target system, but the condition is product-based if the CA file isn't being installed to the system and is consequently stored in the Binary table.

This behavior of deferred CAs and the use of CustomActionData also applies to VBScript CAs. This VBScript CA shows how to retrieve the CustomActionData property, and also how to write data to the log in the same way that you did with the LogMessage function in the CA DLL earlier in this chapter:

```
option explicit
dim inst, rec
set inst = CreateObject("WindowsInstaller.Installer")
set rec=inst.CreateRecord (2)
rec.StringData(1) = "Logging call from " & property("CustomActionData")
Session.Message &H04000000, rec
```

After creating a record and adding text to it, the Session.Message function logs it if logging is in effect. That first parameter is the msiMessageTypeInfo constant, which makes this a message for the log.

Note that I explicitly created an Installer object using CreateObject. You can also do this by using the built-in Installer property of the Session object. In short, you can use Session.Installer to get an instance of the Installer object in a CA script such as this.

Executable Programs As Custom Actions

The ability to fire off a program as a CA is clearly useful, although the fact that it's a separate process means that the CA doesn't have access to the properties of the installation. In other words, the separate process doesn't get passed an MSIHANDLE to access installation properties. You'll proceed as before, using VS to add an executable in the same way that you added a VBScript file or a DLL. In this case you'll add an executable called GetUser.exe, one of the book's sample programs. GetUser.exe has the Exclude property False so it is installed on the target system. The Install CA to run this is shown in Figure 5-13.

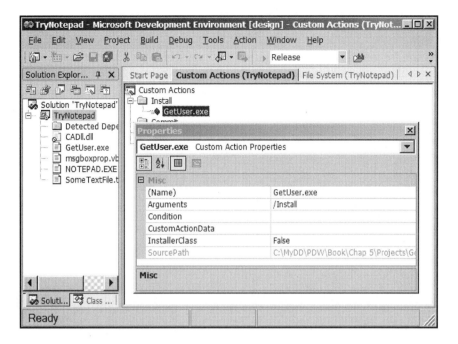

Figure 5-13. CA executable in VS

Note that VS added a default Argument of /Install (if you'd made this an Uninstall CA you'd see /Uninstall). Build this and run the installation, and this program shows a message box, the caption of which is the current domain name and the text of which is the installing user account. I'll come back to this later, but notice for now that the installation stops until you OK the message box. One reason you might use this type of CA is to install a product and then launch one of the programs to start the client using the product. However, this won't work if the installation has stopped during the call to the CA, which it has.

Going back to Orca and looking at the Type of the CA, Figure 5-14 shows that this is a Type 1042 CA, which decodes as 1024 (deferred) + 18 (launching a file installed with the application), where the Source column is a key into the File table. It's time to introduce the CA Return Processing Options (as they're described in the SDK), which are the bits that affect whether the installation will wait for the program to finish or not. As you might guess from the default behavior and the Type value of 1042, the default is that none of these bits are set in the CA. You have a number of choices here, but going with the scenario of launching the installed application, the most useful choices are the bits that cause the installation to continue and the program to be asynchronous from it. These bits are msidbCustomActionTypeAsync + msidbCustomActionTypeContinue, for a total of decimal 192, giving 1234 for your Type, adding to 1042. With this value in the Type field in the CustomAction table, the program does indeed proceed independently, allowing you to close the installation while leaving the program running. That's a useful capability to have after you've installed a product. Look at the later section "Commit Custom Actions" for what might be a better way to accomplish the same thing. Why did the program display user information? Because it shows the Windows account the program was running with, which brings me to security in the context of CAs.

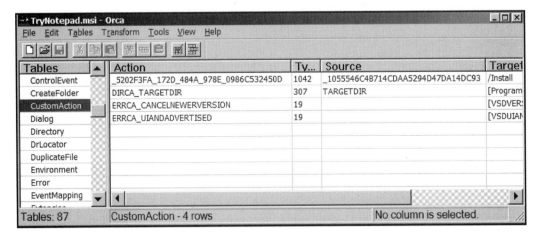

Figure 5-14. Executable CA in Orca

Security and Custom Actions

Apart from showing the general principles of programs as CAs, the point of the previous exercise was to demonstrate that even though Windows Installer runs as a Service, the CA ran with the installing user's account. This makes a great deal of sense as the default behavior. When the installer creates entries that are user-related (such as HKEY_CURRENT_USER Registry entries or profile folders), the consistency between what the installer does and how a CA behaves means that they'll be using the same data. From a security aspect, this impersonation of the installing user means that an installation doesn't violate security by allowing non-privileged users to run with elevated privileges. But you can cause a CA to run in a system context by setting the msidbCustomActionTypeNoImpersonate bit in the Type value. As you just saw, running the GetUser.exe program as a CA was a Type 1042 CA: a deferred launch of a program installed with the application. VS has no way in the IDE to change this Type, so to run the program with no impersonation, add hex 800 (decimal 2048) to get a value of 3090 for the Type. If you change the CustomAction table Type to this value with Orca and run the installation, you should see that the domain name displayed in the caption is NT_AUTHORITY and the account name is System. Incidentally, only deferred CAs can run with the System account.

Use of the msidbCustomActionTypeNoImpersonate bit requires Administrator privilege, or for an administrator to have blessed the package:

- The elevated privilege is allowed if an administrator is performing a per-machine install (typically by double-clicking the MSI package).

- Per-user installs that have been advertised by an administrator can run with elevated privileges; this is key to the idea that non-admin users can install packages that otherwise they wouldn't have the privilege to install.

- An administrator can set the AlwaysInstallElevated policy for the machine and the user. This effectively means that the user has elevated privileges during the course of an install. This policy is a security hole and should be avoided. For example, a user familiar with VBScript can arrange to have a script run with elevated privileges as a CA. Chapter 13 discusses this more fully.

Preserving the Installation Location with a Custom Action

It's quite common to want to know the main application folder where a product has been installed. Although you can do this in a number of custom ways (such as writing your TARGETDIR to the Registry), the installer way to do this is to set the standard installer property ARPINSTALLLOCATION with a Type 51 CA. You set it to the TARGETDIR value. The reason for this particular method is that setting ARPINSTALLLOCATION has the effect of propagating the installation location such that you can obtain it using the installer APIs and COM interfaces into Windows.

Figure 5-15 shows the way to define this CA with Orca. You then add it to the InstallExecuteSequence; adding it somewhere between InstallInitialize and InstallFinalize but before RegisterProduct is fine. It makes sense to call this CA only if the product isn't already installed, so a condition of Not Installed makes sense. After you install the product, the programmatical interface to find this location is the MsiGetProductInfo API, passing the ProductCode GUID and INSTALLPROPERTY_INSTALLLOCATION as parameters. This is the equivalent to the following WSH VBScript:

```
option explicit
dim installer, msg
Set installer = CreateObject("WindowsInstaller.Installer")
msg = installer.ProductInfo("{B3E1B56E-D853-4780-BF62-47B95195CD6B}",
"InstallLocation")
msgbox msg
```

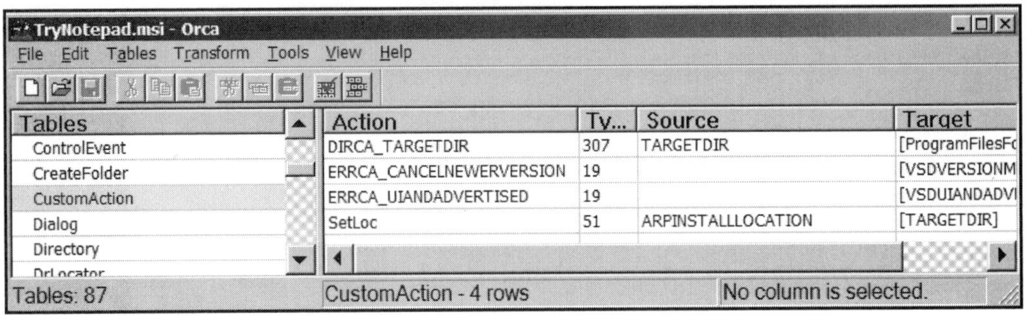

Figure 5-15. Type 51 definition in Orca

As noted in Chapter 4 in the description of using a Windows Installer Component search, the files installed with your product might be installed in folders other than just TARGETDIR. So it makes sense to evaluate whether you need to preserve TARGETDIR, or whether you can locate a previously installed component using its installer component GUID. In the context of APIs rather than searches, you'd use the Installer.ComponentPath method in the scripting automation environment, or MsiGetComponentPath in the Win32 environment.

Custom Actions in the UI Sequence

All the CAs you've looked at so far have been in the InstallExecuteSequence, and this is the right place to put CAs that might change the system. However, it can be useful sometimes to put CAs in the InstallUISequence. These CAs shouldn't update the system, but sometimes you need them to initialize properties used elsewhere in the installation. One way this can be useful is when using a property as a LaunchCondition or in an AppSearch, or when initializing a standard property such as TARGETDIR. For example:

- You want to install a product in the same location as another product that's already installed.

- You want to search for a file that your product might have installed in the product's installation directory.

As an example, suppose you wish to install your product in the same folder as some other product. Take a look at this VBScript CA:

```
option explicit
dim installer, msg
Set installer = CreateObject("WindowsInstaller.Installer")
```

```
msg = installer.ProductInfo
    ("{60600409-EA9B-45E9-A468-2C68C8DE70DF}","InstallLocation")
Property("TARGETDIR")=msg
Set Installer=Nothing
msgbox msg
```

That ProductCode GUID belongs to VS 2003; you get its install location and set your installation's destination folder to be the same by setting the TARGETDIR property. You can add this VBScript file to the installation as an Install CA using VS. If you add this CA script file to the installation, marking the VBScript file properties as Exclude set to True, VS will create a Type 1030 CA in the InstallExecuteSequence. This is just a way of having VS provide you with the foundation for your CA. In the CustomAction table, the Type 1030 VBScript means that it's a deferred CA with the VBScript stored in the Binary table; changing to a Type 6 makes it immediate. In the InstallExecuteSequence, find the CA and delete it (Drop Row in Orca), then copy the name of the CA and insert it (Add Row in Orca) into the InstallUISequence table. If you were going to use the TARGETDIR property, or any other property for that matter, in a LaunchCondition or AppSearch, you would need to sequence it before these actions. Assuming you've got that VS ProductCode GUID installed, you'll see its installation location show up as the default destination in the UI. That's because the content of that dialog box is defined as the value of the TARGETDIR property.

If you look at the way VS sets the value of the TARGETDIR property, you'll find that there's a CA (DIRCA_TARGETDIR in VS 2003) that sets TARGETDIR from the usual concatenation of the ProgramFilesFolder, Manufacturer, and ProductName properties (see Figure 5-16). DIRCA_TARGETDIR appears in the InstallUISequence and the InstallExecuteSequence with a Condition of TARGETDIR="". This Type 307 CA is a Type 51 CA with the msidbCustomActionTypeFirstSequence bit set, meaning that it will run once if present in both tables. Like the AppSearch and LaunchCondition actions, this is a way of getting a CA into both sequences and having it called just once. The reason for this is that the InstallUISequence won't be processed in a silent install (such as running Msiexec.exe with a /q option), so always keep this in mind with CAs in the InstallUISequence and arrange to have the CA in both sequences. How about that TARGETDIR="" condition on the DIRCA_TARGETDIR CA? That's there so that you can do a command-line installation specifying the value of TARGETDIR, and the CA won't override the command-line specification.

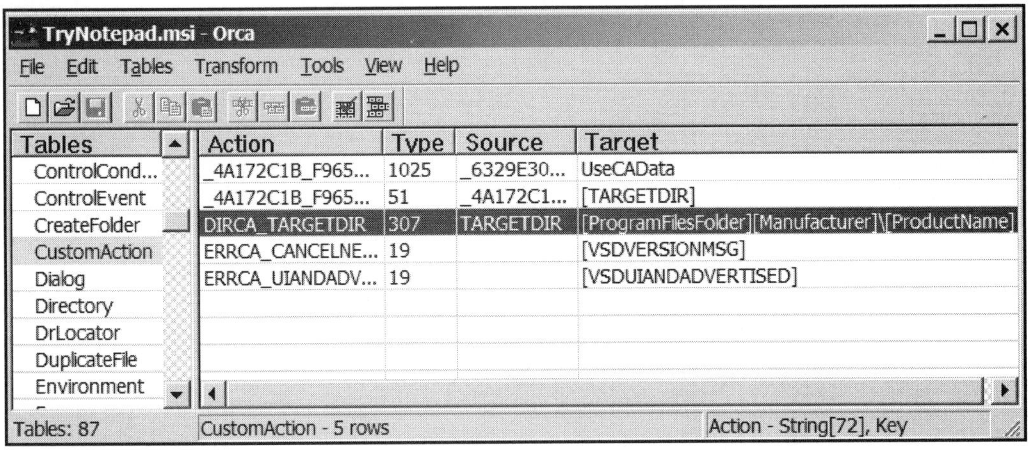

Figure 5-16. How VS sets TARGETDIR

You can trigger CAs that need to run while the install is showing the UI by controls on dialogs. Figure 5-17 shows an event triggered off the Next button in the FolderForm (the one that lets you choose the installation folder). The Event column value of DoAction means that an action is to be called, and the Argument column value is the name of the action. In this case it's FindRelatedProducts, a standard installer action, but you can add your own CAs and have them called with a DoAction in the same way.

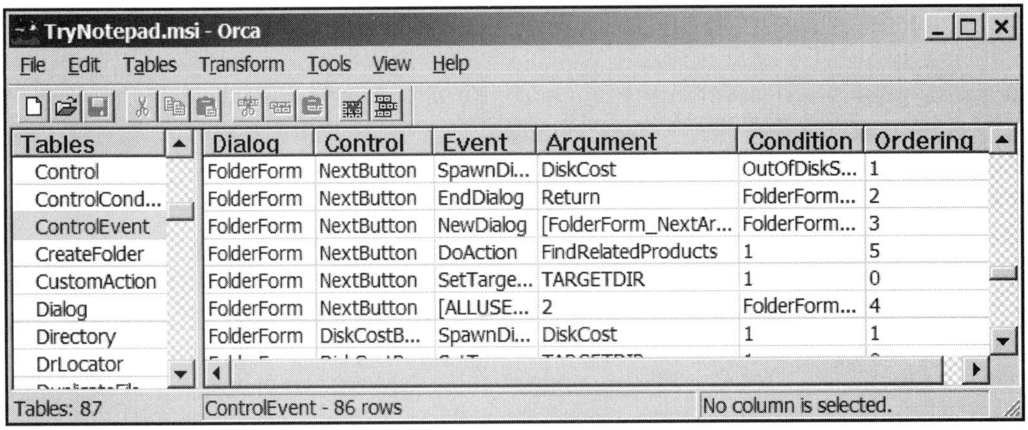

Figure 5-17. Calling a CA from a UI button

Custom Action Scheduling

You can have CAs in the UI sequence and in the execute sequence. VS's IDE builds deferred CAs in the execute sequence, so this fact isn't readily apparent. When a CA is in both sequences you can specify whether it should run twice (once per sequence) or just once; this is determined by the CA scheduling options. The default is to run twice, once per sequence. However, many CAs need to called just once when first encountered; the msidbCustomActionTypeFirstSequence bit specifies this in the Type field in the CustomAction table. Recall from Chapter 2 that properties created in the UI sequence must be public (an upper-case identifier) for their values to be propagated into the execute sequence. Also keep in mind that you might have to specify property names in the SecureCustomProperties property for them to be transferred to the execute sequence. You'll see an example of this in Chapter 6 when I discuss major upgrades.

Uninstall Custom Actions and Conditions

In the same way that there is no such thing as an Install CA, there is no such thing as an Uninstall CA. There are only CAs in VS that are conditioned on a state change for an installer component or the product itself. VS chooses a component-based condition when the file is being installed on the system. It uses a condition based on the product state (based on the value of the REMOVE property) when the file isn't being installed or uninstalled, and in fact runs the CA from the Binary table. When multiple features are in a product, you can con-dition a CA on what happens to a feature. For components, these conditions are based on $ComponentName, as you saw with some of VS's Install and Uninstall conditions. For features, the conditions are based on &FeatureName and have the same values for the resulting state: $MyComponent=2 is a condition that evaluates to true if MyComponent is being uninstalled. Similarly, &MyFeature=2 is a condition that evaluates to true if MyFeature is being uninstalled, so that you can condition a CA on what will happen to a particular feature.

Commit Custom Actions

A Commit CA gets called when the installation script (the second phase of the InstallExecuteSequence) has been completed successfully. This installation script consists of the actions scheduled between InstallInitialize and InstallFinalize, so a Commit CA is called only when InstallFinalize is reached successfully. This is clearly useful because there will be things you want to do if the installation is successful. If the installation process rolls back because of an error, the Commit CA won't be called. Back in the section "Executable Programs as Custom Actions" you looked at launching a program when it's been installed. If this is the main product executable, a help file, a "read me," or a run of a con-figuration program, it makes sense to launch a program only if the product has been installed successfully. A Commit CA can be ideal for this situation. This design choice can also be dependent on the tool you use to build your setup. Some tools let you edit dialog boxes and attach CAs to button clicks, so with these development tools you could choose to run a program as a result of clicking the "Install Complete" button. However, VS doesn't let you do this with its IDE, so you'll use a Commit CA as an example way to launch a program after a successful install.

VS builds a Commit CA for an executable as a synchronous action, so it prevents the installation from proceeding until the program finishes. As you did in the "Executable Programs as Custom Actions" section, set the msidbCustomActionTypeAsync and msidbCustomActionTypeContinue bits (adding 192 to the Type of the CA) to cause the CA to be asynchronous from the installation.

The preceding examples of launching installed programs are the safest uses for Commit CAs because they're free from rollback considerations. It's not a good idea to alter the system during a Commit CA when the installation has completed successfully and it's highly unlikely that a rollback will occur. That's because there's very little scope to undo whatever you do in the CA.

As you can see, Commit CAs are a special type of CA because the msidbCustomActionTypeCommit bit is set. They don't work using install or uninstall conditions like Install and Uninstall CAs do, and additionally they're called only if rollback is enabled for the installation. You can control rollback with the DISABLEROLLBACK property, the DisableRollback system policy, or by inserting the DisableRollback standard action in the sequence table. Windows Installer might also disable rollback if there's insufficient disk space.

Rollback Custom Actions

Rollback CAs are more or less the opposite of Commit CAs. A Rollback CA is executed when the installation has failed and the system is being restored to what it was before the installation started. This is your opportunity to undo anything you might have done with an Install CA. You need to sequence Rollback CAs before the action they're intended to undo, so that there's never a point in the execution where a change has been made to the system without having the corresponding Rollback CA already in the script and ready to run if necessary.

Type 19: Terminating the Installation

Occasionally there's a need for the installation to terminate itself, which is the purpose of a Type 19 CA. Typically, something like a CA sets a property value, then you condition the Type 19 CA on the presence (or the value) of that property. Type 19 CAs are always immediate, so there are no issues here with visibility to installation properties and states.

The easiest way to define a Type 19 is to add its name to the Action column of the CustomAction table and insert some error text in the Target column, although there are other ways to display the error message; refer to the SDK documentation.

The text in the Target column of the CustomAction table for a Type 19 is the Formatted Type, which means you can do things such as put property values there in square brackets and they'll be resolved when the text is shown. Figure 5-18 shows the Endit CA in Orca, together with some others generated by VS, which doesn't offer explicit support for creating Type 19 CAs.

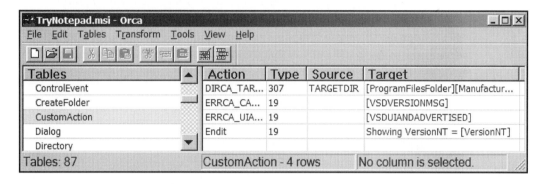

Figure 5-18. Type 19 CA

Installing and Embedding Other MSI Packages

The SDK documentation describes three ways of installing another package from a parent installation (Types 7, 23, and 39), but they're not the only ways. You'll start by looking at Type 7 and then look at another way of doing this: a Type 50 CA.

Using Type 7 and Type 39

Type 7 is a nested installation of a package residing in a substorage within the parent package. Orca doesn't show the storages within a package, so they're not obvious. However, a _Storages table in the package contains two items: a Name for the storage, and Data, the binary data.(The _Storages table isn't an actual table; it's a virtual table, a view into the database to make management of the embedded substorages a bit easier.) To get your external package MSI file inside the parent package for the Type 7 CA, you must update the database with a storage consisting of the external MSI file, but before doing that, the overall scheme needs looking at.

In the Type 7 CA, the Source column of the table is the name of that sub-storage, but the Target column is more interesting because it's where you get the opportunity to propagate attributes from the parent installation into the nested installation. Now note that this CA installs a separate nested MSI package embedded in the parent package. "Embedded" means that you don't see the UI, which means that you want to make sure that the embedded installation has some of the same installation properties as the parent. In many cases, the embedded installation should probably have the same TARGETDIR and the same ALLUSERS values as the parent. You specify these values in the Target column. The behavior of an embedded installation in Add/Remove Programs is also perhaps not what you might expect—although the embedded product shows up in Add/Remove Programs as a product, you can't remove it from there. Attempting to do so will tell you that removing is only valid for products that are installed. (If you right-click the external package and attempt to uninstall it, you'll be told that the system administrator has set policies to prevent this installation.) You could hide this Add/Remove Programs entry with the ARPSYS-TEMCOMPONENT property, by adding ARPSYSTEMCOMPONENT=1 to the embedded install Target shown in Figure 5-19.

It turns out that these embedded products get uninstalled when the parent product is uninstalled. To do this there is a CA, Type 39, which in this case is the opposite of Type 7. This Type 39 CA has the ProductCode of the embedded package in the Source column and a setting for the REMOVE property in the Target column.

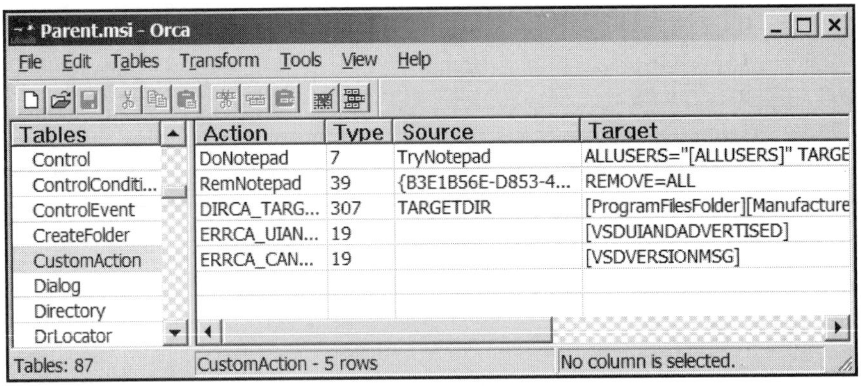

Figure 5-19. Type 7 and Type 39 CAs

When you put these two CAs together, they look like Figure 5-19, where DoNotepad is the Type 7 and RemNotepad the Type 39. DoNotepad gets the embedded package from a substorage (not yet created) called TryNotepad, and passes the values of ALLUSERS and TARGETDIR from the current installation to the embedded one, setting the Target column to:

```
ALLUSERS="[ALLUSERS]" TARGETDIR="[TARGETDIR]" ADDLOCAL=ALL
```

It also sets a standard public property called ADDLOCAL. The ADDLOCAL property names a list of the features that are to be installed (in some ways, the opposite of REMOVE), and ALL is a way of saying that all features are to be installed. For the Type 39 CA RemNotepad that uninstalls the embedded product when the parent product is uninstalled, the Source column contains the ProductCode GUID of the embedded product package (truncated in Figure 5-19), and Target sets REMOVE=ALL. Finally, these CAs need inserting in the InstallExecuteSequence table with appropriate conditions. You should sequence both CAs between InstallInitialize and InstallFinalize, as the documentation says. You should condition the Type 7 on Not Installed so that it's called when the parent product isn't already installed, and you can condition the Type 39 on REMOVE="ALL" to be called when the parent product is uninstalled. Notice that there seem to be inconsistencies here regarding when quotes are needed around ALL. The rule of thumb is that when you're using the REMOVE property as a condition, the quotes are required, but they're not required when you're using it as part of a command line to the installer.

You insert the external package into a storage in the parent package with the same APIs and automation interfaces you first used in the "Into the Package with Programming" section in Chapter 2. In fact, a VBScript in the Windows Installer SDK—WiSubStg.vbs—does exactly this. You can run this VBScript with three parameters: the name of the parent installation package, the name of the package to be embedded, and the name of the substorage. You can rewrite this script down to the basics and tailor it to your specific needs here. This condensed script is in the book's code: the file SetStream.vbs. The key parts of this script (omitting some setup code, error checking, and declarations) are as follows:

```
sqlQuery = "SELECT `Name`, `Data` FROM _Storages"
"" Open database in transacted mode
Set database = installer.OpenDatabase(<path to parent MSI>, 1)
Set view = database.OpenView(sqlQuery)
Set record = installer.CreateRecord(2)
record.StringData(1) = "TryNotepad"
view.Execute record
' The field within the record is 2
record.SetStream 2, <path to MSI file to be embedded>
' update with msiViewModifyAssign
view.Modify 3, record
database.Commit
```

Having opened the database in transaction mode and opened a View based on a query to the _Storages table, the script creates a record containing two fields corresponding to the storage name and the storage data. It sets the first field to the storage name TryNotepad and it assigns the second field—the actual binary data of the external package—by calling the SetStream method on the Record object. Finally the script code modifies the View object and commits the changes to the database, the parent package.

After running this script and embedding the package, the parent package is complete and ready to install.

Embedded MSI files ("nested installs") have their uses because of the Windows Installer rule that disallows two simultaneous MSI installations. However, there are limitations with nested installs when the product needs updating. Minor upgrades and patches (Chapters 6 and 12) aren't possible with nested installs. The best approach to installing multiple MSI files is to build a launching program or WSH VBScript that installs each of the packages sequentially. You can design the launch program to uninstall previous products if some of the installs fail.

Using Type 50: Launching an Executable to Install a Package

Type 50 is a generic CA to run an executable, a variation on the earlier topic "Executable Programs As Custom Actions." In the CustomAction table, the Source column is a key to the Property table, naming a property value containing the full path to the executable. You put any command-line arguments in the Target column.

To use a Type 50 CA to launch another package, the plan is to use Msiexec.exe as the executable program that you'll run with a command line that points to the external MSI package you want to install. You could perhaps use this scenario when several installation packages are on a CD and you want one to launch the others. This is also a general technique that you can use any time you need to launch an executable that's already on the target system because, for example, the program is a standard part of the operating system, such as Msiexec.exe. Using Type 50 turns out to be less than optimal for installing other packages, as you'll see when it comes to uninstalling these other packages.

Because the Source column names the property that's the path to the executable, you need to name Msiexec.exe. All you put in the Property table is the name MSIEXEC with a Value of Msiexec.exe; this is sufficient to locate the file. In the CustomAction table, the Target value is where you pass the arguments, which must include the location of the external package. As before, you should arrange to propagate the values of ALLUSERS and TARGETDIR from the parent installation into this external one. This gives you a Target value of the following:

```
/i "[SourceDir]trynotepad.msi" ALLUSERS="[ALLUSERS]" TARGETDIR="[TARGETDIR]" /q
```

SourceDir is a standard installer property that names the folder from which the package is running, so you can use it to locate your external package (trynotepad.msi) in the same folder as the parent package. You pass the ALLUSERS and TARGETDIR properties in the same way as the Type 7; this time you append a /q to make the external package install without showing any UI.

The Uninstall CA has the standard command line to uninstall a product by passing the ProductCode GUID to Msiexec.exe:

```
/x {B3E1B56E-D853-4780-BF62-47B95195CD6B} /Q
```

There's a /Q to do it quietly. This CA is conditioned on REMOVE="ALL" so that it runs when the product is being uninstalled.

The disadvantage of using Type 50 to install an external package stems from the fact that only one installation at a time is allowed to be in the execute sequence. This is turn means that you must place both the Type 50 CAs to install and uninstall the external package in the UI sequence, inside the InstallUISequence table. Because this table doesn't get used during silent installs, the CAs won't get called in silent mode where the UI has been suppressed. This isn't much of a problem for an installation where you could be reasonably sure that the user will run the package and interact with the UI. However, uninstalls from Add/Remove Programs are silent, so you're in the situation where the uninstall of the other product isn't called because the Uninstall CA isn't called. The UI sequence does get called if you attempt to reinstall the parent package again. It goes into a maintenance mode dialog (offering Remove or Repair in VS-generated packages), and in the Remove choice the UI sequence runs and the Uninstall CA gets called. Keep in mind that silent installs are common in many system management and group policy distribution scenarios, so in most cases you must assume that your package will be installed silently. Therefore, you cannot rely on running CAs in the UI sequence.

To summarize, a Type 50 CA might be a useful way to install a collection of packages from a CD, by using a parent install to launch them all when you know there will be a UI. But it's not so useful for uninstalls (or installs) where the UI has been suppressed.

Calling Custom Actions with MsiDoAction

You can use the Win32 API MsiDoAction to call CAs:

```
UINT MsiDoAction (MSIHANDLE hInstall, LPCTSTR szAction)
```

The first parameter to this API is a handle to an install. This is the handle that's passed to CAs, either as an explicit parameter to a CA DLL function or as an implicit one via the Session object to scripts. The second parameter to this call is the name of the action. Within a script, you invoke this call using Session.DoAction.

Perhaps the most useful cases when you can use MsiDoAction are those where the conditions on calling the CA are more complicated than can be easily expressed using conditional expressions. You can also become more independent from conditions and actions based on property values by customizing the tables in the MSI package. For example, when the package is created you could populate the Error table with your own data or, perhaps a cleaner design, create your own custom database table and populate it. During the install, you can call a CA to examine the custom data that's specific to the package and use it in your CAs. You can even use your custom data to decide which CAs are to be called using MsiDoAction. In other words, you can build a data-driven approach to installing a package instead of relying too much on combinations of properties and conditions that could be complex and cumbersome to use.

Conditions on Custom Actions

CAs nearly always need conditions because you typically want to run them when the product is being installed or uninstalled, or when a component is being removed or added. The most useful conditions are therefore often based on the following properties.

Installed

The Installed property is initialized if the product is already installed on the system. If you want to run a CA only when the product is first installed, you can use Not Installed as a condition.

REMOVE

The REMOVE property is set when all or part of the product is being removed. It's a list of features, and you use the REMOVE="ALL" condition when the entire product is being used. It's not until after the InstallValidate action that you can safely use a condition based on the REMOVE="ALL" condition, because the REMOVE property isn't fully set until InstallValidate.

Component and Feature Conditions

When you want the CA to be associated with a component (in practice this means a file), you can condition the CA on whether that component is being added or removed. With VS setup projects this type of condition isn't very useful because the component name isn't visible in the IDE, and the generated MSI package isn't one that lets you pick and choose individual components or features. But if you use a tool that does let you choose features to be uninstalled, it's often the case that CAs shouldn't be conditioned on the product as a whole but on the features that are being installed or removed. The most useful conditions for these situations are the action conditions, which tell you what's going to happen to a feature or component in the current install. The most useful values are 2 (INSTALLSTATE_ABSENT), meaning that the feature or component is being uninstalled, and 3 (INSTALLSTATE_LOCAL), meaning that it's being installed. You use the $ and & characters as a prefix to denote a component name or a feature name.

A condition of $ComponentName = 3 is true if the named component is to be installed, and $ComponentName = 2 is true if it's to be uninstalled. Similarly &FeatureName = 2 is true if the named feature is to be uninstalled and &FeatureName = 3 is true if it's to be installed.

Note that the component conditions are based on the intent of the install. If you have a condition such as $ComponentName = 3, this is true if the component is marked to be installed, but the actual file in the component might not be installed if, for example, the Key Path file of the component is of a lower version than an existing one on the target system. Note also that there are sequencing restrictions on use of component and feature conditions in CAs: You cannot safely use them until after the CostFinalize action has run.

The Interaction of Properties, Conditions, and Installation State

If you think about dialogs you've seen that let you pick and choose features, it's obvious that conditions relating to the installation of features and components aren't initialized until after these choices have been made in the UI. In a silent installation where no UI is shown, the features to be installed might have been specified on the command line using ADDLOCAL to name a list of features. Therefore, you must sequence any CAs that are conditioned on feature or component transitions (installed to uninstalled or vice versa) after these determinations are made. In practical terms, this means you must sequence them after the CostFinalize standard action.

The same type of situation happens with some Windows Installer properties. Standard properties associated with the operating system are initialized as the install starts, so checking a property such as VersionNT is always safe. Properties you set up with an AppSearch are available after the AppSearch action. Others need care. You cannot use the SourceDir property until after a ResolveSource action has been done. The installation folder TARGETDIR has a default value that might be changed by the user in the UI. Because most conditions use property values, be aware of the sequence progression of an install and that properties might not contain the values you expect until after some standard action in the sequence sets them.

Summary

You add your own functionality to an install using CAs. Not only is it important to choose the type of CA that best accomplishes the task, but also where you sequence a CA is critical, although VS shields you from these choices by making them deferred at specific places in the execute sequence. CAs are highly dependent on properties because this is how data is passed to them.

CAs do have disadvantages, especially when you can obtain the same result using the standard Windows Installer tables. As discussed in Chapter 1, there are disadvantages to running code during an install because of DLL dependencies, COM dependencies, and the simple fact that your code can crash. It's also true that a CA is a black box to a system administrator, and running black box code with Administrator privilege during an install isn't secure. Add to this the fact that CAs might alter the system, and it's up to the package author to ensure that there's a corresponding Rollback CA. You should get the idea that CAs are very flexible but need to be used responsibly and carefully.

CHAPTER 6

How Do You Fix It?

IT'S SAFE TO ASSUME that at some point you'll need to ship fixes or updates to your application. In this chapter I'll examine some of the ways you can do this. I'm going to start with perhaps the simplest type of upgrade that you can do with VS. In Windows Installer terms, the simplest type of upgrade is a major upgrade, which you trigger in a VS Setup and Deployment project by setting the RemovePreviousVersions project property to True. Later on I'll discuss minor upgrades, and in Chapter 12 I'll describe patches, which are usually the preferred way to ship fixes to a product.

The Major Upgrade

A major upgrade takes the position that the simplest way to update an installed product is to completely uninstall the old version and then install the new version. Windows Installer supplies an automatic mechanism to make this seamless; installing the new version also removes the older one. In Chapter 2 you looked at the GUIDs that are used to define a product and its packaging. In particular, the UpgradeCode GUID is intended to be common across all versions of an upgradeable product, even though the Product code can change. The UpgradeCode is the key to a major upgrade.

A major upgrade requires three key changes to the installation package:

1. The ProductCode GUID must change.

2. The PackageCode GUID must change.

3. The ProductVersion must be changed (and this means incremented).

The UpgradeCode GUID stays the same as previously mentioned.

Internally, in the MSI package, the Upgrade table (together with some standard actions) makes the major upgrade remove the prior version of the product as it installs the new version, but you'll get to that by using VS.

Looking at Notepad's project properties in Figure 6-1, you can see there's a RemovePreviousVersions property. Setting this to True is the way you tell VS you want a major upgrade. Changing the Version property prompts you with a message box confirming whether the ProductCode and PackageCode GUIDs should be changed, and they should. Building this project gives you a completely new product that removes a previous version at install time. Following your usual methodology, look at what was generated in the Upgrade table using Orca, and decipher what VS created here (see Figure 6-2).

Figure 6-1. RemovePreviousVersions property

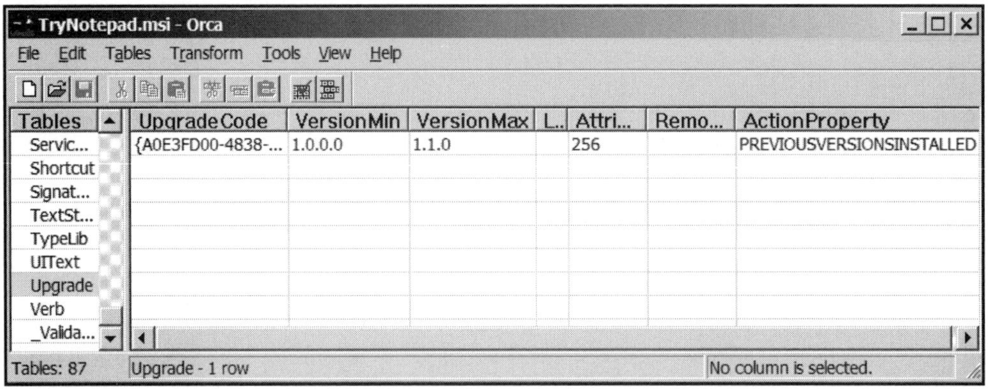

Figure 6-2. The Upgrade table

The UpgradeCode column contains the UpgradeCode GUID that Windows searches for among the products installed on the system. The VersionMin and VersionMax values define the range of versions that, if found, means that there's a prior version to uninstall. The Attributes column refines exactly what is meant by VersionMin—the minimum version—and what to do if a previous product version is found. In this particular case, the value 256 is a flag meaning that VersionMin is included in the range of values that are detected; in other words, version 1.0.0.0 is detected. Similarly, the VersionMax value is the highest version that's searched for, but in this particular case the flag bit (msidbUpgradeAttributesVersionMaxInclusive, 512) isn't set, leaving a search for everything greater than or equal to 1.0.0.0 but less than 1.1.

One of the flags that's conspicuous by its absence is the msidbUpgradeAttributesOnlyDetect flag, which (when set) means that the only purpose of the Upgrade table entries is to detect other versions and not to uninstall them. Whether it uninstalls or not, the key to the mechanism is that detection causes the property named in the ActionProperty column to be set, PREVIOUSVERSIONINSTALLED in this case. VS does one other thing: It adds an entry to the Property table of the package with SecureCustomProperties as the property name and PREVIOUSVERSIONINSTALLED as the value. The purpose of this is to ensure that the PREVIOUSVERSIONINSTALLED property is one of the properties that a non-privileged user can pass to the installation sequence Service process.

When these flags and table entries are in place, this is what happens:

1. The FindRelatedProducts standard action uses the contents of the Upgrade table to search for products with the UpgradeCodes in the table. If a match is found, the ActionProperty value is set. FindRelatedProducts is in both the InstallUISequence and the InstallExecuteSequence so that it's performed when the UI is suppressed, but it's performed only once.

2. The RemoveExistingProducts action uninstalls the previous version of the product if the Attributes value in the Upgrade table attribute isn't marked with the "detect only" flag, msidbUpgradeAttributesOnlyDetect.

Note that VS setups have a single feature, so the MigrateFeatureStates standard action isn't relevant. In a multifeature install, this action is useful because it preserves the features that were already installed. This action uses the Upgrade table to match the new incoming product with the prior one being replaced. When the msidbUpgradeAttributesMigrateFeatures bit is set in the Attributes value of the matching product in the Upgrade table, MigrateFeatureStates causes the features installed by the new product to match the features that were installed by the old product.

That's the big picture, and as far as using VS to perform a major upgrade that's about it. However, there are some details to look at.

If you look at the documentation for the RemoveExistingProducts action, it talks about a number of places that this action can be sequenced within the installation. VS sequences it just after the InstallInitialize action; one of the other choices is between InstallValidate and InstallInitialize. Both of these places have the same overall result for a successful install: The previous product is uninstalled and then the new incoming version is installed. This is the straightforward approach, compared to the other possibility of sequencing the action after InstallFinalize. The documentation describes this as the most efficient place to sequence RemoveExistingProducts because the major upgrade replaces only the files that need updating (because the new file versions are higher).

One of the difficulties with sequencing RemoveExistingProducts after InstallFinalize relates to CAs. RemoveExistingProducts effectively runs the uninstallation of the previous product, including any CAs. If there are CAs that are specifically designed to clean up at uninstall time, you don't want them to run after InstallFinalize on a newly installed version of the product—they'll most likely remove something that's just been installed. This means that you need to be careful when putting conditions on these uninstall CAs. This is where the UPGRADINGPRODUCTCODE property is useful, and there's an example of its use in the next section, "Preserving Data Across Major Upgrades."

Another point to keep in mind about this efficient sequencing of RemoveExistingProducts is whether you need it or not. The efficiency is based on the idea that some of the files in the new product are the same as the ones in the product being replaced and therefore might not need replacing. I suspect that in most cases you will have a newer product that has rebuilt a substantial number of the program files and given them higher versions, so they'll replace all the older versions anyway.

The result of a major upgrade rollback is highly dependent on the sequencing of the RemoveExistingProducts action. The entire major upgrade has two steps: removing the old product and installing the new one, although not necessarily in that order. When considering the result of a rollback of a major upgrade, the key point is whether you sequence RemoveExistingProducts between InstallInitialize and InstallFinalize, which is where the audited script actions are generated (see the section "The Execute Sequence" in Chapter 5). If RemoveExistingProducts is audited for recovery when the new product is being installed, the rollback restores the old product. Take a look at the four possible positions where you can sequence RemoveExistingProducts, and its effect on a rollback:

1. You sequence RemoveExistingProducts *before* InstallInitialize, and it therefore isn't audit scripted in the new product's execute sequence. This sequencing means that the old product is removed in its entirety before the new product is installed. If the uninstall of the old product fails, the uninstall rolls back (using the *old* product's rollback), and the entire major upgrade finishes. This leaves the old product on the system. If the old product removal is successful and then the new product install fails, the new product install rolls back (using the new product's rollback), and leaves the system with none of the products installed. The rollback does *not* roll back the removal of the old product and reinstall it. Note that because these two steps are an entire uninstall followed by an entire install, this process is potentially inefficient because files that haven't changed versions are removed and reinstalled.

2. You sequence RemoveExistingProducts *after* InstallFinalize, and therefore it isn't audit scripted in the execute sequence. This means that the new product is installed, and then the old product is uninstalled. This is potentially more efficient because files that haven't changed versions aren't copied twice. The install of the new product could roll back; this leaves the old product on the system because RemoveExistingProducts hasn't yet removed the old product. However, if the removal of the old product then fails, this removal rolls back (using the old product's rollback) and restores the old product. At this point you now have the new product and the old product installed, and this is how the system remains.

3. You sequence RemoveExistingProducts *after* InstallInitialize but before any of the actions that generate script actions. This means that the old product is uninstalled, then the new product is installed. Note that the removal of the old product is now in the audit-scripted part of the new product install. So, if the old product removal rolls back (using its own rollback), it restores the old product and the major upgrade terminates, leaving the old product on the system. If the new product install (after removal of the old product) fails and rolls back, the new product's rollback includes RemoveExistingProducts in its audit script, so the old product is restored because RemoveExistingProducts is rolled back.

4. You sequence RemoveExistingProducts after InstallInitialize, but between InstallExecute (or InstallExecuteAgain) and InstallFinalize, and therefore it's still within the audit-scripted part of the new product install. The new product is installed, then the old product uninstalled. If the install of the new product fails, it rolls back and the major upgrade terminates, leaving the old product on the system. If the old

product removal fails after the new product has successfully installed, the new product install rolls back. This rollback includes RemoveExistingProducts in its audit script, and therefore the old product *is* restored.

There's no *functional* difference between the preceding cases three and four; the result is the same no matter what rolls back. However, case three, where RemoveExistingProducts is sequenced before any scripted actions in the execute sequence, is potentially less efficient than case four because case three uninstalls the entire old product. Compared with case four, there's no optimization for files that don't need replacing.

VS's implementation of the major upgrade assumes that the previous version has a major version of 1, as you can see from Figure 6-2. It can't know the version of the product that's already installed and that will be replaced, and it doesn't give you an IDE choice to specify it. So, it assumes that the original's major version is 1, and that's what it looks for. The major upgrade therefore won't work if your original version is something like 0.9.

Something else to watch out for is whether the product has been installed for the current user ("Just me" in the install dialog) or for all users ("Everyone" in the install dialog). If you install the first version for Everyone and then install your major upgrade for Just me, you'll find yourself with two versions of the product on the system. That's because a per-user install doesn't upgrade a per-system install (and vice versa). At the time of writing this is an issue with VS.NET setup projects, but not VS 2003. If you generate a setup project with VS.NET and use your trusty friend Orca to look at the InstallUISequence, FindRelatedProducts is sequenced up front, just after AppSearch. But at this point there has been no user dialog asking whether this is a per-user or per-machine installation. The Windows Installer default is per-user, and I've just said that a per-user install won't upgrade a per-machine install. Whatever you say in the Everyone/Just me dialog, it's too late because FindRelatedProducts has already decided that it won't upgrade. So if you're trying a major upgrade to a per-machine setup in VS.NET, you'll need to update to VS 2003 to detour this problem. Now that you understand the mechanism behind the major upgrade, the most straightforward way of fixing this in a VS.NET MSI package is to move FindRelatedProducts. I said that FindRelatedProducts is in the wrong place, so go to the InstallUISequence table with Orca and juggle the sequence numbers to put FindRelatedProducts just before ExecuteAction. That causes FindRelatedProducts to take account of what was specified in the Everyone/Just me dialog.

By the way, if you take a look at the InstallExecuteSequence table, you'll see that FindRelatedProducts is sequenced before the LaunchConditions action, as is AppSearch. The advantage of this is that sometimes it can be useful to have FindRelatedProducts *before* the LaunchConditions action so that you can have a Launch Condition based on the properties created by FindRelatedProducts when it processes the Upgrade table. In other words, both AppSearch and FindRelatedProducts can be used to set properties that can in turn be used in the LaunchConditions action. The Upgrade table is far more flexible than just a mechanism to perform a major upgrade: It can detect other versions of your own (or other) products on the system, as you'll see next.

As well as the RemovePreviousVersions property in Figure 6-1, notice that there's a DetectNewerInstalledVersion property. When set to True, this works in exactly the same way as the detection of older versions that you used to trigger a major upgrade (VS adds another entry to the Upgrade table), but this one is designed to prevent you from installing an old version of the product over a newer version. The assumption here is that it's probably a mistake for a user to attempt to install an old version when a newer version is already installed. In any case, if that's what you really want to do, then it just means prompting the user to uninstall the new version, if that's the intent.

The contents of the Upgrade table are the same UpgradeCode repeated (see Figure 6-3). However, the contents of the VersionMin column (1.1.0) and the Attributes column are set to detect a version greater than the VersionMin value, and VersionMax is null, meaning any higher version is detected. This is the entry generated by the DetectNewerInstalledVersion property in VS. Notice also that the Attributes column has the value 258 that includes the msidbUpgradeAttributesOnlyDetect bit. As the name implies, this bit causes only detection of the corresponding UpgradeCode to occur; no removal is done.

Tables	▲	UpgradeCode	VersionMin	VersionMax	Attribut...	Remo...	ActionProperty
TypeLib		{A0E3FD00-4838-...	1.1.0		258		NEWERPRODUCTFOUND
UIText		{A0E3FD00-4838-...	1.0.0.0	1.1.0	256		PREVIOUSVERSIONSIN...
Upgrade							
Verb							
_Valid...							

Figure 6-3. Upgrade table detecting newer version

These values in the Upgrade table don't accomplish anything except the setting of the ActionProperty NEWERPRODUCTFOUND, but if you go to the CustomAction table and the InstallExecuteSequence, you'll see that VS generated a Type 19 CA (ERRCA_CANCELNEWERVERSION) that's called if NEWERPRODUCTFOUND is set. A Type 19 CA terminates the installation with an error message. This is where you could put your message telling users that if they really want to install the older version of the product, they should uninstall the newer version first. The text of this message is in the Property table, associated with the property VSDVERSIONMSG.

Note also that the Property table has a SecureCustomProperties value that contains both of the properties named in the Upgrade table, separated by a semicolon: PREVIOUSVERSIONSINSTALLED;NEWERPRODUCTFOUND. This allows the properties named in the list to be transferred from the UI sequence into the server stage of the install.

These are the advantages of a major upgrade:

- Because it's an entirely new product, you're free to change the name of the product package MSI file (not the case with a minor upgrade).

- It's easier for the end user because the installation process simply involves installing the package, which detects older versions and replaces them if necessary.

- The content of the package—its features and components—might be completely different. You can use a major upgrade to replace a product with a new and completely different one, or you could use it as a convenient way to update an existing product. If you do a total replacement (the sequencing of RemoveExistingProducts is what determines this), the new product can have completely different component GUIDs, subject to any component sharing with other products.

The main disadvantage of a major upgrade is that you're shipping the entire product to your customers, which might be inconvenient for Internet deployment. It's a heavyweight solution compared to some of the more advanced methods of shipping fixes.

Preserving Data Across Major Upgrades

A major upgrade to an installed product is for all intents and purposes an uninstall of the existing product, followed by an install of the new product. There's a subtle issue here. An uninstall is supposed to remove the entire product—its files and Registry entries—but in the major upgrade situation you might need to preserve some of these. The user might have updated Registry entries or modified data files that need to be available to provide a seamless transition to the newer version.

You can prepare for this in the original install by using the UPGRADINGPRODUCTCODE property, the property that means the product is being removed because of a major upgrade. Windows Installer sets this property to the ProductCode GUID of the product that's replacing it, and it isn't set during a remove from Add/Remove Programs or any other type of standalone uninstall. This means that if you have CAs that remove data that the incoming product needs, you can condition them on a condition such as REMOVE="ALL" AND NOT UPGRADINGPRODUCTCODE. The other approach you can take here is to have a CA conditioned on UPGRADINGPRODUCTCODE that preserves data in some well-known location where the incoming product can find it.

CAs that run during an uninstall usually work best when they're immediate CAs. This is because the actual process of removing the pieces of the product doesn't happen until the deferred phase, when the uninstall script is being processed (see Chapter 5). Therefore, if you need to preserve anything from the original product, it's best to use an immediate CA sequenced, for example, just after InstallInitialize in the InstallExecuteSequence table. Although VS's uninstall CAs are deferred, they're sequenced early enough in the InstallExecuteSequence that the product's files and Registry entries are still on the system when the CA runs.

One of the ways to preserve Registry entries across a major upgrade is to use regedit.exe in a CA. Although regedit.exe is usually associated with a GUI to look at the Registry, it has a silent mode and command-line options to create a REG file containing a Registry key. To save the data to a known location, use a Type 50 CA to run regedit.exe with a command line such as this:

```
regedit /e yoursettings.reg HKEY_LOCAL_MACHINE\Software\YourKey
```

To restore the entries later, you can use the equivalent of this, where the /s switch means to be silent and not display a confirmation dialog:

```
regedit /s yoursettings.reg
```

To be explicit about the location of the created file, prefix the file name with the installer property [TempFolder], which is resolved at run time to the actual "temp" path.

Minor Upgrade by Reinstalling

Instead of performing a major upgrade, you can use a minor upgrade to update the existing product on the system by reinstalling it. Because this is an update, the ProductCode stays the same, but you must change the PackageCode and ProductVersion. In addition, you cannot change the name of the package: the MSI file. You need to be careful in the VS environment because changing the Version in the project's properties, which becomes the installer's ProductVersion property, prompts you to change the ProductCode—which you don't want to change—and the PackageCode—which you do want to change. The safest course of action is to increment the project's Version property, accept the changes of those codes, and then set the ProductCode property back to the same value as the original product you're updating.

If you run the resulting package, you'll see the standard message box reporting that another version of the product is already installed, because a product with the same ProductCode is already installed and this product you just built has a different package code. The way to install these updates is with a command-line run of the Windows Installer executable Msiexec.exe, passing some properties that specify what's being updated and how. Here's a typical command line to do this:

```
Msiexec /I <path to new MSI package> REINSTALL=ALL REINSTALLMODE=vomus
```

It's worth noting before you examine this command line that it says nothing about file locations or where the product is installed. You might also have a product containing multiple features, some of which aren't installed. The way this update works is that for this particular ProductCode, Windows looks at each feature and component to see if it's installed on the system. It knows where each component is located because of the KeyPath settings for each component.

The REINSTALL property is the most straightforward. It's a list of the features that are to be reinstalled, meaning they'll be updated. The word ALL means that all the features are to be updated, but if you happen to know the features that have been updated, you can list them here, separated by commas. In VS setup projects there's only one feature anyway, so ALL is the only practical choice. In multifeature packages, if you knew exactly which features had been updated in the new package, you could explicitly name them as an optimization. In tools that let you build multifeature packages, Windows Installer allows addition of a new feature, but to install a new feature in a minor upgrade you need to name the feature with the ADDLOCAL property as well as explicitly list all the features in the REINSTALL property.

The REINSTALLMODE property consists of a list of attributes that specifies how the updates should be installed, where each letter defines some behavior of the installation. Most of this behavior deals with the replacement (or not) of files that the prior version of the product installed. The letter o in that list is one of several choices in this area of file replacement, and it's the most reasonable choice, given the scenario that you're updating an existing product. The o means that files from the updated package are to be installed if the version already on the system has a lower version or is missing. The other choices for file replacement are *p, e, d, c,* or *a.* These are documented in the Windows Installer SDK, but briefly the *p* means reinstall if the file is missing, the *e* means reinstall if the file is missing or is equal or older in version, the *d* means reinstall if the file is missing or is a different version, *c* causes a reinstall if the file is missing or corrupt as defined by its checksum, and a causes an unconditional reinstall of all files no matter what version the prior one is. The big picture here is that for each component in the new package, Windows Installer decides whether to replace the existing file already present on the system based on the REINSTALLMODE specification and the file versioning and overwrite rules.

The m and u values cause Registry updates to be performed. In particular, u applies to entries in the Registry table that are targeted at the HKEY_CURRENT_USER or HKEY_USERS keys, and the m applies to more of the package tables that update the Registry, such as the Class table. The s marks shortcuts to be updated and the v indicates that the package is to be recached. This recaching is important because it's at the heart of the way Windows Installer packages are managed. If you don't recache the package, Windows Installer runs the cached MSI package for the already installed product with this same ProductCode instead of using your new package.

The behavior of a minor upgrade is somewhat like a merge of the installed product with the new version of the product, although the analogy isn't exact. The contents of the incoming package are "merged" with the existing product installed on the system in the sense that files and Registry entries are replaced (or not) depending on the settings of REINSTALLMODE. This all works at the installer component level, and consequently it's a bad idea to reorganize or change components. After all, this is a minor upgrade that's intended to replace some of the files with newer versions. Adding files to existing components, deleting components, or reorganizing the arrangement of components within features isn't appropriate for a minor upgrade. Once you've installed a product with a set of components (with their KeyPaths) and features, it's then dangerous to update that product with a different arrangement of components and features, or missing or altered components. The Windows Installer section of the Platform SDK documents how to organize applications into components and discusses the consequences of breaking component rules.

When you perform a minor upgrade with a VS setup, the upgrade's behavior can be confusing. It displays a maintenance dialog showing Repair or Remove choices, with Repair selected as the default. In fact, this is the minor upgrade taking place, even though it looks like a repair. Unfortunately, it isn't clear from this dialog whether you have correctly configured the minor upgrade, because you'll see this dialog if you're in maintenance mode, as opposed to performing a minor upgrade to update the product. VS doesn't expose the Maintenance form (the source of this dialog) in the user interface, so there's not much you can do to correct this confusion. But if you know that the new package correctly does a minor update of the installed product, you can append /q to the Msiexec command line to suppress all user dialogs, or /qb to show a progress bar during the update.

Component Rules and the Minor Upgrade

One of the major areas of difficulty with new versions relates to components. Windows manages an installed product in terms of the product's components, features, and their relationships and reference counts. A major upgrade is usually less troublesome because you can arrange for the new incoming product to replace the older one completely, but the minor upgrade you're about to look at is more fragile. You should see a minor upgrade primarily as a replacement of existing components, although it can also add new components. The component's GUID is critical here, because it's what identifies a component. Because VS doesn't expose component GUIDs in its IDE, it can be easy to create a minor upgrade that breaks component rules and consequently leaves reference counts broken with unpredictable effects. In VS you might start with the original setup project and decide to add a new version of a file to replace an older version. VS is good at preserving component GUIDs when you add and delete files, so the best approach is not to create a minor upgrade by creating a brand-new setup project, but to start with the previous one and simply put new files at the location where the build expects them. Although it's true that a minor upgrade will replace files if needed, it's more important to realize that you're really replacing components of the previously installed product.

Before Windows Installer 2.0, there was no support for adding a component to an existing feature, and VS setup projects have only one feature. This means that if you add a new file—or in fact anything, such as a Registry entry, that results in the creation of a new component—to a setup project and try to use it for a minor upgrade, you need to ensure that you do this with a minimum Windows Installer version of 2.0.

Similarly, you shouldn't delete files (and therefore components) during a minor upgrade. Presumably the file is being deleted because it's no longer used, so just keep on installing it to preserve the component rules, and delete it at your next major upgrade.

VS setups help you obey component rules by not exposing too much of the inner mechanics in VS's IDE. Other tools that build MSI packages might give you more flexibility in the construction of components, and expose the details of components. You still need to apply component rules, and when you're working at that level you need to understand some of the exceptions to these rules. For example, you can add new files to a component with these tools. This does break the component rules even though technically you can do this if you're sure that the component isn't shared with any other products.

Versions and Version Lying

A lower version of a file won't normally replace an existing higher version on the target system. It's probably fair to say that the entire infrastructure of updating versioned files onto a system has always depended on the rule that a higher-versioned file replaces an existing one with a lower version. This is why you should avoid using the *a* option in REINSTALLMODE, because it causes all existing versioned files to be replaced, regardless of versioning rules.

A technique to force installation of a lower (or same) versioned file is to change the file's version in the Version column of the File table. The installer uses this version when deciding to replace or not, so you can manipulate this to achieve the desired result. However, the version of the file that gets installed on the system using this technique doesn't match the version in the File table— that's what you've lied about—so Windows Installer attempts to repair the file if a repair or reinstall occurs. There's nothing inherently wrong with this, but note that the repair operation needs access to the source MSI package to reinstall what appears to be an incorrectly versioned file.

Minor Upgrades and Data Files

You can find two contradictory situations when you ship a new version of a product that you want to update with a minor update.

1. The user might have updated the prior version of the product-shipped data (for example a database), and you don't want the new version to replace it.

2. You *do* want to replace the prior version of the product-installed data files but they aren't versioned, so how can you replace them?

You generally don't need to worry about the first case because of the Windows Installer overwrite rules as they apply to data files: A file isn't overwritten if its modification time is different from its creation time (my use of time here includes the date). The assumption here is that a user has modified the file so it shouldn't be replaced. The other assumption here, which isn't quite so obvious, is why the creation and modification time would be the same anyway. The answer to that is that Windows Installer installs the file with identical modify and create times. (If the modify and create times are different when you add the file to the setup project, the modify time is typically after the create time, so an installed data file has modify and create times that are identical, and the same as the file's original modify time.)

However, the second case, replacing a file that might have been updated, is more problematic. The overwrite rules as they apply to data files take place in the context of REINSTALLMODE=vomus, where the "o" effectively means to reinstall files using the standard overwrite rules as they apply to versioned and nonversioned files. If you want to replace data files during a minor update, you could substitute "a" for "o," which would result in unconditional replacement of all files, not just data files. This has the potentially undesirable effect of replacing higher-versioned files with lower versions from the new incoming package.

One solution is to alter the dates of the data files in the installed product. This isn't particularly elegant, but it's fairly straightforward to run a program that uses the SetFileTime Win32 API, as in the following example code:

```
int _tmain(int argc, _TCHAR* argv[])
{
FILETIME willbeNow = {0};
SYSTEMTIME st = {0};
GetSystemTime (&st);
SystemTimeToFileTime (&st, &willbeNow);
HANDLE hFile = CreateFile (TEXT("sometextfile.txt"), FILE_WRITE_ATTRIBUTES,
FILE_SHARE_READ, NULL, OPEN_EXISTING, FILE_ATTRIBUTE_NORMAL, NULL);
if (hFile == INVALID_HANDLE_VALUE)
{
    DWORD gle = GetLastError();
    return gle;
}
BOOL res = SetFileTime(hFile, &willbeNow, &willbeNow, &willbeNow);
// Error checking code omitted
CloseHandle (hFile);
return 0;
}
```

Doing this to the data files before the minor upgrade sets the dates to identical values, so you could make this code part of a launch program that resets the dates and then launches the installation of the minor upgrade. You need to know where the files are installed, so this is another place where the component GUID is your friend because you can use the MsiGetComponentPath Win32 API call to retrieve its location on the system.

Your distribution medium and mechanism are important in these kinds of scenarios. It's relatively easy to alter files on the system from a program if you distribute your minor upgrade as a CD or self-extracting package so that you can run your program before you perform the actual minor upgrade. But in a software distribution system that uses only the MSI package, you can't run your program.

You could also add a CA to remove the data files early in the installation, or change the dates using the preceding code in a CA. However, the problem with this approach is that VS's install CAs are not only deferred, but are also sequenced toward the end of the install process, and the decision not to overwrite the data files has already been made by the time your CA runs. This means you must use Orca to resequence the CA so that it takes place before the overwrite decisions are made, which means before InstallFiles in the InstallExecuteSequence table. Also, don't forget that there are always security issues when you access the system from a CA, so you need to be sure that your CA (running by default under the installing user's account) has the privilege to alter the installed files. It might be necessary to make your CA run without impersonation in the system context by using the msidbCustomActionTypeNoImpersonate bit in the Type value of the CA. However, see the section "Security and Custom Actions" in Chapter 5 that details the conditions under which you can do this.

The best way to force removal of files is to use the RemoveFile table. You can populate this table with the files you want to remove during the minor upgrade. The reason it works is that this table is processed during the RemoveFiles action, which is sequenced during the first part of the execute sequence before any new files are installed. Figure 6-4 shows the RemoveFile table values to remove the data file called Sometextfile.txt during a minor upgrade. The reasonable value to put in the Component_ column is the one associated with the new version of the file being removed. The FileName column contains the file name, the DirProperty has the containing folder name as a key into the Directory table, and the InstallMode value of 1 means that this particular row of the RemoveFile table is processed only during an install. If you take an installer log of the removal you'll see something such as this:

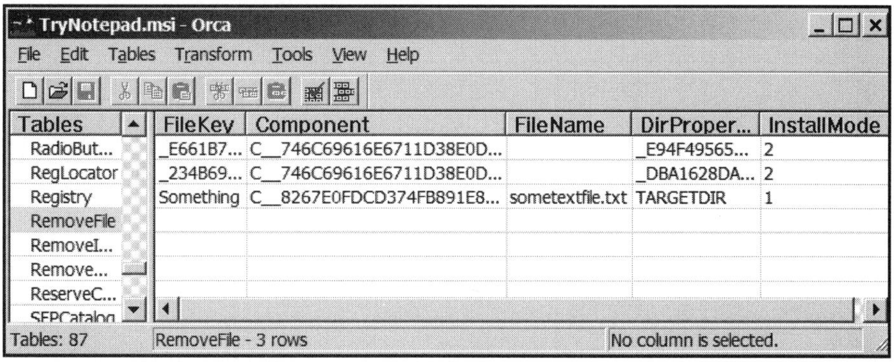

Figure 6-4. RemoveFile table

125

```
MSI (s) (CC:9C): Executing op: SetTargetFolder
                (Folder=C:\Program Files\Phil\TryNotepad\)
MSI (s) (CC:9C): Executing op: FileRemove(,FileName=SomeTextFile.txt,,)
RemoveFiles: File: SomeTextFile.txt, Directory: C:\Program Files\
                Phil\TryNotepad\
MSI (s) (CC:9C): Verifying accessibility of file: SomeTextFile.txt
MSI (s) (CC:9C): Executing op: ActionStart(Name=InstallFiles,
        Description=Copying new files,Template=File: , Directory: , Size: )
Action 15:43:05: InstallFiles. Copying new files
```

Companion Files

Companion files are a mechanism to derive the overwrite rules for a particular file from another file. This means that you could force installation of a data file by having it be a companion of a versioned file that you know is going to be installed. To illustrate this, you can combine the companion files mechanism with version lying for a minor update of the Notepad installation, as seen in Figure 6-5.

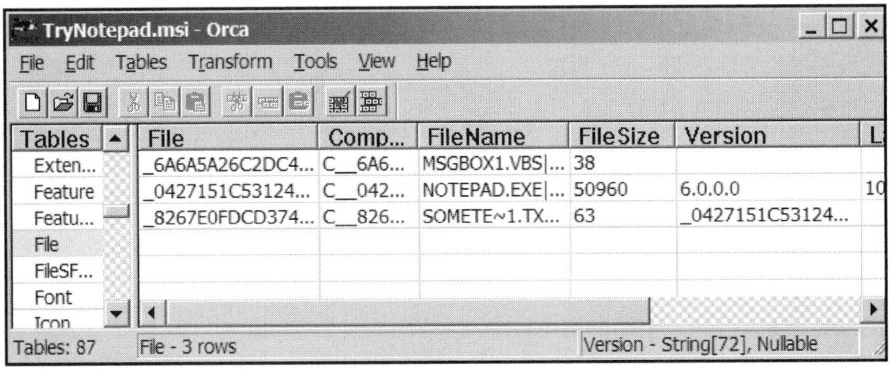

Figure 6-5. Version lying in the File table

The version of Notepad.exe has been increased beyond its actual version, and the Version column for the text file contains the File key for Notepad.exe. There's an issue here related to VS's creation of components and key paths that you must correct: A key path file must not derive its version from another file. But the file Sometextfile.txt is the key path of its own component. The easiest way to resolve this with a VS-generated package is to go to the Component table for Sometextfile.txt and make its KeyPath column null. If you do this and perform a minor upgrade with REINSTALL=ALL and REINSTALLMODE=vomus, the text file is replaced even though the user might have updated it and made its modify time different from its create time. If you produce a log during the minor upgrade, you'll see something like this code saying that Notepad.exe will be overwritten:

```
FileCopy(SourceName=NOTEPAD.EXE|NOTEPAD.EXE,SourceCabKey=_0427151C53124
FC691215A79025A4B10,DestName=NOTEPAD.EXE,Attributes=512,FileSize=50960,PerTi
ck=32768,,VerifyMedia=1,,,,,CheckCRC=0,Version=6.0.0.0,Language=1033,
InstallMode=1 26091264,,,,,,)
MSI (s) (98:B0): File: C:\Program Files\Phil\TryNotepad\NOTEPAD.EXE;
                 Overwrite;  No patch;  Existing file is a lower version
```

And this is where the version lying about Notepad.exe caused it to replace the already installed version:

```
MSI (s) (98:B0): Executing op: SetCompanionParent
  (ParentPath=C:\Program Files\Phil\TryNotepad\,ParentName=NOTEPAD.EXE,
                 ParentVersion=6.0.0.0,ParentLanguage=1033)
MSI (s) (98:B0): Executing op:
                 FileCopy(SourceName=SOMETE~1.TXT|SomeTextFile.txt,
                   SourceCabKey=_8267E0FDCD374FB891E8BAC45218DB0B,
                   DestName=SomeTextFile.txt,Attributes=512,FileSize=63,
                   PerTick=32768,,          VerifyMedia=1,,,,,CheckCRC=0,
                   Version=_0427151C53124FC691215A79025A4B10,,
                 InstallMode=126091264,,,,,,)
MSI (s) (98:B0): File: C:\Program Files\Phil\TryNotepad\SomeTextFile.txt;
                 Overwrite;  No patch;  Existing file is a lower version
                 (Checked using version of companion:
                   C:\Program  Files\Phil\TryNotepad\NOTEPAD.EXE)
```

This is where the log confirms that SomeTextFile.txt has Notepad.exe as its companion, and that it will be installed because Notepad.exe is being installed. That's because the incoming Notepad.exe has a higher version (the version lying value) than the Notepad.exe on the system.

Uses of Minor Upgrades

Just like a major upgrade, a minor upgrade is a heavyweight solution when perhaps there are only a few changes between the older version and the new one. However, a minor upgrade consists of the entire product, so you could ship it together with a launching program that detects whether an older version of the product is already on the system. The launching program then launches the MSI package as a minor upgrade if it's already installed, or installs it as new product if there is no older product. On the other hand, the MSI package might be intended strictly for use as a minor upgrade only. If this is the case, then you can prevent it from being used as a fresh install of the product in several ways: You can search for the previously installed product or its components, and add launch conditions and CAs (such as a Type 19 error) to terminate the install.

Summary

You can update a product by rebuilding the install package with the product's updated files and then reinstalling the entire package with either a minor upgrade or a major upgrade. These methods aren't the most efficient in some ways, primarily because the entire package must be supplied, but they're relatively convenient for the developer. When the size of the change is small compared to the original product, Windows Installer lets you create patches, the subject of Chapter 12.

CHAPTER 7

ASP.NET Setups

IN THIS CHAPTER, you'll build a basic ASP.NET Web page application, and then create a VS Web Setup and Deployment project for it. As in Chapter 2, after the build you'll dissect the setup and see how it works underneath and how you can use what you learn.

The Web Project

The ASP.NET sample project is just a basic form containing a textbox and a button; clicking the button displays the current time in the textbox. You add a Web Setup project to the ASP.NET solution by selecting the solution in the Solution Explorer, choosing Add New Project, and then selecting Web Setup Project as shown in Figure 7-1.

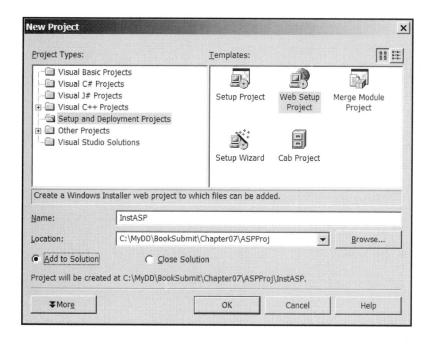

Figure 7-1. VS's Web Setup Project wizard

You need not specify the input to the Web Setup project as files—you can say that the output from the ASP project is the input to the Setup project.

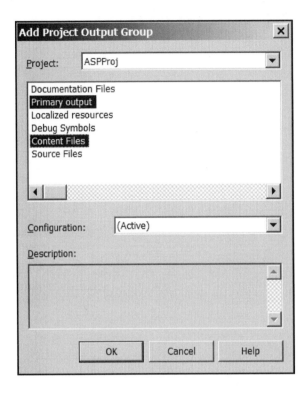

Figure 7-2. Adding Primary output to the Setup project

You do this by selecting the Setup project in the Solution Explorer and then choosing Project ➤ Add ➤ Project Output, as in Figure 7-2. Select Primary output and Content Files (use the Control key to select more than one). Selecting only Primary output includes the generated DLL but not the Web pages.

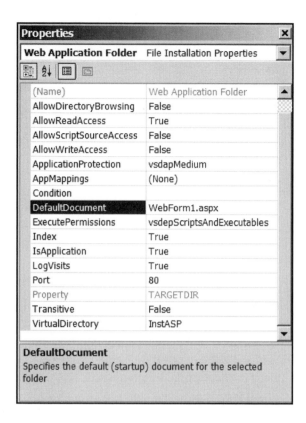

Figure 7-3. Web Application Folder properties

You need to specify the default properties for the Web Application Folder, in particular the default document, which appropriately enough is default.aspx unless you change it. Figure 7-3 shows these properties, with the name of your form in the DefaultDocument property. Note that there's a VirtualDirectory property where the ASP.NET project will be installed.

At this point you can build the solution. Note that VS doesn't seem to mark the Setup project to be built as part of the solution's build, so use the Build menu's Configuration Manager to mark the Setup project to be built. In addition, you're assuming you don't need a bootstrapping executable to install the Windows Installer Service, so in the project's Property Pages select a Bootstrapper value of None.

To understand how this setup works, you'll examine the package using Orca. Starting at the beginning, there's an entry in the AppSearch table and a corresponding search in the RegLocator table to get the version of Internet Information Services (IIS).

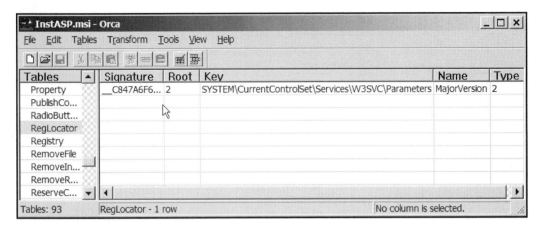

Figure 7-4. Searching for the IIS version

A Registry search here looks at the value of MajorVersion in the HKLM key shown in Figure 7-4. This search sets the IISVERSION property to the value found there. Examining the LaunchCondition table reveals that this install won't proceed unless the condition IISVERSION >= "#4" is met. Notice that the # is present because that MajorVersion value in the Registry is of type REG_DWORD and is therefore returned to the install in that format. In other words, the install won't start unless the system is using IIS version 4 or greater.

If you run this setup, notice that there isn't the radio button choice in other deployment projects that asks whether this install is being done for Everyone or Just me. If you look in the package's Property table, you'll see an entry ALLUSERS with a value of 2. This value means that a per-machine install is done if the installing user is an administrator, otherwise a per-user install is done. Because you probably don't want a per-user install of an ASP.NET application, it might be useful to add your own LaunchCondition of Privileged to ensure a per-machine install.

Another thing to notice is that the install doesn't give you a choice of where to install the application. Clearly the ASP.NET application will be installed into the IIS folder, but what if you have other files you want to install somewhere? If you go to the VS Setup project and right-click the File System on Target Machine text, you'll see an Add Special Folder choice that offers a list of the well-known standard folder locations, such as Common Files Folder, User's Desktop, and User's Application Data Folder. If your other files belong here, go ahead and use them. However, you can also use the Custom Folder choice for more flexibility. Figure 7-5 shows the properties of a custom folder named MyLoc.

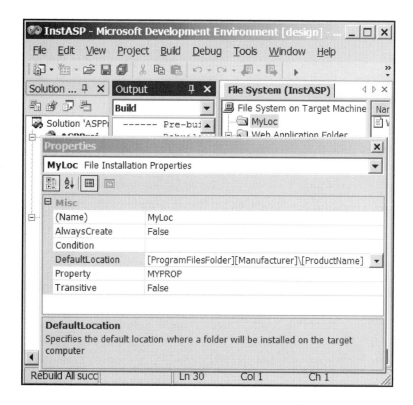

Figure 7-5. Custom folder properties

The DefaultLocation value is a concatenated list of standard installer properties in square brackets, most notably Manufacturer and ProductName, the values of which you can define in the project's properties. If you're wondering why no slash follows [ProgramFilesFolder], it's because installer folder properties already include the trailing slash. There's also a Property specification there, MYPROP.

The DefaultLocation value is resolved at install time to the actual location on the target system, but what's MYPROP for? The way it works is that the location specified in DefaultLocation is indeed just the default. For example, you can use a command-line install to set the MYPROP location:

```
msiexec /i  "C:\MyFiles\InstASP\InstASP.msi" MYPROP=c:\TEMP\MYFOLDER
```

This causes the install location of your custom folder to be C:\TEMP\MYFOLDER instead of that default. You can also get a value into MYPROP by using a search technique that gets a folder path from the Registry with a Registry Search or a Windows Installer Search for an installer component (see Chapter 4).

You can see how MYPROP is put together by looking at the package with Orca. In the CustomAction table there's an entry:

```
Action            Type    Source   Target
DIRCA_MYPROP      307     MYPROP   [ProgramFilesFolder][Manufacturer]\[ProductName]
```

This is a Type 51 CA with the "execute once" option (51+256) so that it's only performed once if the CA is present in both InstallUISequence and InstallExecuteSequence tables, which it is. This CA sets the value of MYPROP to the Target value. In the sequence tables VS generates a call to the CA like this:

```
Action            Condition        Sequence
DIRCA_MYPROP      MYPROP=""        754
```

This means that this CA is called only if MYPROP hasn't been initialized, which is how you get the choice to set it in some other way. Because MYPROP is a directory, there's also an entry in the Directory table, and the Component table has an entry for files in this folder with a Directory value of MYPROP.

Looking at the CustomAction table in this setup, it's clear that a lot of functionality is being performed by calls to a DLL (Type 1) in the Binary table (see Figure 7-6).

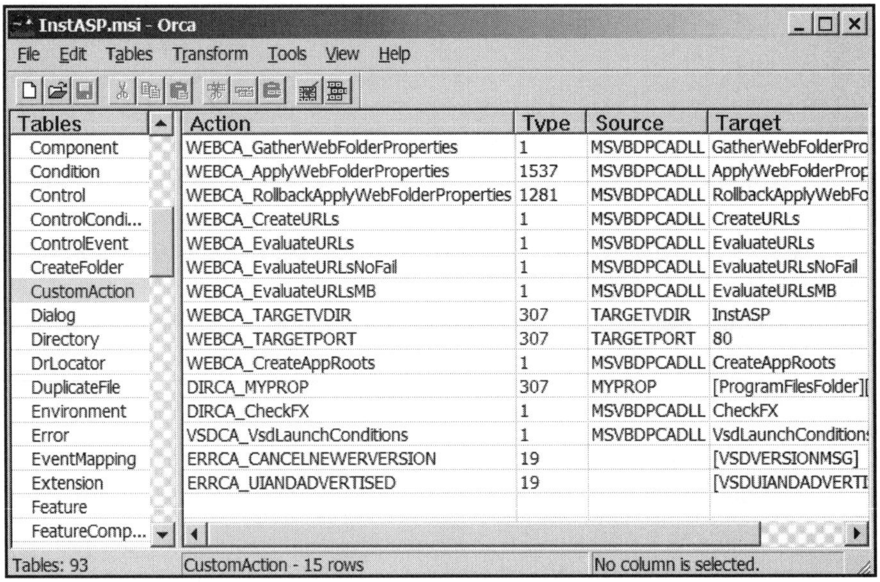

Figure 7-6. CAs in Web setup

Although you cannot do much about what happens inside those CAs, you can use some property names, TARGETVDIR and TARGETPORT, that are set to the default values shown, InstASP and 80. If you look in the InstallExecuteSequence and the InstallUISequence tables for the two CAs—WEBCA_TARGETVDIR and WEBCA_TARGETPORT—you'll see that they're both conditioned like this:

```
Action                 Condition          Sequence
WEBCA_TARGETVDIR       TARGETVDIR=""         750
WEBCA_TARGETPORT       TARGETPORT=""         750
```

These have the same format as the MYPROP example you just looked at, so you can set both of these properties in the same ways. If you wanted to perform a silent install of this Web application and specify Virtual directory or Port values other than the defaults, you can specify new values on a command-line install. Incidentally, those CAs do have the same sequence value of 750 in a package generated with VS 2003. Although the sequence value doesn't matter in this case because they have no dependency order, having the same value isn't good practice.

I can't mention TARGETVDIR and TARGETPORT without looking at the UI dialog where you can set them (see Figure 7-7).

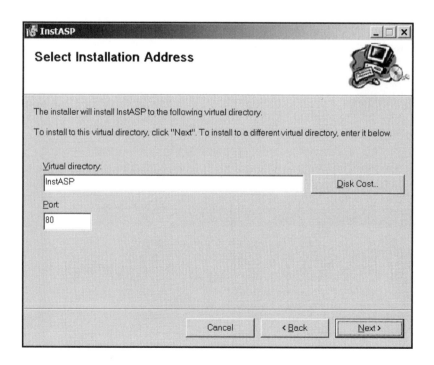

Figure 7-7. Selecting Virtual directory and Port

In the package, this is the WebFolderForm dialog; it has an entry of this name in the Dialog table. It's more interesting to note that in the Control table, those two property names are associated with the contents of the VDirEdit and PortEdit controls on the WebFolderForm dialog (see Figure 7-8).

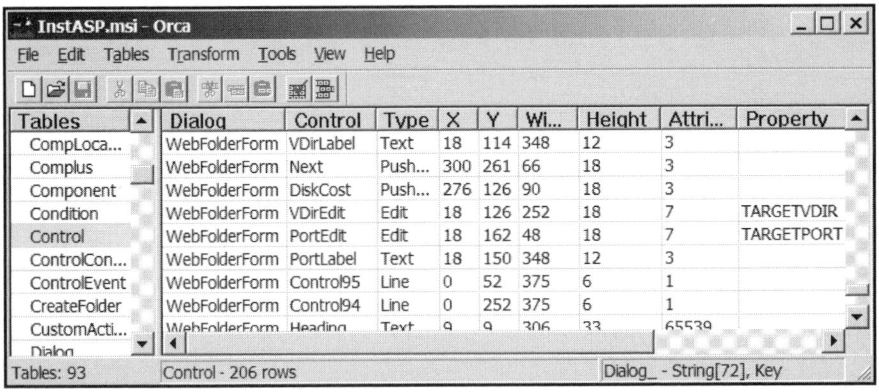

Tables	Dialog	Control	Type	X	Y	Wi...	Height	Attri...	Property
CompLoca...	WebFolderForm	VDirLabel	Text	18	114	348	12	3	
Complus	WebFolderForm	Next	Push...	300	261	66	18	3	
Component	WebFolderForm	DiskCost	Push...	276	126	90	18	3	
Condition	WebFolderForm	VDirEdit	Edit	18	126	252	18	7	TARGETVDIR
Control	WebFolderForm	PortEdit	Edit	18	162	48	18	7	TARGETPORT
ControlCon...	WebFolderForm	PortLabel	Text	18	150	348	12	3	
ControlEvent	WebFolderForm	Control95	Line	0	52	375	6	1	
CreateFolder	WebFolderForm	Control94	Line	0	252	375	6	1	
CustomActi...	WebFolderForm	Heading	Text	9	9	306	33	65539	

Tables: 93   Control - 206 rows   Dialog_ - String[72], Key

Figure 7-8. TARGETVDIR and TARGETPORT in the Control table

Up to this point during the install:

- The user has set the values of these properties, such as with a command line specifying TARGETPORT and TARGETVDIR values.

- The CAs WEBCA_TARGETVDIR and WEBCA_TARGETPORT have set the values of these properties, if the values weren't previously set.

If the installing user changes the contents of the edit boxes shown in Figure 7-7, the values should clearly be propagated into those properties. Figure 7-9 shows that a DoAction ControlEvent is associated with the Next button on the WebFolderForm.

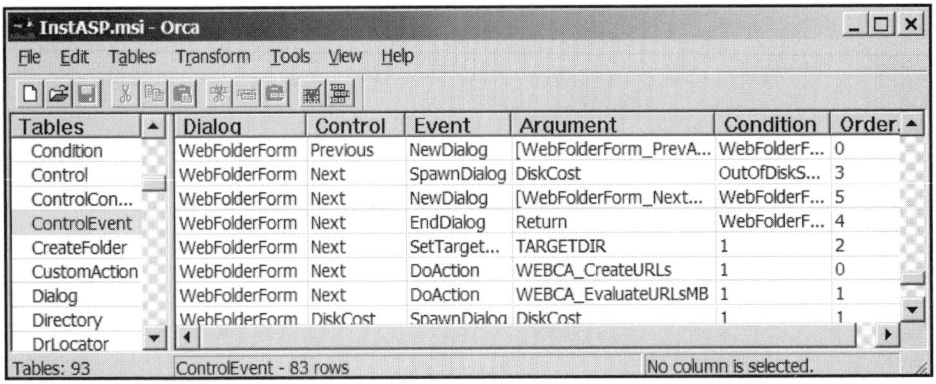

Tables	Dialog	Control	Event	Argument	Condition	Order.
Condition	WebFolderForm	Previous	NewDialog	[WebFolderForm_PrevA...	WebFolderF...	0
Control	WebFolderForm	Next	SpawnDialog	DiskCost	OutOfDiskS...	3
ControlCon...	WebFolderForm	Next	NewDialog	[WebFolderForm_Next...	WebFolderF...	5
ControlEvent	WebFolderForm	Next	EndDialog	Return	WebFolderF...	4
CreateFolder	WebFolderForm	Next	SetTarget...	TARGETDIR	1	2
CustomAction	WebFolderForm	Next	DoAction	WEBCA_CreateURLs	1	0
Dialog	WebFolderForm	Next	DoAction	WEBCA_EvaluateURLsMB	1	1
Directory	WebFolderForm	DiskCost	SpawnDialog	DiskCost	1	1
DrLocator						

Tables: 93   ControlEvent - 83 rows   No column is selected.

Figure 7-9. CA called from Next button

In other words, when the user clicks the Next button on this form, a series of events takes place, two of which are DoAction events that are calls on the CAs named in the Argument column. You can assume that the WEBCA_CreateURLs CA is the code that creates the URLs associated with TARGETVDIR and TARGETPORT, and you'll see the WEBCA_CreateURLs CA called in the InstallExecuteSequence where it's needed for installs that suppress the UI sequence.

The other CA that gets called after WEBCA_CreateURLs is WEBCA_EvaluateURLs, which checks that the URLs are valid. In the call from the WebFolderForm dialog, the call is made to a slightly different DLL function: WEBCA_EvaluateURLsMB. If you type a 0 into the Port number box during the install (see Figure 7-7), you'll realize that the MB suffix on the function name means "MessageBox," because you'll see one telling you that the resulting URL is invalid. During the UI sequence it's reasonable to show a message box if incorrect values are entered, but during the InstallExecuteSequence an invalid URL simply results in a failing install. Say that you run the install in a silent mode with a command line that causes the URLs to be invalid:

```
msiexec /i "InstASP.msi" TARGETVDIR=Fred TARGETPORT=0 /qn /l*v failasp.log
```

This example runs with no UI, produces a log file called Failasp.log, and specifies an invalid port number value. The error shows in the log file together with the URL that was constructed:

```
MSI (s) (D8:B0): Doing action: WEBCA_CreateURLs
Action start 12:11:35: WEBCA_CreateURLs.
MSI (s) (D8:B0): Creating MSIHANDLE (30) of type 790542 for thread 1456
Action ended 12:11:35: WEBCA_CreateURLs. Return value 1.
MSI (s) (D8:B0): Doing action: WEBCA_EvaluateURLs
Action start 12:11:35: WEBCA_EvaluateURLs.
MSI (s) (D8:B0): Creating MSIHANDLE (34) of type 790542 for thread 1456
Error 1314. The specified path 'http://MachineName:0/Fred' is unavailable.
        The Internet Information Server might not be running or the path exists
        and is redirected to another machine. Please check the status of this
        virtual directory in the Internet Services Manager.
Action ended 12:11:36: WEBCA_EvaluateURLs. Return value 3.
Action ended 12:11:36: INSTALL. Return value 3.
Property(S): UpgradeCode = {218E3F44-88FB-4568-8DD9-7F222C7075AB}
Property(S): TARGETVDIR = Fred
Property(S): TARGETPORT = 0
Property(S): TARGETURL = http://MachineName:0/Fred
```

The moral of this story is that it's always a good idea to create a log file when you're doing a silent install, because failing CAs don't always display messages describing their failures, but they often produce log entries that tell you what went wrong.

Which Web Site Is Used?

Given that a system might be hosting several Web sites, you might have noticed that there's no way to specify which Web site your setup installs into. It installs to the Web site that matches your port number. If multiple sites are on that port number, the setup chooses the first active site it finds.

But I Don't Want to Use the IIS WWWRoot Folder

The setup installs into the system's IIS Web publishing folder, typically something like C:\inetpub\wwwroot. If you want to use a different location, you might be thinking that you could manipulate TARGETDIR to some other location, but this doesn't work. Installing into another folder location requires the location to be a virtual directory, and you must create this virtual directory before running your setup. The following section shows you the VBScript you can use for this.

IIS and Its WMI Provider

You aren't forced to use a Web deployment project to install an ASP.NET application, although it's clearly convenient to do so. You might have an application to install that's primarily an application like the Notepad installation in Chapter 2, where a choice of installation folder is a more useful option than a choice of virtual directory or port number. IIS is a WMI provider, and you can use VBScript to create IIS virtual directories to install the Web part of the application.

MSDN documentation has examples of how to do this, but the key points to creating virtual directories using VBScript (for example, in a CA) are:

- Check that your virtual directory doesn't already exist with this type of code:

```
On Error Resume Next
Set IIS = GetObject("IIS://localhost/W3SVC/1/Root/" & VDirName
If Err.Number = 0 then ….. <it already exists>
```

- Ascertain the path to the virtual directory with code like this:

```
Set IIS = Nothing
Set IIS = GetObject("IIS://localhost/W3SVC/1/Root")
VDirPath = IIS.Path & "\" & VDirName
```

- Create the resulting path if it doesn't exist. You can do this with the FileSystemObject in this general way:

```
Set ofs = CreateObject("Scripting.FileSystemObject")
On Error Resume Next
Set folder = ofs.GetFolder(VDirPath)
If Err.number = 76 Then ' 76 means it does not exist
    ofs.CreateFolder VDirPath
End If
```

- Create the Web directory like this:

```
Set oVDir = IIS.Create("IISWebVirtualDir", VDirName)
```

- Set the path and appropriate attributes:

```
oVDir.Path = VDirPath
oVDir.AccessScript = …
oVDir.AccessRead = …
oVDir.AccessWrite = ….
oVDir.SetInfo
```

You can customize the virtual directory settings in the context of a Web setup by using a CA based on a .NET Installer class. The MSDN article "Modifying Internet Information Services During Deployment with Custom Actions" describes using the IIS WMI provider from a CA Installer class. This article is targeted at setting the AuthAnonymous property for the virtual directory, but it also shows you how to use a custom UI dialog to collect other settings and pass them to your code in the Installer class methods.

Summary

VS Web Setup projects can conveniently deploy ASP.NET applications and Web Services; the principles are the same. You can extend Web setups and add your own files to the install, but by default you don't get much choice of where the non-Web files are to be installed. Most of the code to install the virtual directories is in a CA DLL in the Binary table, in an interesting contrast with the use of .NET installer classes for installation of Windows Services and some other items.

CHAPTER 8

Installing .NET Assemblies

IN MANY WAYS, installation of a basic .NET application consisting of a client program and one or more code libraries is a return to the pre-COM world. You can
install the client program and the code libraries to an application folder and the
application just works. Assemblies are different though—you can strongly name
them, they can have a special shared location (the GAC), and there are enough
XML configuration opportunities that you could be forgiven for thinking that
DLL Hell has been replaced by XML Hell. In the Windows Installer world, there
are new tables that install assemblies, as well as deployment choices, such as
whether you should install an assembly in the GAC or not.

Assemblies and Sharing

One of the main deployment issues has always been sharing. Building code
as shareable components is a useful paradigm for building applications;
deploying them can be extremely difficult. Microsoft has tried to sidestep the
deployment issue by hinting that sharing is dead in the .NET world (or at least
obsolescent), and that you don't need to install one system-wide component
for all users to share. Instead, you can install a private copy for each application. This is recognition of the fact that sharing code isn't the same as sharing
the same physical instance of the code on a particular system, which in
practice is how most people deploy COM servers, despite COM's side-by-side
capabilities.

The simplest type of application that this nonsharing model applies to consists of an executable that the user runs, which uses some shared code in one or
more class libraries installed in the same application folder. These same class
libraries might well be installed with other applications on the system, also in
their own private application folders, which is the model that Microsoft calls
side-by-side. The point of this model is that applications can bind to the specific
class libraries that they've been tested against, rather than use a sharing scheme
that requires new versions of libraries to be backwards-compatible with existing
clients.

The sample projects for this chapter include ClassLib, whose solution file includes projects for the ClassLib C# class library; a VB.NET client program; and a setup project to install them. The VB.NET program has a reference to the class library ClassLib, from which it instantiates a class and calls a method. To deploy this simple application, all you need to do is copy the VB.NET client and the ClassLib class library to the application folder. If you add the VB client program to the application folder in the setup project, VS will detect that it has a dependency on ClassLib.dll and automatically add it to the installation's application folder.

Installer Tables and Assemblies

Although you can install assemblies—both executables and DLLs—like normal files, most installation building tools recognize that they're assemblies, not just traditional code files. These tools therefore populate two Windows Installer database tables that are specific to assemblies, MsiAssembly and MsiAssemblyName, which this section describes.

The MsiAssembly table has the following columns (see Figure 8-1).

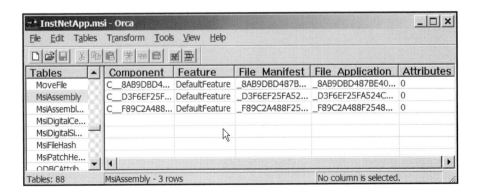

Figure 8-1. The MsiAssembly table

Component

This is the link to the installer component to which the assembly belongs.

Feature

This is a link to the containing installer feature, of which there is only one in a VS setup. The FeatureComponents table describes the relationship between a component and a feature, so it's a little unusual to name a feature and a component explicitly in a table, as you see here. However, if you look at the other tables where a feature is referenced explicitly, you'll see that these tables are associated with items that can cause repair and that can be advertised. When Windows accesses shortcuts, COM components, and files (through their extension) and finds an installer descriptor, it uses this descriptor to perform a health check of the component and its owning feature. Assemblies have the same behavior, and consequently VS added a feature name here.

File_Manifest

In many cases, this is a link to the File table, and File_Manifest therefore refers explicitly to the actual assembly. However, strictly speaking, this refers to the assembly's manifest, and .NET manifests are embedded in the actual assembly code file. However, this File_Manifest linking does allow for a manifest to be separate from the code file.

File_Application

This is a link to the file table that identifies the actual file. If you specify a value here, it means that the assembly will be installed in the private application folder named by the component. If you don't specify a value, it means that the assembly will be installed into the GAC.

Attributes

This contains zero for a .NET assembly and 1 for a Win32 assembly.

The other table is the MsiAssemblyName table, which consists of a Component column naming the component containing the assembly, and then pairs of Name and Value columns, each describing the Name of an attribute and its corresponding value (see Figure 8-2). As you see from Figure 8-2, the Component/Name/Value entries are repeated as many times as necessary to contain the data. This is a flexible design because it allows Windows Installer to add new attributes for new versions of the .NET Framework without adding new tables or otherwise changing the database schema. In Figure 8-2, the two class libraries were compiled with a key file and therefore have a PublicKeyToken entry, whereas the VB.NET program wasn't compiled with a key file, and contains just Version and Culture entries. Note that this version is from the AssemblyVersion specification and not from the file version.

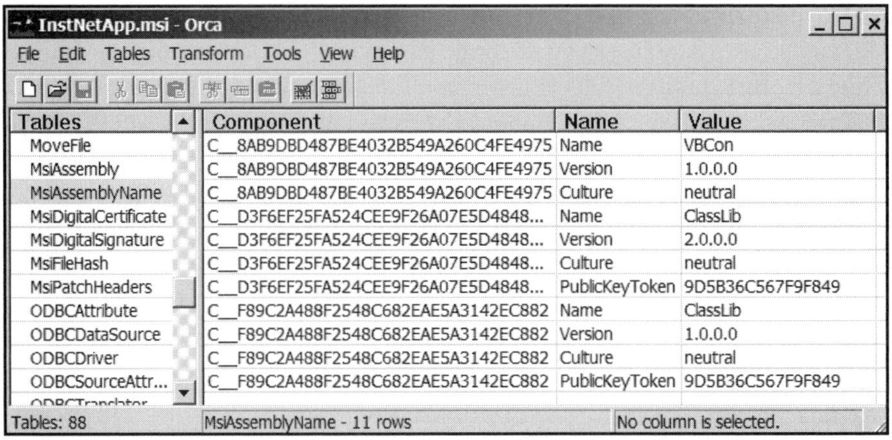

Figure 8-2. The MsiAssemblyName table

Installing Assemblies

VS allows you to build an installation for your .NET application, and when you install the client program and its class library in the same folder, "it just works." This is exactly what side-by-side installation is about—the application always has its own private copy of the class library. This is sometimes referred to as "xcopy deployment," meaning that installation of the product involves simply copying the files to the destination folder on the target machine. The product's installation folder is on the default search path for the assemblies required by the client program.

However, there's a potential problem here that I can illustrate with some code in the class library. When your sample class library is called, it returns a string that contains the file path from which the assembly's code is running:

```
Module mod = Assembly.GetExecutingAssembly().GetModules()[0];
return "Here's the string from " + mod.FullyQualifiedName;
```

The example ClassLib solution contains a setup project, InstNetApp, that includes a shortcut to the VB.NET executable. After installing the MSI package from this InstNetApp project and using the shortcut to the VB.NET client, you see a message saying that the ClassLib.dll being used is running from the application's installation folder, exactly as you'd expect.

However, the default assembly search path includes the GAC before it searches the client's application folder. So if another application chooses to install ClassLib.dll into the GAC, and if you then use the shortcut, you'll see that the class library is now running from the GAC. (You can do this as a test by doing a drag and drop of ClassLib.dll into the Windows assembly folder in <WindowsFolder>\assembly.) The message is something like this:

```
Here is the string from
c:\windows\assembly\gac\classlib\1.0.0.0__9d5b36c567f9f849\classlib.dll
```

This behavior might surprise you. You could have assumed that side-by-side sharing means that the application should always use the version of ClassLib.dll that's installed in the application folder. On the other hand, the fact remains that by all the criteria that matter, the version of the class library in the GAC is identical to the version in the application folder. The short answer to dealing with this behavior is that if you've changed the behavior of a class library, you should change enough (such as the assembly version or the public key) so that the client program won't find an inappropriate class library in the GAC.

Installing into the GAC

If you choose to install an assembly in the GAC, remember that it needs signing with a strong name. Also, in VS setup projects, the GAC doesn't show by default in the list of possible destination folders. However, if you right-click File System on Target Machine in the File System view, you'll get an Add Special Folder choice that includes the GAC, and then you just need to put your assemblies there.

During the installation process, assemblies don't get installed into the GAC at the same time that other files are copied to other folders. They're actually committed to the GAC during the InstallFinalize action. In the context of a VS setup project that creates install CAs in the execute sequence (and recall that these are deferred), these CAs are sequenced after most changes have been made to the target system. Therefore, these CAs cannot use files that have been copied to the application folder. However, these CA programs cannot use assemblies in the GAC because they aren't yet installed into the GAC. (In case you were looking at the InstallExecuteSequence table and wondering if resequencing the MsiPublishAssemblies action to occur before the install CAs makes a difference to this behavior, it doesn't. The MsiPublishAssemblies action advertises assemblies; it doesn't install assemblies physically.) In other words, if you run an executable .NET program as a CA, and this program has references to assemblies being installed into the GAC, the program will fail because its referenced assemblies haven't yet been installed into the GAC.

Another area where you might run into problems is when Services reference assemblies in the GAC. The StartServices action in the InstallExecuteSequence table is prior to where VS sequences install CAs, so if an assembly isn't in the GAC for an install CA, it's not going to be there when Services start either. This might well be an issue for .NET Services that have references to assemblies in the GAC.

Assemblies are in the GAC by the time that Commit CAs are called. The two-phase commit mechanism that installs assemblies into the GAC is required so that Windows Installer can remove assemblies from the GAC if the install fails. In this scheme, assemblies are committed in the GAC during the InstallFinalize action, and Commit CAs are called toward the end of the InstallFinalize action. This means that you can run CAs that reference GAC assemblies as Commit CAs. But you must beware that Commit CAs aren't called if rollback is disabled (see the section "Commit Custom Actions" in Chapter 5). So alternatively, you can sequence these CAs *after* InstallFinalize, but this in turn means that you cannot mark them deferred. So, in a VS setup project, you need to edit both the CA Type (making it immediate) and its sequence to have it run after InstallFinalize. For an executable assembly installed with the product and used as a CA, this means changing the Type of the CA from 1042 (1024 deferred +18 Executable installed with the product) to 18. Remember that CAs sequenced after InstallFinalize aren't rolled back, so if your CA program fails for some reason, the product nevertheless will still be installed.

Assemblies in the GAC are protected from removal. If you use Windows Explorer to navigate to the Windows\assembly folder on your system (the GAC), and attempt to remove an assembly (such as one installed by chapter's samples) you'll see a message box such as, "Assembly 'CLVer1' could not be uninstalled because it is required by other applications." This is because a reference-counting scheme keeps track of clients using the assembly. This is no different from the reference counting used for Windows Installer component GUIDs, but there's an added complication because you can also install assemblies into the GAC using Gacutil.exe (see the following sections). Using Gacutil.exe adds one reference, and each install by Windows Installer adds a reference. You can run Gacutil.exe with the /lr option to list client references.

The GAC can be quite difficult to deal with from an installation perspective, and I'll explain this in Chapter 11.

What About Gacutil.exe?

Most developer documentation talks about installing assemblies into the GAC using the tool Gacutil.exe. However, this is a developer tool and isn't always available on target systems that have only the .NET runtime installed. Gacutil.exe wasn't part of the original 1.0 runtime, but it's part of the 1.0 SP2 update. However, it isn't part of the 1.1 Framework runtime. In any case, Gacutil.exe doesn't appear in the list of redistributable components, so if it isn't part of the redistributable .NET runtime, you can't redistribute it to perform your installs.

Why Use the GAC at All?

Installing assemblies in the GAC rather than into a private application folder has some eerie echoes of the reasons people choose COM singletons. One of the reasons that designers might choose a single copy of an object, whether it be a COM object or an assembly in the GAC, is that they want a single copy of something. The interesting question is what that something really is. Are you forcing a single copy of the code so you can implement a requirement for a single copy of some data? Clearly, you can put an assembly in the GAC and use that single copy to contain application-wide data. However, if the requirement is truly for a single copy of some data, other solutions permit multiple copies of the code to access a single copy of the data. An alternative design would be to have that data stored in a database, or perhaps the Registry or some other resource to which access can be single threaded or locked. Consequently, there's no longer any need for a singleton object to manage the data. This design choice is critical because it determines whether you can deploy your application into private application folders in a side-by-side mode, and this significantly impacts your options when the application needs fixing or updating.

Runtime and Design-Time References

When you build a VS assembly (an executable or a library), it usually has references to standard Microsoft assemblies and perhaps to other assemblies you've built. These design-time references are different from the referenced assemblies that are used when the application runs after being deployed to a client system. In many ways, the relationship between an assembly at design time and run time is similar to the relationship between a C++ program that references a LIB file at build time and the actual DLL that's used when the code runs. The presence of a design-time assembly reference, just like the LIB file, says nothing about how the program finds the assembly at run time and what its location is expected to be. You need to consider deployment of assemblies separately from their design-time references. Although VS releases are tied to a version of the .NET Framework (VS.NET to 1.0, VS 2003 to 1.1), this doesn't require a VS.NET application to use the 1.0 Framework when it's deployed. That's because most applications developed for 1.0 run successfully on the 1.1 Framework. In fact, the default behavior of Windows Server 2003 with only the 1.1 Framework installed is to redirect references for 1.0 to the 1.1 runtime.

You can install the .NET runtimes side by side on the same system; the 1.1 runtime isn't an update to the 1.0 Framework but a new version. You can configure your application to use one or both in some preferred order. As of Windows Server 2003, the .NET runtime is part of the operating system (it shipped with only the 1.1 version). Whether you need to install a particular version of the .NET runtime depends on whether your application runs correctly on other versions of the Framework that might already be installed on the target system.

You can indicate a preference for a .NET runtime version with a client configuration file of this form:

```
<configuration>
    <other directives>
<startup>
    <supportedRuntime version="v1.1.4322" />
    <supportedRuntime version="v1.0.3705" />
</startup>
    <other directives>
</configuration>
```

You can also apply this kind of redirection to your assemblies. The following configuration file redirects a client request for version 1.0.0.0 of an assembly to version 2.0.0.0.

```
configuration>
    <runtime>
        <assemblyBinding xmlns="urn:schemas-microsoft-com:asm.v1">
          <dependentAssembly>
            <assemblyIdentity name="SomeAssembly"
                          publicKeyToken="a3e5f6aed4fb91db"
                          culture="en-us" />
            <bindingRedirect oldVersion="1.0.0.0" newVersion="2.0.0.0"/>
          </dependentAssembly>
        </assemblyBinding>
    </runtime>
</configuration>
```

Although this example shows redirection of a single assembly version to a different assembly version, the bindingRedirect syntax also allows you to specify a range of older versions, effectively allowing redirection of every older assembly to use a new one without changing the client program.

I show these examples of redirection because they have an important effect on deployment. Traditionally, to make a client program use a different version of a DLL, you'd probably have to change the client program, or in the COM model, ship a new version of the COM server that maintained its interfaces to existing client programs and replaced the previous version. The use of configuration files (policy files) gives more flexibility in deployment choices, primarily because you don't need to replace existing files on the target systems. Instead, you can install configuration files that redirect client programs to use the appropriate versions of assemblies in a side-by-side manner.

Serialization and Assembly Dependency

You can build .NET classes with the [Serializable] declarative attribute, which allows clients of the object to use streams and formatters, such as the BinaryFormatter, to serialize the object to disk. You can instantiate the object from disk by deserializing it. The definition of the object and its structure might be in a class library assembly, described by metadata. When you serialize that object to disk using this technique, the file contains not just the serializedobject, but also the attributes of the assembly that contains the definition of the object, which you can retrieve using .NET reflection. Therefore, files that you create by serializing an object are tied permanently to a specific assembly that contains the metadata for that object, and this assembly is required to deserialize the object. This means that you always need to deploy the assembly—or more accurately, an assembly with the same name, assembly version, strong name, culture, and so on—that contains the object's metadata description to serialize or deserialize the object. This has the potential to become a development and deployment nightmare because your files (your serialized objects) are tied permanently to a specific assembly whose attributes you cannot change.
For example, you can't change the assembly version because then you can't deserialize your existing serialized objects from disk. That's because the .NET deserialization routines want the specified version. In the assembly itself, you can't seriously alter the structural definition of the objects because they will no longer deserialize correctly.

Some of the approaches to avoiding this are as follows:

- Use assembly-specific serialization only for temporary files or similar situations.

- Use neutral serialization that isn't tied to a specific assembly (generic XML, for example).

Exposing .NET Class Libraries to COM Clients

It's fairly straightforward to expose class library methods to COM clients. The class library in the sample project you're using here is set up to do exactly that. Here are the key ingredients from a "good practices" point of view:

- Use interface-based programming. Declare the interface explicitly, give the interface a name, mark it as ComVisible, and give it a GUID using the GuidAttribute. Most opinions recommend a decleration of [ClassInterface(ClassInterfaceType.None)] to prevent the compiler generation of a default class interface.

- Be explicit with a GUID for the class definition; give the class a ProgId to enable its use from scripting clients.

- Scripting clients require you to give some thought to parameter types. As a generalization, stick to strings and integers.

- The default setting for the AssemblyVersion in the AssemblyInfo.cs file contains a value with an asterisk in it. This causes the assembly version to change every time it's built. As you'll see later, you use this assembly version to locate the specific assembly. The attempt to locate an assembly can create havoc when the version changes at every build, so specify it exactly.

In your sample project, this gives you this code:

```
[ComVisible(true), GuidAttribute("E51820EA-B647-463D-91FB-80A5AB2A97A0")]
public interface IDoThis
{
    string GetAString();
}
[ComVisible(true), GuidAttribute("D1D38EB0-0210-479A-B8B5-48ADB897A610")]
[ProgIdAttribute("PDWClass.Class1")]
[ClassInterface(ClassInterfaceType.None)]
public class Class1 : IDoThis
{...
    public string GetAString ()
    {
    Module mod = Assembly.GetExecutingAssembly().GetModules()[0];
    return "Here's the string from " + mod.FullyQualifiedName;
    ....
}
```

You have an interface IDoThis that implements the GetAString method, and a class that implements this interface and is therefore required to implement the GetAString method. This method returns a string consisting of the path to the executing assembly module (the code file), which helps you be sure in this test case that your client programs are calling the installed assembly from the location you intended for it.

The way that most documentation describes how to install a .NET COM assembly is to use the Regasm.exe utility to create the COM registration entries at installation time. You won't do that here because you'll be doing things the Windows Installer way. Instead, you'll use a VS setup project, with a little help from Regasm.exe to help you see what's happening.

There seems to be a common belief that you must install an assembly into the GAC for COM clients to use it. This isn't true, as evidenced by the /codebase option to Regasm.exe, which allows the assembly to be outside the GAC by referring to its actual location. It's highly recommended that you strong name these assemblies that aren't installed to the GAC because the codebase entry is a hint, not an absolute rule. The GAC is still a candidate location to find your assembly, so unique strong names prevent an assembly in the GAC from taking precedence over the one at your codebase.

For this example, you'll take your existing class library and add the Registry entries that expose it as a server to a VBScript client, and later to a C++ client program. You can get a good idea of the registration entries that are required to expose a COM interface from a .NET class library by running Regasm.exe against the class library, using the /regfile:<file name> and /codebase options. This creates a REG file that contains most of the data you need to put in the target system's Registry, plus it shows you what a codebase entry should look like. Remember that COM clients will be calling into your class library, so you should expect to see some traditional COM registration entries with CLSID entries and some way to locate your class library.

The REG file that Regasm.exe creates contains the Registry entries; these are the more interesting ones:

```
[HKEY_CLASSES_ROOT\CLSID\{D1D38EB0-0210-479A-B8B5-
48ADB897A610}\InprocServer32]
@="mscoree.dll"
"ThreadingModel"="Both"
"Class"="PDWClass.Class1"
"Assembly"="ClassLib, Version=1.0.0.0, Culture=neutral,
PublicKeyToken=9d5b36c567f9f849"
"RuntimeVersion"="v1.1.4322"
"CodeBase"="file:///C:/MyDD/PDW/Book/CHAP8~1/Projects/
            ClassLib/bin/Debug/ClassLib.DLL"
```

```
[HKEY_CLASSES_ROOT\CLSID\{D1D38EB0-0210-479A-B8B5-
48ADB897A610}\InprocServer32\1.0.0.0]
"Class"="PDWClass.Class1"
"Assembly"="ClassLib, Version=1.0.0.0, Culture=neutral,
PublicKeyToken=9d5b36c567f9f849"
"RuntimeVersion"="v1.1.4322"
"CodeBase"="file:///C:/MyDD/PDW/Book/CHAP8~1/Projects/
                 ClassLib/bin/Debug/ClassLib.DLL"
```

Note that

1. There's indeed a traditional COM CLSID entry that refers to Mscoree.dll as the server. From the associated Registry entries you can deduce that Mscoree.dll has code to locate your class library by version and location and instantiate it, providing marshaling support in a COM-callable wrapper. The specification for the required assembly is precise; it names the assembly version and the public key token. These must match; otherwise the runtime reports that it couldn't find the right assembly.

2. There are two general sets of entries here. The first, where Mscoree.dll occurs, is a generic entry, whereas the second adds a version key, 1.0.0.0, to the InprocServer32 key. Under this key, entries duplicate the previous entries. These version-dependent keys allow multiple versions of a class library each to be exposed as COM servers. If you run Regasm.exe from the 1.0 .NET Framework, you won't see these version keys; they're new with Regasm.exe from the 1.1 Framework. You'll look at them in more detail later on.

3. The format of the codebase entry is a URI pointing to the file. This URI format isn't an absolute requirement, as you'll see in Figure 8-4.

You're not going to use this REG file; you're just using it as a clue to what you expect the resulting Registry entries to look like when you use VS to generate the registration entries for you.

Getting this assembly registered for COM clients is straightforward in VS. The properties for the assembly include a Register value that you set to vsdraCOM (see Figure 8-3). In this example, you're installing the assembly into the Application Folder, so you expect to see some kind of codebase reference when you install the resulting package.

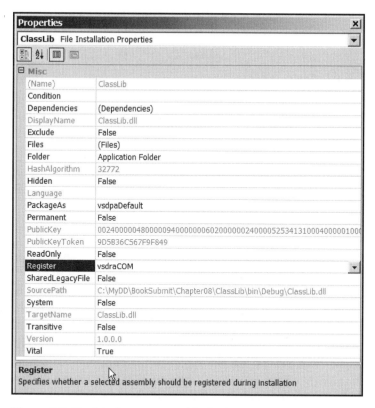

Figure 8-3. Registering an assembly for interop

If you're set up to monitor assembly loads with Fusion Log Viewer (Fuslogvw.exe), you'll notice that Regasm.exe appears when you build the setup project. You can surmise that VS is using Regasm.exe to extract the relevant assembly registration data.

Installing the package and inspecting the Registry settings that are created shows what you expect. The most important entries are those under the InprocServer32 key, shown in Figure 8-4.

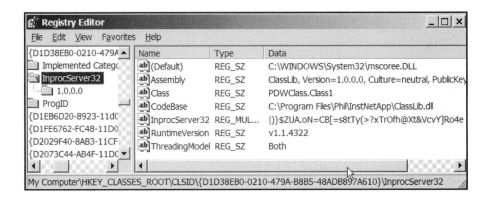

Figure 8-4. Codebase Registry entries

The way that these registration entries work is that a COM program requests a class in the usual way, and internally this becomes a request to the required COM function DllGetClassObject. This request is routed to Mscoree.dll. It's the job of Mscoree.dll to create an instance of the COM class described by the InprocServer32 Registry entries and to provide a COM Callable Wrapper (CCW) for the COM client. Mscoree.dll locates the assembly using the standard assembly location rules, looking for the specific version, public key token, culture, and assembly name. Mscoree.dll uses the codebase entry as a hint to find the assembly. Note that there's still the Windows Installer repair descriptor in the InprocServer32 item that you saw in COM entries in Chapter 3. The GUID underneath the Implemented Categories key, {62C8FE65-4EBB-45E7-B440-6E39B2CDBF29}, means that this COM server is a .NET component. If you run the Platform SDK's OLE/COM Object Viewer you see this COM class there, together with a collection of other .NET assemblies.

The sample project included with this chapter includes a shortcut to a simple VBScript, Callit.vbs, that calls the GetAString method. You can verify that the installation has worked by using this shortcut. The VBScript itself is exactly like any other VBScript that uses a ProgID and automation-compatible parameters to call COM methods:

```
dim obj,amsg
set obj = CreateObject ("PDWClass.Class1")
amsg = obj.GetAString
msgbox amsg
```

Errors with COM clients using .NET COM assemblies generally fall into two areas:

1. Traditional COM error HRESULTs relating to classes or interfaces not being registered. These are the types of errors that any COM client can get, and they indicate that the first COM stage of instantiation has failed.

2. HRESULTs thrown by the .NET Framework during the attempt to locate and instantiate the assembly and the required class. For example, if your .NET COM class contains initialization code in its constructor that faults, it will throw a .NET exception, and this exception will be reported as the kind of HRESULT that you wouldn't get from traditional COM servers written in unmanaged code.

The distinction between these types of errors tells you where to start looking for registration or instantiation problems.

Downstream Dependent Assemblies

Just like any other assembly, a class library installed as a COM server might have dependencies on other assemblies you've created. You should install these into the same location as the .NET COM assembly. What happens is that the code-base specification remains in effect while the class library is initializing, and is used as the application base (AppBase) for loading dependent assemblies.

Creating Side-by-Side .NET COM Components

Earlier on, you ignored the fact that Regasm.exe created a 1.0.0.0 subkey under the InprocServer32 key, but you'll use it now to look at side-by-side configuration.

To illustrate the way multiple side-by-side versions work, you'll do the following:

1. You'll add a C++ COM client program to the solution. This is just an ordinary COM client program that calls a method on the COM interface exposed by the class library.

2. You'll add another class library to the solution. This is identical to the 1.0.0.0 class library you're already using except that the GetAString method now returns text describing it as version 2.0.0.0 of the object, and in the AssemblyInfo.cs file you mark it as version 2.0.0.0. This is the new version that you're shipping to install side by side with version 1.0.0.0.

3. You'll add everything to the installation so that your COMClient uses a particular version of the class library. Apart from installing the new version of the class library, the key item you install is a configuration file to make your COM client program use a specific version of the class library. Note that this new version of the class library has the same name as the original, so you install it into subfolder "Version2" of the application.

This entire VS ClassLib solution is in the code for this chapter.

To recap: You're installing two versions of a .NET class library that both expose the same COM interfaces, you install them in side-by-side mode, and you use a configuration file to direct a COM client program to use a particular version of the class library. You expect to find Registry entries for InprocServer32\1.0.0.0 and InprocServer32\2.0.0.0 that provide side-by-side installation of different versions of the class library. The latest version, 2.0.0.0, is in a subfolder "Version2" of the application installation folder.

The COM Client

You need a type library to generate the appropriate header files for the C++ client program, and you build this by running Tlbexp.exe on the original class library. You then import the generated TLB file into the COM client; here's the code:

```
#include "stdafx.h"
#import "classlib.tlb" raw_interfaces_only no_namespace
int _tmain(int argc, _TCHAR* argv[])
{
CoInitialize(0);
HRESULT hr = 0;
CLSID cls;
CComPtr< IDoThis> idt;
hr = CLSIDFromProgID (L"PDWClass.Class1", &cls);
if (SUCCEEDED(hr))
  {
    hr = CoCreateInstance (cls, NULL, CLSCTX_INPROC_SERVER, __uuidof(IDoThis),
          (void**)&idt);
    if (SUCCEEDED(hr))
     {
      CComBSTR mystring;
      hr = idt ->GetAString(&mystring);
      if (SUCCEEDED(hr))
         {
```

```
        MessageBoxW  (NULL, mystring, L"Call Returned", MB_OK);
        idt.Release();
    }
  }
}
}
```

Configuring the Updated Class Library

You also need an updated class library with an AssemblyVersion of 2.0.0.0 (the Classlib2 project in the ClassLib solution). This library uses entries beneath the InprocServer32\2.0.0.0 Registry entries describing the assembly and its location. You'll install this library into a subfolder called Version2 of the Application Folder. If you add the assembly to this new folder, set the Register property to vsdraCOM and perform the build, you'll see an issue with VS 2003:

```
ERROR: Unable to build assembly named 'ClassLib.dll', HRESULT == '0x8007065B'
```

This error is documented as "Function failed during execution," and even though the MSI package is successfully built, attempting to install it results in error 2920: "Source directory not specified for file [2]." A log of the install expands this error to name the key into the File table for version 1.0.0.0 of ClassLib.dll. It's not that this particular assembly has a problem, because it installed correctly when it was the only assembly with COM registration specified. Rather, the issue appears to be that the two nearly identical assemblies, version 1.0.0.0 and 2.0.0.0, create conflicts in VS's scheme for getting the registration information. If you set version 2.0.0.0's Register property to vsdraDoNotRegister, you'll find that the build of the MSI package succeeds. Needless to say, this means you don't have the required registration entries, so you need to add them manually.

There's no need to type those Registry entries into VS's IDE. You saw before that you can run Regasm.exe against an assembly to create a REG file, and you can do this with version 2.0.0.0 of the assembly. You know that most of the default Registry entries are created by registration of version 1.0.0.0 using the vsdraCOM property, so you can edit that REG file down to just the essentials for version 2.0.0.0:

```
REGEDIT4
[HKEY_CLASSES_ROOT\CLSID\{D1D38EB0-0210-479A-B8B5-
    48ADB897A610}\InprocServer32\2.0.0.0]
"Class"="PDWClass.Class1"
"Assembly"="ClassLib, Version=2.0.0.0, Culture=neutral,
```

```
PublicKeyToken=9d5b36c567f9f849"
"RuntimeVersion"="v1.1.4322"
"CodeBase"="file:///C:/MyDD/PDW/Book/CHAP8~1/Projects/CLASSL~1/bin/
    Debug/ClassLib.DLL"
```

VS's ability to import REG files simplifies getting this REG file into VS in a state that you can use. If you right-click Registry on Target Machine, an Import selection lets you browse for REG files. Having imported the REG file that Regasm.exe made for you, you'll make the entries match the target machine instead of the settings on the development machine. The entries in the VS IDE look like Figure 8-5.

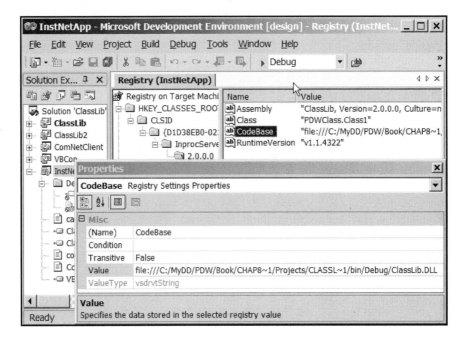

Figure 8-5. After importing the REG file into VS

The only thing wrong with the entries you added from the REG file is that the codebase entry needs to point to your updated ClassLib.dll that you'll install into subfolder Version2 of the Application Folder. The most convenient way to do this is to use the TARGETDIR property and append the Version2 subfolder and the name of the assembly. As an aside, this method is convenient but not necessarily foolproof. There's a Windows Installer format for specifying the actual location of a file: You specify [#FileKey] as part of the codebase, where FileKey stands for the value in the file's File column of the File table, because that resolves to the file's actual installation path. But that means knowing File table keys, which means you need to be comfortable with the innards of MSI packages and understand that a File Key value might change. You could also tweak this codebase string to use the Directory table entry that refers to the \Version2 subdirectory, but you can't manipulate that from VS's IDE. So stick with your TARGETDIR approach to the codebase, and change the contents of the codebase entry to this:

```
{file:///[TARGETDIR]Version2\ClassLib.DLL}
```

Those curly braces in the Value property in Figure 8-6 enclose the entire string. However, they're removed when the TARGETDIR property is resolved at install time, so the result in the Registry after the installation is in the required format.

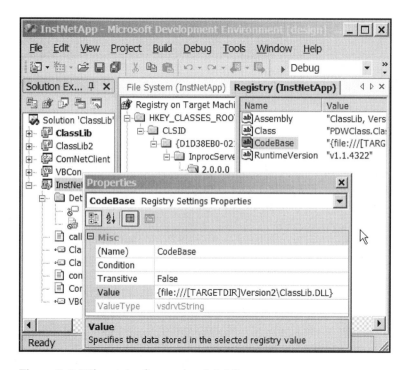

Figure 8-6. VS's entries for version 2.0.0.0

At this point you now have the version 1.0.0.0 assembly being registered with vsdraCOM (you don't see any Registry data for that in the IDE). You also have your IDE Registry entries that register version 2.0.0.0 in the Version2 subfolder.

If you install this project, you can again use the shortcut to the VBScript file to see what happens. What you'll find is that the message now indicates that the assembly being called is the one you added in the Version2 folder. This is an important part of the behavior: By default, applications are directed to the latest version of the .NET assembly.

So what do those version-dependent keys have to do with this? The answer is nothing so far, because the VBScript client doesn't indicate that it cares about version choices here, so it gets the latest version. To see how multiple versions work, you need a COM client program with some way to specify that it does require a particular version, which is what our program in the preceding section "The COM Client" will be used for.

Redirecting the Default Behavior

You know that the default behavior is to connect to the latest version, 2.0.0.0 in this example. To direct a COM client program to use a particular version (you'll redirect back to 1.0.0.0), you need to install an application configuration file, named as the client program name suffixed with .config. You redirect back to the old version with this configuration file, ComNetClient.exe.config:

```
<configuration>
    <runtime>
        <assemblyBinding xmlns="urn:schemas-microsoft-com:asm.v1">
            <dependentAssembly>
                <assemblyIdentity name="ClassLib"
                    publicKeyToken="9d5b36c567f9f849" />
                <bindingRedirect oldVersion="2.0.0.0"
                                 newVersion="1.0.0.0"/>
            </dependentAssembly>
        </assemblyBinding>
    </runtime>
</configuration>
```

The key part of this code is the bindingRedirect specification that says the assembly location code in .NET should redirect requests for version 2.0.0.0 to use 1.0.0.0. If it seems unusual for a COM client program to be using .NET configuration files, remember that this standard .NET redirection occurs when the .NET Framework loads the assembly for the COM client.

Running the Client Programs

You now have all the ingredients to put this example together and install it. The shortcut to the VBScript file causes the assembly loader to use the default version 2.0.0.0 of the class library, but the shortcut to the ComNetClient.exe program uses version 1.0.0.0. It's instructive to look at the Fusion Log Viewer for this latter case. (If you haven't used this viewer before, look up the documentation for Fuslogvw.exe.) This is an example of the Fusion Log Viewer detailed output for the redirected COM client:

```
Assembly manager loaded from:
C:\WINDOWS\Microsoft.NET\Framework\v1.1.4322\fusion.dll
Running under executable  C:\Program Files\Phil\InstNetApp\ComNetClient.exe
--- A detailed error log follows.

=== Pre-bind state information ===
LOG: DisplaName = ClassLib, Version=2.0.0.0, Culture=neutral,
PublicKeyToken=9d5b36c567f9f849
 (Fully-specified)
LOG: Appbase = C:\Program Files\Phil\InstNetApp\
LOG: Initial PrivatePath = NULL
LOG: Dynamic Base = NULL
LOG: Cache Base = NULL
LOG: AppName = NULL
Calling assembly : (Unknown).
===

LOG: Processing DEVPATH.
LOG: DEVPATH is not set. Falling through to regular bind.
LOG: Attempting application configuration file download.
LOG: Download of application configuration file was attempted from
 file:///C:/Program Files/Phil/InstNetApp/ComNetClient.exe.config.
LOG: Found application configuration file
        (C:\Program Files\Phil\InstNetApp\ComNetClient.exe.config).
LOG: Redirect found in application configuration file:
        2.0.0.0 redirected to 1.0.0.0.
LOG: Publisher policy file is not found.
LOG: Host configuration file not found.
LOG: Using machine configuration file from
 C:\WINDOWS\Microsoft.NET\Framework\v1.1.4322\config\machine.config.
LOG: Post-policy reference: ClassLib, Version=1.0.0.0, Culture=neutral,
     PublicKeyToken=9d5b36c567f9f849
LOG: Cache Lookup was unsuccessful.
LOG: Attempting download of new URL
        file:///C:/Program Files/Phil/InstNetApp/ClassLib.DLL.
LOG: Assembly download was successful. Attempting setup of
        file: C:\Program Files\Phil\InstNetApp\ClassLib.DLL
LOG: Entering run-from-source setup phase.
```

Notice particularly the prebind state information where the Framework is already looking for version 2.0.0.0, and note that it successfully locates the configuration file and redirects to version 1.0.0.0. You can see how the Fusion Log Viewer can be useful in debugging installation issues involving missing assemblies.

For good measure, a VB.NET client references the class library in the usual .NET method. This doesn't go through COM, so the client uses whichever library it finds in the standard assembly location algorithms.

Type Libraries

Although you used Tlbexp.exe to generate a type library to import into your COM client, you didn't install this type library. Whether you need to install it depends on your COM clients and whether you need to access the COM server with COM marshaling. If you do need to install your generated type library, just add it to the setup project and VS will mark its Register property as vsdrfCOM. After the build you'll see the Interface entries in the package's Registry table.

COMRegisterFunctionAttribute

One of the ways you can mark your assembly for COM interop is to set the COMRegisterFunctionAttribute attribute on a .NET class and implement RegisterFunction and UnregisterFunction methods that perform COM registration. Regasm.exe calls these methods when you run it against the DLL. You'll probably find sample code that uses these methods to create COM Registry entries and remove them at install time, but I don't recommend running Regasm.exe to do registration when you can use vsdraCOM in your setup project. It's also nontrivial to locate Regasm.exe on client systems and run it—you'd need to find it in the Windows Microsoft.NET folder under the latest Framework version and run it as a CA. Also, remember that it's more robust and secure to update the system from the standard Windows Installer tables when compared with running code in a CA.

Assemblies and CAs

Starting with a class library project in VS, you can select Project ➤ Add Class from the main menu, and then choose Installer Class. This adds some boilerplate code for a .NET installer class. The class heading looks like this:

```
[RunInstaller(true)]
public class Installer1 : System.Configuration.Install.Installer
```

The RunInstaller attribute setting of true says that this class is intended to be instantiated and its methods called during various install steps, although I must admit that it's not obvious to me why you would have an installer class that you didn't want to be used. You override the Install, Uninstall, Commit, and Rollback methods with your own code. Note that these four methods are exactly the choices that VS gives you with CAs in setup projects.

To have the installer call the methods in your installer class, you:

- Add the installer class to your project.

- Override the methods where you want your own code to be called (Install, Uninstall, Commit, Rollback). A good citizen of the installation world should always undo any actions performed during the install process, so if your code in the Install method changes the system you should also have code in the Uninstall method restore the system to its previous state. The same is true for rollback; you should supply Rollback CAs that undo whatever your Install CA did to the system in case the install fails and does a rollback.

- In your setup project, add your assembly to the Application Folder in the project's File System view, and then use the CA editor to browse to the assembly and add it at the required stage (Install, Uninstall, Commit, Rollback).

Note that this final step describes browsing to the specific assembly code file and adding it as a CA. I find this more flexible than the case where the input to a setup project has been defined as the Primary output of an assembly project.

Following these steps for an Install CA gives you the view shown in Figure 8-7.

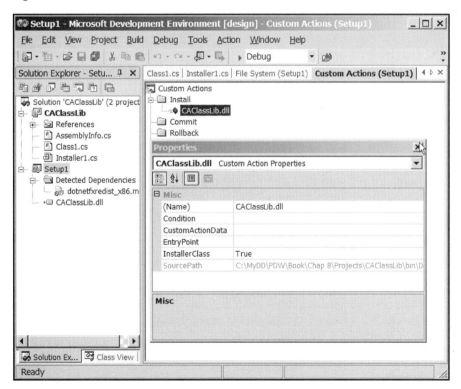

Figure 8-7. Installer class CA

Notice that the properties here show InstallerClass to be True, meaning that this is a call to a .NET installer class rather than what might be called a more traditional call to a CA. Note also that there's a CustomActionData property where you can pass data into the chosen method.

It helps to understand how this works if I outline the mechanism used to call the methods in your class. VS doesn't generate a CA that Windows Installer calls directly. Instead, VS generates a call to a DLL stored in the package's Binary table, passing parameters that include your CustomActionData properties. This DLL, called InstallUtilLib.dll, contains code that locates your assembly and then uses .NET reflection to instantiate your installer class and pass your CustomActionData to it. The System.Configuration.Install class contains an InstallContext member called Context, which is how InstallUtilLib.dll passes your CustomActionData to your methods. This is the same general way that the .NET Framework utility InstallUtil.exe works, and the parameters that you pass via CustomActionData have the same format:

```
/Item=<value>
```

The InstallContext object has a member named Parameters that's a StringDictionary. Therefore, it has a collection of keys and values corresponding to some built-in parameters and the ones you pass in. This code in the overridden Install method shows the entire collection:

```
public override void Install(IDictionary savedState)
{
    base.Install(savedState);
    StringBuilder sb = new StringBuilder();
    foreach (DictionaryEntry de in this.Context.Parameters)
    {
        sb.AppendFormat ("Key = {0}, Value = {1}\n", de.Key, de.Value);
    }
    MessageBox.Show(sb.ToString(), "Context Keys and Values");
}
```

When passing data in the CustomActionData property, you can pass more than one parameter at a time, and the data must be contained in quotes if it contains spaces. Figure 8-8 shows two strings being passed into the Install method.

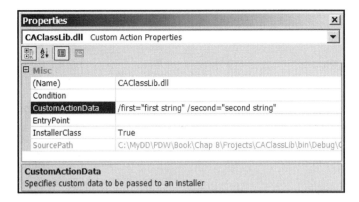

Figure 8-8. Passing two strings to an installer class method

When you call the code in the Install method, the resulting message box shows each key of the Parameters collection and its value (see Figure 8-9).

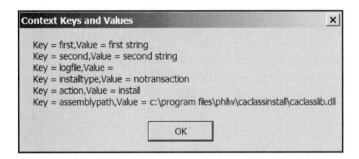

Figure 8-9. The context parameter contents

You can see that the quotes around the strings have been removed, probably because their purpose is to enable the internal parser to separate out each string. You also can see that some other parameters are passed into InstallUtilLib.dll as well as the ones you specified. It's probably safe to assume that the "assemblypath" value is passed into the DLL so that it can use reflection on the file and instantiate your installer class.

Now, although passing strings illustrates how to pass values via CustomActionData, it's not very practical because in most cases you can just use hard-coded strings in the Install method itself instead of passing them in. It's much more useful to pass Windows Installer properties such as the application's installation folder: the value of the TARGETDIR property. When these Windows Installer properties are folder locations, VS requires you to pass them in a quoted form with a trailing backslash:

```
/location="[TARGETDIR]\"
```

Presumably, this format exists so that the internal parser can figure out how to delimit the value. You can pass multiple folders in the same way, so if you need to pass both the TARGETDIR and SourceDir properties to the method, you would specify the CustomActionData string as this:

```
/location="[TARGETDIR]\" /source="[SourceDir]\"
```

In the Install method displaying the preceding data, this gives you a message box showing the appropriate values associated with the keys "location" and "source" (see Figure 8-10).

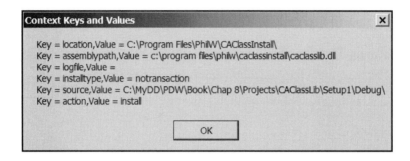

Key = location,Value = C:\Program Files\PhilW\CAClassInstall\
Key = assemblypath,Value = c:\program files\philw\caclassinstall\caclasslib.dll
Key = logfile,Value =
Key = installtype,Value = notransaction
Key = source,Value = C:\MyDD\PDW\Book\Chap 8\Projects\CAClassLib\Setup1\Debug\
Key = action,Value = install

Figure 8-10. TARGETDIR and SourceDir in the Install method

Internally, installer class CAs work in the same general way as other deferred CAs that use CustomActionData. A Type 51 CA sets a property, with the same name as the CA itself, to the list of parameters delimited with the forward slash. VS also generates another CA that's the actual call to InstallUtilLib.dll, a Type 1024 CA. I'll look at this in more detail in Chapter 10, where you'll see how to use this installer class mechanism to install .NET Windows Services.

What if the code in the method needs to terminate the installation? That's what you use the InstallException .NET class for. Your code should throw this exception if it must terminate the installation.

Finally, there's an important restriction on calling installer classes in this way: The destination folder of the assembly must not be the GAC.

Summary

Installing .NET assemblies, either into the GAC or into private application folders, is relatively straightforward. In this chapter, you dug deeply into exposing .NET components to COM clients. The key point is that COM clients do what they have always done until the .NET runtime takes over. From that point on, the behavior is pure .NET as it locates assemblies in its usual way, including use of configuration files to redirect to other versions of the .NET assembly.

The use of .NET assemblies as COM servers to legacy COM clients is an extremely useful feature in its own right. I think that being able to use .NET assemblies as COM servers side-by-side for legacy COM clients and use .NET configuration files to direct to appropriate versions is an astounding combination of old and new technologies.

Installation Design

IN THIS CHAPTER, I'll examine some design issues and challenge some assumptions about what installation programs should or shouldn't do. These issues generally fall into three main areas:

1. What items should the installation program require the system to have? In other words, should it check for things such as service packs, drivers, hardware, and Internet Explorer (IE) levels, and perhaps refuse to install unless these prerequisites are met?

2. What should the installation program do about installing components that aren't part of the application being installed? Should it fire off other installation programs? Create databases?

3. What is the relationship between the application and the installation? To what extent should the installation deal with the application design, and vice versa, to what extent should the application be designed to deal with the installation?

I'll examine these areas and discuss the implications.

Installation Prerequisites

It's not unusual to find an installation that refuses to start unless a particular piece of software is installed, such as a Windows Service Pack. You need to ask a couple of key questions here, discussed in this section.

Does the Application Need It or Does the Installation Program Need It?

If you think about something like a service pack, the answer most of the time is that the application needs it. The same is typically true of IE versions, hardware, perhaps even other servers on a network, or hardware components. In other words, the application needs the particular item and wants the installation program to perform checking on the application's behalf. There's something slightly odd about this situation. If you went to a co-worker and said, "Look, my program requires IE 6.0, but your program always runs before mine so I want you to check IE 6 for me," you might get some strange looks and get told that it's your responsibility. But when the first program to run is the installation program, somehow it's considered normal to ask the installation program to do the checking.

In some cases it's downright pointless for the installation to check for this kind of thing. For example, a Windows Service Pack can be uninstalled, so checking once at installation time doesn't solve the problem. In these plug-and-play days it seems equally pointless to require some hardware item to be present at installation time if the application needs it and the hardware item can be installed later.

There are cases where the installation process needs prerequisite software, and therefore this software must be installed before the installation can proceed. These cases need careful evaluation, particularly when a prerequisite is required for code you're running during the installation. For example, if you're running CA code that requires one or more dependent DLLs that aren't on the system, you'll need to get those dependent DLLs on the system. This might well lead you down the path of adding other CAs to install those DLLs before your code runs, and consequently makes your installation more and more unreliable. This is one of the reasons why performing COM registration from the installer tables is more reliable than getting the code to self-register. In many cases it's safer to finesse the issue by finding another way to solve the problem. In the cases where your VS C++ code really does need to run during the installation and can't find its dependent DLLs, check if the /DELAYLOAD switch can reduce your dependency on external DLLs.

People sometimes resort to extracting a dependent DLL programmatically from the Binary table so a CA that needs it can load successfully. This assumes that you have the security privileges to store the extracted DLL on the target system where your CA code will find it. This location is typically the Windows System folder because it's in the default PATH for searching for DLLs, and it's difficult to figure out where Windows Installer will temporarily store your CA DLL code when it calls it. It's by no means certain that you have the privilege to create a file in the Windows System folder, and you have to deal with the fact that the DLL might already be there. The PATH environment variable can sometimes have so many folders specified that it's not clear whether your DLL in the Windows System folder will be the one that's loaded. This might seem to be an artificial scenario, but people do sometimes try this kind of thing during an install, and this shows some of the complications that can arise out of dependencies.

What Does the Application Do If the Prerequisites Aren't Met?

This is really a question about degrees of failure. If, after installation, the application programs can start up and run, but at some point they fail because a service pack or version of IE is missing, I would argue that the application should be checking for such items when it starts up. This is essential if users could remove or downgrade the dependent software after your product's installation has been done.

On the other hand, the application being installed might not start at all, perhaps because it requires the .NET Framework. Or there might be some other situation where the application simply can't proceed for as long as it takes to display an error message. In these cases, the installation program has to step up and check for required prerequisites.

Redistributables As Programs

It's common to find that installation programs try to fire off other installation programs that are built as self-extracting executables that extract and install their contents. Examples of these are the .NET Framework runtime and its service packs, Acrobat Reader, the Microsoft Data Access Components (MDAC), and so on. These programs are usually explicitly designed to be the correct (and required) way to install the required files—they don't have a UI and often have options for silent installation. If you're going to install these as CAs from your install, watch out for some of these issues:

- Some of these redistributables might have prerequisites of their own, so you fire them up and they won't run (see what needing prerequisites gets you into?). They might also have security requirements. The user performing a product installation might have sufficient privileges to install an application because the product's installation doesn't require elevated privileges. But installing the redistributable might well require privileges that the user doesn't have—many of these redistributables install shared system components.

- They might require a reboot to complete. The only mechanism that most of them have to tell the user about a reboot is a message box. Programmatically, it's often impossible to know if the redistributable installation programs want to reboot after you've fired them up. Some have a command-line option that suppresses the message box asking about the reboot, but even if you know a way to suppress a reboot, you're stuck wondering whether a reboot will be required at the end of your installation. Needless to say, your choices here are limited. If you don't reboot, that installation might not be complete, and any use you're about to make of it might fail. Or you can just unconditionally reboot anyway. Apart from the unfriendliness of an unconditional reboot, you also have to worry about the timing. If you're relying on something from this external setup during the installation (such as a CA or starting a Service), then you can't complete the installation. You'd need to reboot, then restart your installation. A reboot that occurs in the middle of your install might require you to design it so that it doesn't repeat actions that have already been done, which is what the installer property AFTERREBOOT is intended for.

- If you build applications intended for other parts of the world, you probably shouldn't be installing the English version of a setup when localized versions exist. Many of these redistributables that you install have non-English versions, so you're not going to make many friends installing the English language one where it's not appropriate.

- You often need to understand what's going on inside the redistributable executable. For example, installation of the .NET Framework runtime versions 1.0 and 1.1 uses Windows Installer, and their self-extracting executables also install Windows Installer version 2.0 if required. This means that you can't install the .NET Framework from within an installer package, because you can't have two MSI installations running at the same time. In addition, if the Windows Installer version on the target system is less than 2.0, you'll need 2.0 to install a .NET-based application. So the Windows Installer version needs updating to 2.0 *before* your install starts, not during your install. This example shows that it can be important to understand what self-extracting redistributable packages do, and that you can't treat them as black boxes.

There's no single right way to deal with running these redistributable programs, because it depends on the behavior of each one. However, the short answer is that it's always more robust and less complicated if you don't run these programs from within your install package, primarily because it complicates the entire process, making it unstable and unreliable.

The longer answer is that most developers (and their managers) responsible for building setups would like the client to be able to run one setup and have everything just happen. Note that the preceding short answer didn't say that you shouldn't provide this capability; it just said that you shouldn't do it all from within your application's MSI package. You'll examine some ways to do this.

The Autorun Solution

One of the ways to deal with dependencies, both for the installation and the product, is the Autorun mechanism (sometimes called Autoplay). Most of you are familiar with the idea that you insert a CD and it starts up a dialog to prepare for the installation. When Autorun is disabled, you should just document on the CD how to start the installation manually.

The advantage of an Autorun program is that it can check the system for prerequisites and prompt the user to install them; you can usually arrange to put the required redistributables on the CD. You can make the program itself generic if you encode the requirements somewhere on the CD such that you don't rewrite the Autorun program for every different product CD. For example, if you generate a bootstrap with VS, you'll see that it generates a Setup.ini file that contains parameters such as the name of the package file and the required .NET Runtime version. You could use a similar design, or perhaps add your own settings into this INI file for your Autorun program to read. One of the places you could encode application or installation requirements is in the installation package itself. You could have an encoding of the product's requirements in a number of tables, such as Error and Property, or in your own custom tables. Your custom bootstrap program can extract these encoded prerequisites and check for them on the target system. This approach would be particularly useful if you have a number of installation packages on a CD, each with its own prerequisites.

Even if you're not distributing with a CD, the idea of a separate program that runs before the installation is often better than trying to build everything into the actual installation package itself. Let's admit that installer technology is designed and built to install products, and not necessarily to prepare the system for them. A separate program that advises the customer of the prerequisites and offers to install them is often perceived as safer than an installation that tries to do it all at once. When an Internet connection is available, consider a design that downloads a program to check whether prerequisites are met before the installation is performed.

Here are a couple of tips from the Platform SDK if you write an Autorun program. First, check that the _MsiPromptForCD mutex isn't currently set before starting. When this mutex is in use it means that another installation is running and is prompting for a CD to be inserted, so your Autorun program doesn't need to run. The other mutex you should check is _MSIExecute. If this is in use, this means that an MSI-based installation is already running in its execute sequence, so you should delay your own installation until the mutex is free.

Dealing with the Deployment Scenario

Autorun programs don't solve the privilege issue, where the installing user has the privilege to install the product itself but not its prerequisites. This tends to be an issue in corporate rather than consumer environments because corporate environments often have security and installation policies, and locked-down systems. In this corporate environment, software distribution systems might be used to push product installs to client systems. A corporate distribution can arrange to install prerequisites with the appropriate privileges, and choose to allow users to install the actual products. In other words, CD Autorun programs work well for consumer products, but not well for corporate environments based on software distribution systems that push MSI packages to client desktop systems.

Keep in mind that you cannot separate the design of an installation package from the environment in which it will be used, particularly when dealing with prerequisites and how you install them on client systems.

The Self-Extracting EXE Solution

If you need to install prerequisite applications before installing your actual application, you can combine the prerequisites and your product together in much the same way as the Autorun solution. A single self-extracting executable can contain a number of setup programs, together with a smart installer program that inspects the system, decides what needs installing, and can deal with the possibility of a reboot by putting entries into the RunOnce key of the Registry. This isn't all that different from an Autorun solution. You combine the launching program, the individual install packages, and the self-extracting executables into one program that extracts all the files to a folder on the client system and then starts the launcher program.

Other External Installations

Apart from the self-extracting executables that you use to install support DLLs and so on, you might occasionally be in the situation where you must install a completely separate application with a full UI, perhaps from a CD. These installations aren't simply redistributables that you run to install support DLLs and so on; these are fully featured product installations. Trying to run these separate independent install programs from within your installation package isn't a good idea because of the complications it causes.

You cannot start an external Windows Installer setup from within your own setup because Windows prevents two installs from being in the InstallExecuteSequence at the same time. If the other setup is installer-based, then for this reason you can't start it from within your setup package. Although you can detour this restriction by starting the other install from the UI sequence of your own setup, this in turn means that you're committed to providing a UI from within your own install, which can therefore never be silent. This effectively makes your product nondeployable in software distribution schemes that almost always suppress the UI.

If the other setup is CD-based, you've also got to think about what happens when you ask the customer to insert the other product's CD. Perhaps it has an Autorun and starts automatically, so the customer now sees your setup and also an Autorun asking to start the other one. You could figure out how to suppress Autorun on the target system and temporarily disable it, but then you need to remember you've done this and prepare to restore it if there's a reboot. Disabling Autorun like this is a bad idea, so resist the temptation and don't alter a user setting that has nothing to do with your product's installation. You might also be tempted to check whether the CD inserted by the client is the one you expect, but Murphy's Law means that something on that CD will change (such as the volume name), and your setup will think the client has inserted the wrong CD.

At some point, the perceived benefit to your clients is outweighed by the fragile nature of a complex installation, and if there's one thing most installations need more of, it's simplicity.

Merge Modules

More and more supporting DLLs are being packaged as Merge Modules, particularly from Microsoft but increasingly from other companies with redistributables.

Merge Modules should contain redistributable files and associated data, such as COM registration, together with their destination. You should choose this destination with sharing in mind if it contains COM servers, because you almost certainly want the Merge Modules to be installed at a fixed location so that the sharing rules are followed (see Chapter 3).

You might see Merge Modules that don't contain any files. Setup developers sometimes build Merge Modules that contain only CAs. This is a response to the fact that many redistributables are installed by running a program (see the preceding section, "Redistributables As Programs"), so the Merge Module contains one or more CAs that run these executables. There's no significant advantage to this approach because you still need to run the CA(s) from the embedded Merge Module. For example, you need to evaluate whether adding a Merge Module so that you can invoke its CA to run an executable adds any value compared with your setup running that executable directly as your own CA. However, the Merge Module author can at least standardize the CAs to ensure that all the users of the Merge Module use the CAs correctly.

Although a Merge Module usually contains no UI information because it's used as a standard redistribution method for a shared file, it's sometimes useful to build a standard UI—and nothing else—into a Merge Module so that the same standard UI can be used across a variety of products that are intended to have the same look and feel.

The User Interface

Although the UI is often seen as an essential step when a product is being installed, it shouldn't be. You should design the installation so that it works whether its UI is shown or not. It's not unusual for clients to want a silent installation, perhaps because it's a standard corporate deployment policy, or because your setup is part of a larger installation.

You can use the techniques detailed in the following sections to minimize user intervention during an installation.

Use Windows Installer Public Properties

A command-line install can specify public property names and their values. The installation process works somewhat like a method call if you can parameterize the data passed into it. You can install the package with behavior and options passed in as properties on the command line.

Use Transforms to Specify Install Behavior

Chapter 12 describes how you can use installer transforms to customize an install package. In situations where you know the general installation properties in advance, you can build a transform against the base install package and have it installed silently with the right behavior. This can be useful if the number of changes is significant. For example, you might have designed a flexible package, but the flexibility requires a lot of properties to be initialized that are impractical on a command line. (In practice, the most common use for transforms is localization of the UI, where the functionality of the install package doesn't change, but the UI needs to be shown in another language.)

Delay Collecting Application Data Until the User Runs the Application

If the installation's UI collects data relating to the application or the user, what happens if that data changes? For example, it's no good collecting the client's e-mail address unless you provide a way for it to be changed later. So if you accept that there must be a way for the user to change it later, why not make that the primary means of collecting the data in the first place? The application, when it first runs, can notice that this information hasn't been collected and prompt the user for it. Whenever an installation asks the user for data, many users are left wondering what they do if the data ever changes—maybe reinstall the product?

Apart from allowing a silent installation, collecting this kind of information as part of the application also detours another issue: whether a user will ever install the product personally. It wouldn't be unusual to have a product preinstalled on a system, ready for the client to use, and in these situations there's no alternative but to have the application itself collect the information.

This is also a potential issue with license agreements. These are often shown during the installation and need to be accepted, and again it makes sense for the application to do this, especially if the user of the application isn't the same as the person who installed the application.

Providing Content Dynamically

One of the ways to provide items such as license agreements is to package them in the installation and publish their installer components so that they can be installed if required and the application can find the location. This is exactly what the Win32 APIs MsiProvideQualifiedComponent and MsiProvideQualifiedComponentEx do. Using a localization example with two versions of a Readme.txt where the product has two files (and therefore two installer components) for different cultures, you'll look first at the basic code that would return the file and its location:

```
int _tmain(int argc, _TCHAR* argv[])
{
TCHAR Comp [] = TEXT("{8D8963CB-E9FC-423C-9D8E-A70182694433}");
TCHAR Qualif [] = TEXT("en-GB");
TCHAR Prod [] = TEXT("{FA966279-7BF6-4CB7-9C76-ACC55CA8B50D}");
```

```
UINT res=0;
TCHAR RetPath [_MAX_PATH+1] = {0};
DWORD len = sizeof (RetPath)/sizeof(TCHAR);
res = MsiProvideQualifiedComponentEx(Comp, Qualif, INSTALLMODE_DEFAULT,
    Prod, 0, 0, RetPath,  &len);
TCHAR thing [500] = {0};
DWORD tlen = sizeof (thing)/sizeof(TCHAR);
StringCchPrintf  (thing,tlen,TEXT("Result %d Path %s"), res, RetPath);
MessageBox (NULL, thing, TEXT("Result"), MB_OK);
return 0;
}
```

The input parameters to MsiProvideQualifiedComponentEx include the ProductCode of a package (in Prod) and the GUID of a qualified component (in Comp). Note that this isn't the GUID of an installer component; it's a key into the PublishComponent table in the package.

A number of published components can be in this table, one of which is shown in Figure 9-1. The MsiProvideQualifiedComponentEx API returns the path to the file associated with the installer component identified by the ComponentId and Qualifier columns. Using en-GB returns the path to one file, and using en-US returns the path to the other. Knowing the path to a choice of files is interesting, but you could find the path in other ways. However, the key point here is that you don't need to install those components at all in the product's initial install, because the INSTALLMODE_DEFAULT parameter causes the required component file to be installed automatically if necessary. In any situation in which files to be used depend upon some aspect of the client's environment, you can use this technique to install the file dynamically from your application and find the path to it.

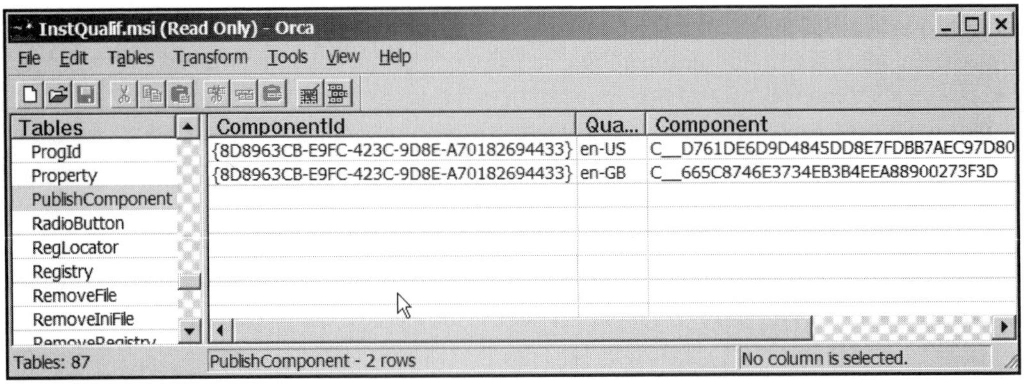

Figure 9-1. The PublishComponent table

Collect the Information Before the Install Runs

If the install needs the user to supply information, another choice is to collect it before running the install. This could be part of an Autorun program or a separate program. The issue here is where the information is intended to be used. For example, if the install is collecting data so that it can be stored in the Registry for the application to use, then the application itself should have a way to collect this data when it runs, perhaps on first use of the application. But if the data needs to be collected for the install, it's sometimes more useful for a preinstall program to collect this and store it for the installation to use. An example of this might be a user account and password that a Service needs to run with. This data can be collected once from the user, stored somewhere (securely if necessary), and used by subsequent installations. This is particularly useful if several applications are being installed that need to share common data.

Finally, don't be tempted to detour a suppressed UI by forcing your own dialogs to show; for example, from a CA. Doing so simply makes it worse when a client requires a silent installation and you ignore that requirement and show a UI.

Application Design and the Install

If you're the developer of a product for which you're building a setup project, you're likely to be biased naturally by the programming development environment. If you're a COM programmer, you probably think of self registration in terms of running Regsvr32.exe. If you're a .NET Framework programmer, you probably think of programs such as Gacutil.exe, Regasm.exe, InstallUtil.exe, and of CAs as being associated with the .NET classes derived from the installer class. In all the cases I've mentioned, these utilities and many installer classes aren't required in the Windows Installer framework. As I've said before, CA code isn't as secure or robust as having the data in the installation package, as it is with data in Service tables and the COM registration tables. You'll need to switch perspectives when you start thinking about the install.

One of the common assumptions about the development of a product and its install is the idea that the product has been completed and works fine, so now all that remains is to build the install for it. There are two major problems with this:

1. The application can't be considered functional until it's been tested after being installed onto a clean system with the install package.

2. The application might have been designed in such a way that it makes the install difficult and unreliable.

This latter point can be illustrated with a few examples:

- Sometimes application designs expect the install to populate the HKEY_CURRENT_USER keys for each user on the system. The idea is that each user has a default set of personal data, stored in the Registry, updated by user activity. Doing this population from an install is extremely difficult, and usually doesn't deal with the case of a new user on the system at a later date. It's a safe bet that changing the application to get default values from HKEY_LOCAL_SYSTEM, and then populating HKCU on first use of the application, is much easier than asking the install to populate multiple HKCU keys.

- A Service that expects the install to populate environment variables for it to use will discover that it can't pick them up until after a reboot. You'll probably find that if you do this reboot and it's unpopular, people will ask why the install requires a reboot. The short answer is that the install doesn't require this reboot; the application design does. Fix the application and the reboot won't be required.

- Occasionally an application will be running a program during an uninstall or an upgrade, perhaps because it's in the Run key in the Registry or in the Startup program group, or it's initiated by another program. At uninstall time or update time, this program needs to be told to terminate, otherwise it can't be removed or replaced. Without a method to terminate this program, you're in reboot territory again. Although there might be some CAs you could use to terminate the program, they'll probably be ugly (as in some kind of "kill program" or Terminate function). It's likely that designing these types of programs as Services would be the correct way, or you could at least design them so they can be told to terminate because the application is being uninstalled.

- You might code your applications to stop and start Services instead of relying on the install. Sometimes this kind of code is useful during development, but not in a customer environment. The issues are the same as usual. If the install is attempting to stop a Service because the product is being updated or uninstalled, the application itself shouldn't be jumping in to start the Service again.

- The application might install data files (perhaps sample HTML, XML, or scripts) that are intended as examples for use by your customers. It's not unusual for these files to be updated to newer versions, and there's a risk that the install will replace files that the customer has used, especially in a major upgrade that uninstalls the old product and then installs the new product. The install is then required to preserve the files that might have been updated by customers by copying them or otherwise preserving them somewhere. In these types of situations, the original application design should ensure that instead of the original files, the customers use copies. Some forceful reminders, such as installing the files as read-only files, would serve to remind customers that they aren't intended to be updated directly.

These examples show that the application and its installation are closely related. In many cases, the install is greatly simplified by a change to the application design. If you're the developer of that application as well as of the install, you're lucky, because making that change should be straightforward. When different organizations do application development and application installation development, you might find it hard to persuade application developers that the best overall course of action is to change the application to simplify the install. This is especially true when a development organization believes its task is complete when the application is handed over to the installation developers. It wouldn't be unusual to find developers who believe that the application and its install are somehow disconnected from each other, and that it's somehow unnatural for the install to have an effect on application design. Nevertheless, they're connected. The payoff during the development process, and later in support, is that the total time and resources expended to build, install, and support the application is less than it would be if the application design remained unchanged, leading to a complex install.

The best solution is to integrate the setup design with the application design, and to have the setup project available from the start of development. The advantages of this are that the setup gets more testing, and the development team needs to specify its software and configuration dependencies from the start of the project.

The Application Must Return Meaningful Error Messages

Sometimes you'll run an application and you'll see a message box "Class Not Registered," or perhaps (especially with Visual Basic programs) "Error 429 ActiveX component can't create object." Similarly, when you start up a Service you might see an error because the Service simply exited without providing any error information. If you look at the code generated by the wizard in VS 6.0 for ATL-based Services and COM servers, this code reads Registry entries to determine whether the process should run as a Service or plain COM server, and doesn't report errors. If the Registry keys are missing, the program just returns. This example shows that Services that just exit when Registry entries are missing might be more common than you suspect.

Thorough error reporting is always important, but the first time you're likely to need it is when you're testing your install packages. You might have just installed your first package to test the application, but all you see is generic error information. Error 429 typically means that a COM class couldn't be instantiated—but which one? A Service might fail to start or it might time out without saying what happened, and it might cause the install to roll back completely. Clearly, errors in the application need to be reported explicitly if you want to have some hope of finding out what exactly is wrong. One of the most difficult and frustrating situations is where an installed application isn't working properly but it doesn't report enough diagnostic information to tell you what's wrong.

Features and Components

I haven't talked much about features because VS's setup projects don't have IDE support for organizing installer components into features. In many ways, features are the most important organizational unit of an install because they're the unit of functionality that the user can choose to install.

The content of a feature is a unit of user functionality, and the rest of the applications function properly in its absence. Internally, a feature is built from a number of installer components that are installed, in the absence of component conditions, when the feature is installed. However, features are useful design units because they can contain multiple components.

If you're designing a client-server install package, you would probably have a feature for the client platform and a feature for the server platform. But it's likely you have some common or shared components that need to be installed on both platforms. If you were to have simply a client feature and a server feature, how would you deal with shared components? You can't easily have the same component in multiple features, and the better design choice is often to have the shared components in a separate invisible feature that isn't shown to the user and is unconditionally installed.

This technique can be extended to the use of redistributables that must be installed on the target system. For example, the Microsoft redistributables that must be installed on the Windows 9x range are different from the NT range, and there are differences even within the NT range. For example, you'd need to install the MFC 4.2 DLLs on an NT 4 system, but not on Windows 2000 or later (they're part of the OS). You can group these redistributables into a feature, hidden from the user, and that includes a feature condition—VersionNT<500— that installs the redistributables only on NT 4 in the MFC case. Internally, these feature conditions are specified in the Condition table, but the development tool allows you to specify this somewhere in the IDE. Should the standard Microsoft Merge Modules have these conditions in them already? Maybe, but they don't. Where Merge Modules do contain a component condition, this condition is generic to the OS and not specific to the level. For example, the ATL Merge Module containing Atl.dll contains two versions of the file, one for the 9x range and one for the NT range (unfortunately with the same name), and the components have conditions of Version9X and VersionNT, the property names that denote these OS versions.

Features in a multifeatured design might need to be installed based on the fate of other features. If a client chooses some number of features to be installed, there could be other supporting features to be installed that you don't need to show to the user. The usual way to do this is to use the INSTALLLEVEL property. Each feature has a Level value specified in the Feature table. A feature is installed if the value of Level in the Feature table is less than or equal to the value of the INSTALLLEVEL property. When the UI shows feature selection, you can set the value of INSTALLLEVEL by using the SetInstallLevel ControlEvent in the UI.

Multifeatured installs might have CAs that must be run when one or more features are being installed, not just because the product as a whole is being installed. You can condition a CA as the feature state of a feature. For example, if a particular CA must be run if either feature Feat1 or Feat2 is being installed, you can have a condition on this CA:

```
&Feat1 = 3 or &Feat2 = 3
```

The condition &FeatureName=3 is True if FeatureName is being installed, 3 being the value of INSTALLSTATE_LOCAL.

Note that you cannot use feature-state conditions (or component-state conditions) until after they have been decided by a UI choice or a default behavior. In practice, this means you cannot use feature-state or component-state conditions until after the CostFinalize standard action.

You can use the same kind of condition when modifying the features in the already installed product. Packages with multiple features typically allow you to go into maintenance mode and add or remove features. If you want a CA to run when a particular feature is uninstalled, use this condition:

```
&FeatName=2
```

This evaluates to true if the feature FeatName is being uninstalled.

Summary

Keep in mind these important points about installation design:

- There's no need to get carried away with the idea that everything must be performed from within a single MSI package. You can initiate prerequisite installation packages separately by wrapping them in an Autorun or similar program.

- Design your installs so that the UI is optional, not mandatory. It ultimately provides more deployment options because it can run silently or in an unattended mode.

- Don't be afraid to go back and change the application design if it makes the install easier, eliminates reboots, or otherwise makes the installation more robust and reliable.

- Windows Installer provides a framework for setups, and although it's true that you can bend the framework somewhat to accommodate your requirements, it's best to use what the framework offers and work within it. Most developers design and build software within the framework of the tools and the architecture in use, particularly in the areas of COM and .NET programming. Installations are no different—working within the constraints of the framework gives you a simpler and more robust installation project. I doubt that many developers would design a COM application without first understanding how COM works; similarly, if you don't know how Windows Installer works, try to avoid a preconceived notion of the installation design until you've looked at the Windows Installer architecture.

CHAPTER 10

Windows Services

WINDOWS SERVICES (sometimes called NT Services) are exclusive to the Windows NT series of operating systems, rather than the 9x and Me range of Microsoft operating systems. Their primary useful feature is that you can configure them to start when the OS starts and before any user has logged on. Other techniques to start programs automatically, such as the Startup group in the Programs menu and HKLM\Software\Microsoft\Windows\CurrentVersion\Run in the Registry, start the program only when a user logs onto the system. In cases where a process should be started whether anyone logs on or not, a Service is usually the answer. This is particularly important with Servers that are unattended.

It's fair to say that there are two types of Windows Service from the developer's point of view: the traditional Win32 Windows Service using the typical Win32 API calls dealing with Services, and the newer programming model based on the .NET Service classes, together with associated installer classes. This chapter treats these two separately because they have some different installation requirements, although the .NET Service classes are really a wrapper around Win32 Services.

Service Installation

The two main database tables that deal with Services are the ServiceInstall and ServiceControl tables. You can look at the first of these tables as the list of the parameters a program would pass into the Win32 CreateService API to create the Service. Because it installs a Service that's a file in the package, the ServiceInstall table also names the component containing the key path file that is to be installed as a Service. The ServiceControl table is more generic. Although it contains a Component_ column, you can use the entries in the table to control any Service on the system, including any Service being installed from within the package itself. This is useful because it's not unusual to need to stop and start system Services as part of an installation.

A number of standard actions process these tables associated with Services, the InstallServices action being the point at which Services get installed. Other actions process the ServiceControl table during the course of an installation or uninstallation. The overall sequence of actions in the order in which they occur follows.

StopServices

At install time and uninstall time, this action stops the Services named in the ServiceControl table that are marked for stopping at this time.

DeleteServices

At install time and uninstall time, this action deletes the Services named in the ServiceControl table that are marked for deletion at this time. This includes the ability to delete a Service at install time.

InstallServices

This action installs the Services in the ServiceControl table.

StartServices

This starts the Services named in the ServiceControl table for starting either at install or uninstall time. This includes the ability to start Services at uninstall time.

This order of the actions is what you'd expect. Clearly a Service needs stopping before deleting, or installing before starting. Remember that the Service tables have component references, and these actions are performed in the context of that named component being installed or uninstalled. It's also important to realize that unlike the behavior of some other installer tables, a Service installed from the ServiceInstall table isn't automatically removed when the product or installer component is removed. There must be an explicit reference in the ServiceControl table to delete the Service.

Installing Win32 Services

VS's installer doesn't support the installation of Win32 Services, so this example uses VS as the base for the installation of a Service, after which you'll update the resulting MSI package with Orca to install a minimal "do nothing" Service. Both projects are part of the code supplied with the book, InstWin32 for the installation project and TestService for the Service itself. You'll be updating the ServiceInstall and ServiceControl tables.

ServiceInstall Table

Some of the columns in the ServiceInstall table are shown in Figure 10-1. Starting with the ServiceInstall column of the ServiceInstall table, you can fill in the straightforward entries, as follows.

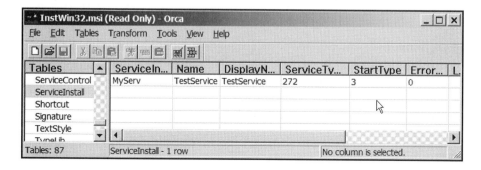

Figure 10-1. ServiceInstall table

ServiceInstall

Use any valid identifier name you like, unique to this table—it's a key for this database table.

Name

This is the internal name that the Service uses.

DisplayName

Use a user-friendly name; this is the name of the Service as shown in UIs to Services.

ServiceType

This is the Win32 Service process type. This value depends on the internals of the Service. Although you could guess, it's best to ask the developer what this value should be. This example uses the SERVICE_INTERACTIVE_PROCESS (only because this is an example with some message boxes) and SERVICE_WIN32_OWN_PROCESS values, giving a decimal value of 272.

StartType

This depends on the needs of the application, such as whether the Service should be started when the system boots (Automatic), or whether it's started by some on-demand method (Manual). A value of 3 installs it as an "on demand" Service.

ErrorControl

This entry is set to zero in this example. This setting usually depends on the needs of the application and how Windows should handle errors in the Service. This doesn't mean error handling by the Windows Installer Service; it means error handling by Windows should the Service fail in some way.

Component_

You must set this to the component containing the Service executable. This executable file, the Service itself, must be the KeyPath of the component.

Description

This is user-friendly text describing what the Service does. By the way, it isn't unusual to see questions about how to give a description to a Service so that it shows up in the Description column of the Services console view—the Service description isn't one of the parameters to the CreateService Win32 API. The long answer is that you can set the description by using the ChangeServiceConfig2 Win32 API. Another long answer is that you can write the description to the Registry entries for this Service. The short answer is that you can set it here in the ServiceInstall table.

Of the other columns in the ServiceInstall table, the StartName and Password are perhaps the most controversial. You can use these to configure the account under which the Service will run. By default (leaving these columns empty), the Service runs with the Local System account. It's probably not a good idea to expose a plain text password in this table, but the data type of this column is Formatted, which means that you could acquire the password via a property or otherwise encode it somewhere in the package. Another issue is that Windows Installer doesn't preserve this password during an uninstall, so if the product's uninstall fails for some reason and Windows tries to restore the product and reinstall the Service, it will be unable to do so because it doesn't know the password that was used at install time. To preserve security, Windows doesn't preserve or expose plain text passwords. For example, the password won't be revealed if you look at a log of the installation. This is a specific case of a more general technique, which is that you can use the MsiHiddenProperties property to specify a list of the properties you don't want exposed in a log. Another approach is to provide for the password to be saved in encrypted form, where you can use it to initialize the contents of the Password value at install time and reinstall time if an uninstall rolls back.

The Dependencies column contains a list of the internal names of the Services that the Service being installed is dependent on. This ensures that Windows starts and stops Services in the required order, as well as shuts down your Service if one you depend on is shut down. For example, if you put MSIServer in the Dependencies column of TestService, manually shutting down the Windows Installer Service will cause Windows to ask if you want to shut down the TestService Service as well.

ServiceControl Table

The ServiceControl table defines what happens to a Service at install and uninstall time. An example is shown in Figure 10-2. You'll go through the column values for your TestService and set the appropriate values.

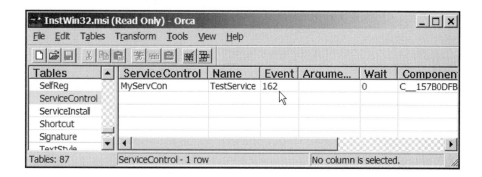

Figure 10-2. ServiceControl table

ServiceControl

Pick an appropriate unique identifier name.

Name

This is required to be the internal name of the Service that's being controlled. This must be an exact match.

Event

This is where you "or" a collection of values together to specify what happens to the Service on an install and an uninstall. The value in your TestService project is 162, meaning stop at install, and stop and delete at uninstall. So, the installation isn't starting this Service when it's installed. At first glance, choices that let you start *and* stop a Service at install time seem a little odd, but keep in mind that you'll need to stop the Service if you're updating it. You might then want to start it again, and being able to start and stop is particularly important so you can minimize reboots caused by the fact that a Service is still running and needs to be replaced or uninstalled. These actions also are happening at different times during the installation process—when the StopServices, StartServices, and DeleteServices actions are performed.

Arguments

This is where you pass parameters to the Service.

Wait

The choices in here are either to wait for the Service Control Manager (SCM) to report that the Service went into a pending state for the required action (set the value to zero), or to wait for the entire operation to complete (set the value to 1 or leave it empty). The documentation describes this last choice as implying that the operation is critical to the install, and therefore an error will fail the install. So if you wait for the entire Service control operation to complete, you're saying in effect that the result is important and that failure of the operation should fail the installation. If the Service control operation isn't important, don't wait for it. Clearly the way that the Service is designed can have a critical effect on the installation. Services are given 30 seconds to respond to control messages, and for any lengthy operations should post the appropriate "pending" state back to the SCM. It isn't unusual to have an install or uninstall fail because a Service isn't following the SCM protocols properly or is timing out somewhere. Note that when the Wait value is 1, Windows Installer still times out even if the Service keeps sending "pending" responses within the SCM's timeout limit. However, an SCM timeout error still causes an immediate timeout error to Windows Installer. See the topic "Service ServiceMain Function" in the Platform SDK documentation for a good summary of the SCM's protocol requirements.

Component_

This is the name of the component associated with this ServiceControl entry, either because the component contains the Service that's being installed or uninstalled, or because the Service control operation is taking place when the install state of that component changes. In other words, you can control Services on the system whether you're installing one or not.

What Could Go Wrong?

These Service tables are pretty straightforward to populate. I've mentioned issues to beware of in connection with the ServiceControl Wait value and with Services running with a named user account, but there are other issues to look out for.

The documentation for the DeleteService Win32 API states that the SCM database entry for a Service isn't removed until all open handles to a Service have been closed. What does this mean in practice? You can find out using the OpenService VS project that's part of the TestService solution in the book's sample code. The code in OpenService opens a handle to the SCM and then to TestService, then does a MessageBox call while owning the handles. When you then uninstall your package containing TestService, while this MessageBox is showing, looking at the state of this Service with Control Panel Services shows that it has been marked as Disabled. That doesn't appear to be a big deal, except that if you now attempt to reinstall your TestService package it fails. You cannot install a Service that would replace one that's Disabled because processes have handles open to that Service. The bad news is this means that your install can fail because some other process on the system has leaked a handle to your Service or has one open for some reason. When the other process closes the handle or terminates, the Service is properly deleted, but until then all you can do is watch out for this scenario. There appear to be other cases where a Service can become Disabled; for example, uninstalling a Service without deleting it leaves a Service entry with no executable associated with it. Attempting to start it returns an error, and attempts to delete the Service programmatically can leave it in a Disabled state until the next reboot, when it's removed.

In the more general case, installing a Service and then starting it during the install violates one of the safety rules discussed early in the book: Avoid running user code during the installation. This is because the Service starts up during the StartServices action. It might be preferable to start the Service from an application program that's part of the product being installed. Also, if the Service has dependencies on CAs, you had better sequence these CAs before StartServices, and you must also mark them deferred because it's not until the deferred phase that the files are on the target system.

The error messages associated with failures during Service control aren't very specific. Most errors report a message saying the Service control operation failed, asking you to be sure that you have the privileges to control Services. Don't treat this message literally, even though it might in fact be the cause of the problem.

Other Ways to Control Services

WMI can be very useful at controlling Services. The following VBScript enumerates each Service on a computer, and stops the Windows Installer Service:

```
option explicit
dim strcomputer, objwmi, servicelist, service, sname
On Error Resume Next
strComputer = "."
Set objwmi = GetObject("winmgmts:\\" & strComputer & "\root\cimv2")
Set servicelist = objwmi.ExecQuery("Select * from Win32_Service")
For Each service in servicelist
    sname = lcase(service.name)
    if left(sname, 9) = "msiserver" then service.stopservice
Next
```

This is just an example, but the Win32_Service class has properties to return the state of the Service (for example, whether running or stopped), as well as methods to stop, start, and delete Services. The Delete method is useful if your Service doesn't uninstall while you're testing an install package. If you use this type of WMI script during a CA, there's the ever-present issue of security to keep in mind, as well as the fact that WMI has security configuration options that can make using WMI more restrictive.

Installing .NET Services

In the context of deployment, the main difference between traditional Windows Services and .NET Services is the addition of installer classes. One of the advantages of .NET metadata and attributed classes is that a setup program can use .NET reflection to find classes, instantiate them, and call their methods. The documentation for .NET Services usually mentions the program Installutil.exe as one of the ways you can install Services by calling the Service's installer class. In the previous section you looked at installing Services using the installer tables, which wasn't particularly difficult. Keep in mind that you used Orca because VS has no built-in support for installing Win32 Services, but fully featured tools from InstallShield, Wise, and others do have support in the IDE for populating the installer tables relating to Services. In light of this, the big question is what you should use .NET's installer classes for. You'll examine this question later after you've used VS to build a C# Service with a setup project to install it, and looked at the resulting package.

VS has wizard support for building a C# Service; just create a new Visual C# project and select Windows Service as the template. By default it's called Service1, and in the design view of the Service, right-clicking the gray panel shows you an Add Installer choice. Choosing this adds a ProjectInstaller.cs file containing an installer class. If you look at the code in the InitializeComponent method, it sets Password and Username properties, which is the account that the Service will be configured to run with (note the overlap with the ServiceInstall table's StartName and Password). To ensure that the Service will run with the LocalSystem account, it's best to go to the design view of the ProjectInstaller class and set the Account property to LocalSystem, which causes the addition of a line of code saying this:

```
this.serviceProcessInstaller1.Account =
                System.ServiceProcess.ServiceAccount.LocalSystem;
```

You can add a Setup and Deployment project to this C# Service using the menu choices File ➤ Add Project, selecting a Setup and Deployment project, and then the Setup Project template. When this project has been added to the solution, select it in the Solution Explorer, right-click, and there's an "Add Project Output" choice (see Figure 10-3, showing how the Primary output of the Active NetService project is added to the setup project).

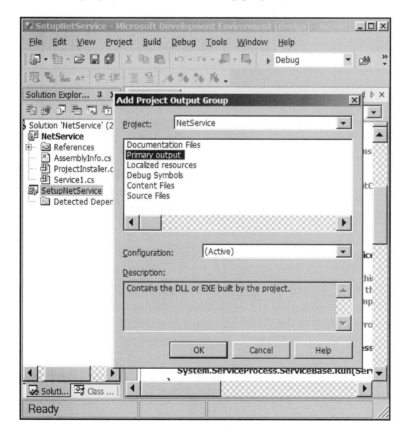

Figure 10-3. Adding Project Output to the install

After adding the Project Output and before building the entire solution of the Service and its Setup project, you might need to go to the build's Configuration Manager and check the Build box to make sure that the Setup project is compiled when the solution is built. So far you've done nothing to install the Service. The ProjectInstaller class does this, but you need to arrange explicitly to have its methods called to accomplish this. As you might have anticipated, these calls are installer CAs.

Figure 10-4 shows the VS view of adding the CAs.

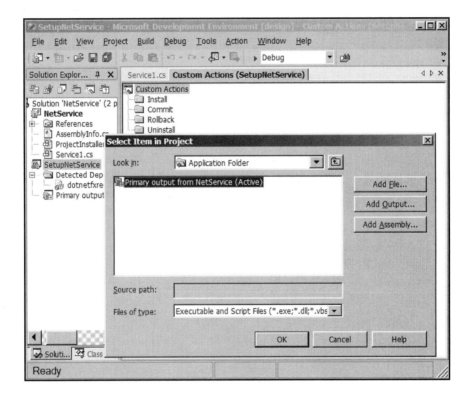

Figure 10-4. Adding a .NET CA

Looking at Figure 10-4, the Custom Action view of the setup project lets you select the Custom Actions text and then browse to the Application Folder that contains the Primary output of the C# Service project. Select this, and you'll find that CAs get added for Install, Commit, Rollback, and Uninstall. Figure 10-5 shows that VS has set the InstallerClass property to be True because these *are* .NET installer classes. Doing a build now results in an installation package that installs your Service.

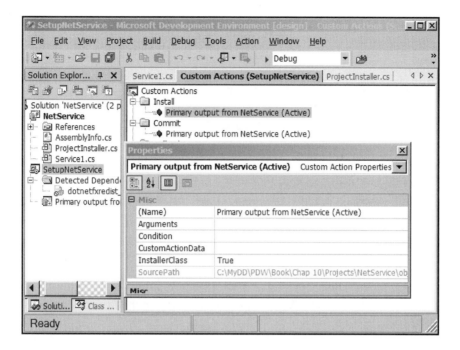

Figure 10-5. The installer CAs in VS

It's instructive to look at the MSI package (Orca again) and see what was generated to perform the tasks associated with installing and uninstalling the Service. You'll see that the ServiceControl and ServiceInstall tables are empty. The InstallExecuteSequence table has CAs at various points, depending on the specific action. Combining entries from both the InstallExecuteSequence and Custom Action tables, these CAs are arranged in pairs of this general form, where <action> is install, uninstall, rollback, or commit:

```
<hex name>.<action>.SetProperty
<hex name>.<action>
```

The <hex name>.<action>.SetProperty form is a Type 51 CA where the Source is the name of the CA sequenced just afterwards, and the Target is a parameter string.

The <hex name>.<action> form is a deferred CA, a Type 1 (call a DLL) where the Source is InstallUtil (a key in the Binary table) and the Target (the function being called) is ManagedInstall.

In other words, the Type 51 is setting the Windows Installer CustomActionData property for a deferred CA. It passes a string such as the following install example to an entrypoint called ManagedInstall in a DLL that VS has added to the Binary table.

```
/installtype=notransaction /action=install /LogFile=
"[#_D3E589ED58B4F1FE93DCAEA2768FA252]" "[VSDFxConfigFile]"
```

Those two pieces in square brackets are installer properties. The first, with the preceding #, is a formatted property that resolves to the installed location of an entry in the File table; in this case _D3E589ED58B4F1FE93DCAEA2768FA252 is the Service executable. The second property, VSDFxConfigFile, is more inscrutable. However, if you install the package you'll see that it creates a file called, for example, netservice.InstallState, so you can surmise that the CA is using the path to the Service executable as the location for a log file.

A bit of detective work shows that the DLL being called is InstallUtilLib.dll from the .NET Framework folder. Orca's Tables menu choice has an Export Tables option, which you can use to export the Binary table, including the binary data as an IBD file. (You can also double-click the cell saying [Binary Data] and select Write Binary to Filename to export the file from the Binary table.) You can look at the properties of this file, as well as look at the exported functions with a tool such as a dependency walker, and see that it exports a ManagedInstall function.

To summarize then, the CA performs the install and uninstall of the Service by calling the ManagedInstall function of InstallUtilLib.dll, passing parameters detailing the action (install, uninstall, and so on) and the location of the assembly executable.

One of the errors you can get when you pass your own CustomActionData into an installer method is shown in Figure 10-6, which shows what happens if you're careless passing properties via CustomActionData. You might mistakenly pass this erroneous string in the CustomActionData property:

```
/TD=[TARGETDIR]
```

As you saw in Chapter 8, you must pass TARGETDIR in this format:

```
/TD="[TARGETDIR]\"
```

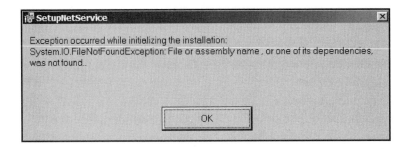

Figure 10-6. CA failure

The reason for this failure is that the internal parsing of the parameter string by the code in InstallUtilLib.dll was unable to resolve the fact that TD is a separate parameter because it has no useful delimiters around it. Oddly enough, if you use Orca to see what the CA looks like with your CustomActionData in it, you'll see the Type 51 CA, suffixed with install.SetProperty, looking somewhat like this:

```
/installtype=notransaction /action=install /LogFile= /TD=[TARGETDIR]
"[#_D3E589ED58B4F1FE93DCAEA2768FA252]" "[VSDFxConfigFile]"
```

As you can see, VS decided to put your CustomActionData string in the middle of the LogFile specification. It does this whether you get the format of your CustomActionData string right or not, so the end result is that the LogFile specification is empty (which you can see if you try to retrieve its value as you did in the code in the installer class). This isn't a particularly great loss because the LogFile specification is intended to be used by the InstallUtil.exe .NET utility, not by the installer classes. However, the main reason for this discussion is to point out that if you see messages such as the one in Figure 10-6, it's highly likely that your CustomActionData string is incorrect and is fooling the internal parser, which seems to trip over the file specification enclosed in square brackets and thinks that the error is due to a missing file. There does seem to be some odd behavior here, so if you can't get around this issue, you can use Orca to rearrange the command-line string, putting your /TD="[TARGETDIR]\" or equivalent immediately after the /action=install part.

Should You Use .NET Installer Classes?

Just in case you're thinking that .NET Services are special and therefore require that you use installer classes, they're not, and you can install .NET Services using the Service tables in the same way that you install a Win32 Service. You can build a deployment project that installs a .NET Service program to some application folder, but don't add any installer class CAs. Just generate the package and then populate the Service tables, illustrated with the NetWithServiceTable project in the chapter's sample code.

Whether to use installer classes or not depends on a number of things:

- If you're just installing a Service that doesn't require any configuration other than the usual things that can be specified in the Service tables, you should use the Service tables instead of installer classes. The ServiceControl table in particular is good at dealing with dependencies and has the ability to control other Services during the install and the uninstall. Should you decide to use .NET installer classes, you can still consider using the ServiceControl table to control other Services during the install or uninstall. And even if you do need to perform extra configuration of your Service, you should realize by now that you can use many types of CAs instead of putting code in an override method of an installer class. In addition, you certainly don't need to use installer classes to create Registry entries that you can specify more easily by using VS's Registry on Target Machine view.

- The reason you used Orca to populate those Service tables is that VS has no support for populating them. This isn't true of some other tools that generate installation packages. If you look at tools from InstallShield, Wise, and others you'll find support in their development environments for specifying the data that ultimately goes into the package's Service tables. So although you might think that using Orca is awkward or difficult, keep in mind that you or your development organization might not need to use Orca to install with the installer's Service tables.

- Microsoft usually supplies a way for developers to install Services on their development systems. The wizards for Win32 Service projects generate code so that you can install a Service by running it with the –Service command-line argument. In the .NET world, perhaps you should consider the installer classes as the equivalent of this: useful for developers with VS who want to install Services on development systems, but not the way to install Services in installation packages shipped to customers.

- The install isn't yet complete when your Install CA is called. Perhaps the most critical issue here relates to the two-phase commit process that Windows Installer uses to install assemblies into the GAC. This means that assemblies haven't yet been committed to the GAC at the time that your CA is called (see Chapter 8). Therefore, your CA won't work if it's dependent on assemblies that you're installing into the GAC. Having said that, it's also the case that assemblies aren't yet committed into the GAC when the StartServices action is performed, so again your Service won't start if it's dependent on assemblies you're installing into the GAC. Taking these factors into account, the best design approach is to avoid dependent assemblies in the GAC, and use Service tables to install your Services.

Summary

Installing Services using the installer's ServiceInstall and ServiceControl tables isn't complicated, especially if you're familiar with the Win32 APIs to create Services. .NET Services are built on top of traditional Win32 Services and have some interesting installer classes that you should evaluate when choosing between ways to install Services. Difficulties when installing Services are often the result of the failure of the Service to start or stop correctly, resulting in the entire installation rolling back. Services installed with Windows Installer generally install and uninstall best when they rigorously obey the protocols of the start, stop, and other Service Control requests.

CHAPTER 11

The GAC and Updating Assemblies

YOU LOOKED AT .NET assemblies in Chapter 8. In this chapter, you'll delve more into the GAC and the issues involved with installing new versions of assemblies. Although I use the generic term "assemblies" here, in practice I'm talking about .NET class libraries.

The GAC

Most file systems intended for use by humans focus on the name of the file. The name makes the file unique, and consequently you can't have two files with the same name in the same location. However, the GAC is designed to solve the problem of having multiple files in the same location that do have the same name but are different in some other way. The GAC treats the combination of name, culture, assembly version, and strong name as defining a unique assembly, so you can install as many assemblies in the GAC as you like as long as they differ in one of those attributes. This is still an evolving framework, so it's likely that there will be additional attributes in the future that describe assemblies. Note that these attributes are in the MsiAssemblyName table; the fact that this is a "name" table should help you understand the idea that these attributes "name" an assembly. In the same sense that a strong name is part of an assembly identity, so are the version and culture. In other words, these attributes contribute to the identity of an assembly.

The main difference in the context of installations between the GAC and conventional file systems is the idea of versions. File versions play a large role in installations because they determine whether an incoming version of a file—a candidate for installation—should replace an existing file at the same location. However, file versions in the GAC are largely subordinate to the idea of assembly versions because the GAC primarily uses the assembly version to determine whether to replace a file or not. Apart from dealing with updating assemblies in the GAC, this can be an issue if you switch to or from using the GAC because the overwrite rules change. If your product installs files to a non-GAC location, you'll be updating the assembly based on file version, but if you switch to installing into the GAC, the assembly version matters, and vice versa. However, you'll see in a subsequent section that you can use the file version to update assemblies in the GAC.

Why Use the GAC?

The GAC is intended as the repository for shared assemblies, and I mentioned the design issues relating to sharing code in the GAC in Chapter 8. But sometimes the decision to install assemblies into the GAC seems to be a consequence of installation difficulties. Here are two of those difficulties:

1. If you're a developer building a class library that exposes COM interfaces, you're probably more familiar with using the Regasm.exe utility than you are with Windows Installer. If you run Regasm.exe and install the class library in the GAC, then it just works. The registration entries specify a particular assembly with no reference to a location, and client programs will find it in the GAC. Although Regasm.exe has a /codebase option that allows you to have the assembly outside the GAC, how do you make that work in the context of an installation? The class library is copied to a user-determined location, because the install offers a choice of installation folder. So, then the install needs to figure out how to run Regasm.exe with text in the /codebase option that points to that install location. This leads many developers to consider the GAC the easiest place to install because these issues don't arise.

2. When you have a self-contained application consisting of executables and class libraries, it's fairly straightforward to have your class library assemblies in the same folders as your client executables. But if Windows calls your assemblies in some way (a more general example of the preceding COM case), it can be much more difficult to use private application folders. If your assembly is called from a management console (mmc.exe) or from any system executable in a non-COM fashion, it's not immediately clear that there's a good solution that doesn't use the GAC. After all, the GAC is among the first places that Windows searches to find an assembly.

Although you can use XML configuration files to redirect assembly versions and locations so that you can avoid using the GAC, there's no good solution to updating these configuration files. If you've installed an XML configuration file with your product and now you want to change a part of it, you need code during the installation that not only can update that part of the XML, but also can undo the change if the installation rolls back. One way to avoid updating a configuration file is to replace it with a new one in your updated install, but there are also difficulties with this approach. You first must deal with the

Windows Installer overwrite rules as they relate to data files (see Chapter 6). Then you need to decide exactly what the content of that configuration file should be. This might be straightforward, but it could equally be nontrivial if you're updating publisher policy files or multiple client configuration files that are potentially scattered around the target system.

Assuming you have a class library assembly already installed in the GAC, look at the ways you could replace this with a newer copy that has the same assembly version, 1.0.0.0, but a higher file version, 2.0.0.0.

Why Is Assembly Version Important?

You're about to investigate ways to replace an assembly in the GAC with a new copy of that assembly with the same assembly version. It's important to understand why you might want to do this instead of simply updating the assembly version and replacing it.

Client References

Client programs with references to an assembly are, by default, tightly bound to a specific version of that assembly. In the absence of configuration files that redirect clients to other versions of an assembly, you need to keep the assembly version constant when you've fixed the code in the assembly and want to deploy the new code to update systems that already have the product installed.

Deserialization

Deserialization of serialized objects requires access to the class library assembly describing the structure of the serialized object (see Chapter 8). If you change the code in a class library and need to update the assembly into the GAC, you have little choice except to keep the assembly version, and some other attributes such as strong name, constant so that deserialization can locate the required assembly.

Major Upgrade into the GAC

You create a major upgrade in the same way as described in Chapter 6; you change the product's ProductCode, PackageCode, and ProductVersion, and you populate the Upgrade table to detect and uninstall the older version. You do this by setting the RemovePreviousVersions project property to True in VS. You expect that a major upgrade will totally uninstall the previous version of the product and then reinstall the new version (remember that this strictly depends on the sequencing of RemoveExistingProducts). This uninstallation and reinstallation behaves exactly as you'd expect with regard to assemblies in the GAC, except for a behavioral quirk. When you perform a major upgrade to replace the existing assembly version 1.0.0.0 with the newer assembly version 1.0.0.0, it appears at first that the assembly hasn't been installed. Looking in the Windows assembly folder shows that it's not there. If you take a Windows Installer log of the major upgrade, you'll find an entry that looks something like this:

```
MSI (c) (D4:1C): skipping installation of assembly component:
{B0C11D1B-882E-1AA5-8222-BF0AFA274DBF} since the assembly already exists
```

Although this behavior appears to be an optimization to prevent an assembly from being replaced unnecessarily, it happens before the RemoveExistingProducts action is performed (the removal of the older product). This action removes the old product's assembly from the GAC. However, the decision that the assembly won't be installed doesn't appear to be reevaluated after RemoveExistingProducts is done, and consequently the assembly doesn't show up in the GAC at all. This behavior is seen in Windows 2000 SP3 and Windows XP SP1, and appears to be a bug. However, if you cause an automatic repair on the newly installed product, by using a shortcut for example, you'll see the Windows Installer progress bar doing the repair to install the file version 2.0.0.0 assembly into the GAC. An explicit repair also puts the assembly into the GAC. So the major upgrade does update the GAC with the newer file version of the assembly, but only after a repair.

Minor Upgrade into the GAC

You can perform a minor upgrade by reinstalling the entire package—a technique you used in Chapter 6—by updating the ProductVersion and changing the PackageCode but keeping the name of the package file the same. Then you usually install the minor upgrade with a command line of REINSTALL=ALL REINSTALLMODE=vomus. That "o" in the REINSTALLMODE string is documented as "Reinstall if file is missing or if an older version is present," which is what a minor upgrade is all about and why "o" is a common and correct choice.

Installing a minor upgrade by reinstalling the package has the same general issue as the major upgrade regarding updating assemblies in the GAC. If you create an updated copy of the assembly that has the same assembly version as the assembly already installed, the existing assembly in the GAC won't be replaced. If you take a log, you'll see the same message that you saw in the major upgrade:

```
MSI (s) (BC:EC): skipping installation of assembly component:
{B0C11D1B-882E-1AA5-8222-BF0AFA274DBF} since the assembly already exists
```

This is reasonable in the context of assembly version, but note that the file version has no effect on this behavior. If the incoming assembly has a higher file version than the one in the GAC, it won't cause the existing assembly in the GAC to be replaced. The "o" choice of REINSTALLMODE applies to assembly version, not file version.

Updating by Incrementing Assembly Version

You can cause a new version of an assembly to be installed into the GAC by incrementing the assembly version of your class library. If you do this with a VS setup project and perform a minor upgrade, an installer log of the minor upgrade will contain a message like this:

```
MSI (s) (E4:18): SELMGR: ComponentId '{B0C11D1B-882E-1AA5-8222-BF0AFA274DBF}'
     is registered to feature 'DefaultFeature', but is not present
     in the Component table.
Removal of components from a feature is not supported!
MSI (s) (E4:18): SELMGR: The feature-component mapping registration is broken for
     feature 'DefaultFeature' of product '{3B9EA0E2-E0D3-4BA0-A373-7181CFFEF81A}'
```

This says that the new package doesn't contain the component identified by that GUID, and that the feature-component mapping is broken. The log reports this error because there's already an installed product with a ProductCode that's mapped to a set of features and components, and a minor upgrade shouldn't delete any components that are already associated with the product. The component that's now missing becomes "orphaned"—it's no longer properly associated with a product. If you uninstall the product after the minor upgrade that broke the mapping, you'd see that the assembly remains behind in the GAC and is extremely difficult to remove. Attempting a manual deletion by right-clicking the file in the Windows assembly folder doesn't let you remove it, and Gacutil.exe doesn't remove it either.

This happened because VS saw that the assembly had a new assembly version and changed the installer component GUID associated with the assembly file. This is perfectly reasonable in the more general sense of what component GUIDs are all about. VS changed the component GUID because the resources in the component changed: You changed the assembly version. This is reasonable behavior for VS because it's the safe default behavior. After all, VS doesn't know that you're intending a minor upgrade, and you don't want a product installation package containing the old version of the assembly to have the same installer component GUID as a different product containing a newer version of the assembly. But it does mean that a minor upgrade of the *same* product leaves you with a problem.

You can correct this by using Orca to go into the package and replace the new component GUID with the one from the original package. In most packages, such as the VS setup projects for this chapter, changing this GUID just means going to the package's Component table, locating the row for the assembly, and changing the GUID in ComponentID to be the same as the GUID for the assembly's component in the original install. After you've done this, the updated assembly will replace the older version in the GAC. To summarize the situation, REINSTALLMODE=vomus won't replace an assembly in the GAC unless the assembly version is incremented, and doing this with VS requires some care because incrementing the assembly version causes its installer component GUID to change in the resulting package. Incidentally, VS isn't totally arbitrary in its choice of component GUID when it builds the package. If you change the assembly version back to the previous version, VS's setup project will remember the installer's component GUID that was used for that assembly version and use it in the resulting package.

Replacing the Assembly with REINSTALLMODE=vemus

To replace an assembly in the GAC with a newer copy of the assembly that has the same assembly version, you could perhaps perform a minor upgrade using "e" instead of "o" in the REINSTALLMODE value. Although this looks promising—the "e" means replace the file if an equal or older version is present—using "e" doesn't replace the assembly. A log of the installation reports "skipping installation of assembly component: {B0C11D1B-882E-1AA5-8222-BF0AFA274DBF} since the assembly already exists." This is somewhat unusual because using "e" with files outside the GAC does cause file replacement when file versions are equal. Again, this reinforces the point that assemblies in the GAC are treated differently from regular files.

Replacing the Assembly with REINSTALLMODE=vamus

The "a" option in "vamus" means that files should be replaced regardless of version, and performing a minor upgrade with this option does replace an assembly in the GAC. This probably isn't a good overall solution because this replacement rule applies to every file in the installation, and as a result there's the risk of replacing existing new versions of files with old ones. See the later section "Using File Version to Update a GAC Assembly" for a caveat to this behavior.

Companion Files and Assemblies

The idea behind companion files, as you saw with updating data files in Chapter 6, is that you delegate the file replacement rules for a particular file to another file by specifying that file's File table key in the Version column. In the situation you're investigating, this means that you could replace the Version value in the assembly's File table with the file table key of your client program (see Figure 11-1). This would potentially mean that the replacement rule for the assembly would be the same as the replacement rule for the client program. However, this isn't what happens. The assembly version still takes precedence and the assembly isn't replaced in the GAC.

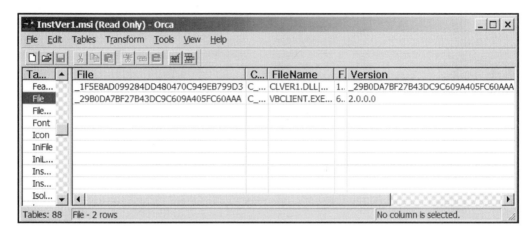

Figure 11-1. Companion file with assembly linked to client program

Replacing the Assembly with Assembly Version Lying

One of the techniques to force replacement, used in Chapter 6, is to make the versions in the package tables different from the actual versions in the files. Using the File table, you can change the Version column value to force replacement of a file that normally wouldn't be replaced because its version isn't the value you put in the table. Using the same principle, the assembly version is one of the items in the MsiAssemblyName table, so you could update the version in this table and see if "lying" about it causes the assembly to be replaced in the GAC.

Figure 11-2 shows the MsiAssemblyName table updated to say that the assembly version is 2.0.0.0. If you perform a minor upgrade (REINSTALL=ALL REINSTALLMODE=vomus) of the installed product using your altered package and look in the Windows assembly folder (the GAC), the assembly isn't there at all. Like a major upgrade, a repair causes the updated assembly to be installed. However, there's a wrinkle to this technique: An uninstall of the product leaves the assembly in the GAC, so it needs removing manually. This occurs because the uninstall process is expecting to remove version 2.0.0.0, but I lied about that—it's really still assembly version 1.0.0.0 in the GAC. When the uninstall sees assembly version 2.0.0.0 in the MsiAssemblyName table and asks the .NET Framework to remove it, the Framework won't have a matching assembly in the GAC to remove.

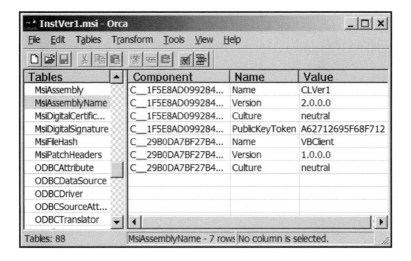

Figure 11-2. Assembly version lying

Using File Version to Update a GAC Assembly

The preceding sections are intended to illustrate the issues you must be aware of when attempting to replace an assembly in the GAC. However, you can use a little-known technique to replace an assembly in the GAC with a new copy that has the same assembly version and strong name but a new file version.

If you look at Figure 11-3, you'll see the MsiAssemblyName table, in which the assembly you're updating in the GAC now has a new entry. The Name is FileVersion and the Value is the file version, 2.0.0.0. Starting with the 1.1 version of the .NET Framework, this causes the existing assembly in the GAC to be replaced by the one with the higher file version. In other words, you can use this technique in a minor upgrade to update an assembly in the GAC that otherwise has the same assembly version, strong name, and other identity attributes. Note that you can use the same Windows Installer component GUID.

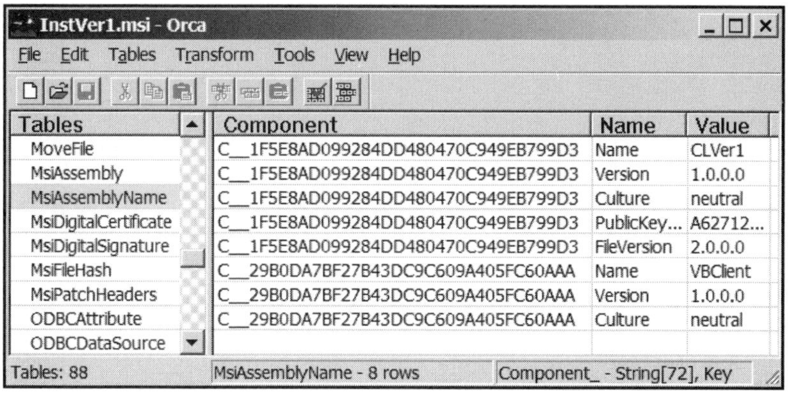

Figure 11-3. Using FileVersion in the MsiAssemblyName table

There's a caveat to using FileVersion in this way. If you perform a minor upgrade with REINSTALLMODE=vamus to overwrite all files (which you shouldn't be doing anyway), FileVersion won't downgrade existing files in the GAC that have a higher file version. In other words, REINSTALLMODE=vamus doesn't replace an assembly in the GAC if you have a FileVersion in the MsiAssemblyName table that's lower than the version of the corresponding file in the GAC.

You can also use this FileVersion technique during a major upgrade. As you saw in the earlier section "Major Upgrade into the GAC," doing a major upgrade with a VS-generated package leaves the product in a state where a repair is need-ed before the assembly with file version 2.0.0.0 is installed into the GAC. If you use FileVersion in the MsiAssemblyName table, you'll get the updated assembly with file version 2.0.0.0 in the GAC when the install has completed.

Policies and Redirection

Although the preceding sections have assumed that assembly replacement is a requirement, assembly redirection is a useful and recommended technique to change the required assembly references. You've looked at changing client-side (application) policy with configuration files (see Chapter 8), but class library assemblies can also redirect client requests to other assemblies; this is referred to as publisher policy. Instead of trying to replace an assembly in the GAC with a new one with the identical assembly version, you could deploy a new version of the assembly with a new assembly version, and install it with a publisher policy file in the GAC that causes client requests to be redirected to the new version. The starting point for this redirection using publisher policy is a text XML file describing the redirection policy. This particular example redirects requests for version 1.0.0.0 to version 2.0.0.0:

```
<configuration>
    <runtime>
        <assemblyBinding xmlns="urn:schemas-microsoft-com:asm.v1">
          <dependentAssembly>
            <assemblyIdentity name="myAssembly"
                              publicKeyToken="32ab4ba45e0a69a1"
                              culture="en-us" />
            <!-- Redirecting to version 2.0.0.0 of the assembly. -->
            <bindingRedirect oldVersion="1.0.0.0"
                             newVersion="2.0.0.0"/>
          </dependentAssembly>
        </assemblyBinding>
    </runtime>
</configuration>
```

You can compile this with the assembly linker program, Al.exe, give it a strong name because it'll be installed into the GAC, and name it:

```
policy.majorversion.minorverion.assemblyname.dll
```

Redirection from 1.0.0.0 to 2.0.0.0 for myAssembly.dll results in the actual name:

```
policy.1.0.myAssembly.dll
```

Publisher policy files are important deployment tools from the class-library assembly point of view. Whether you use publisher policy or application policy (client-side redirection) depends to a large extent on how you choose to package the pieces of an application. If your client applications are packaged separately from the class library assemblies they use, and you wish to deploy a new version of a class library assembly, a publisher policy is useful because all client programs will start using the new assembly as soon as it's installed. It's impractical to attempt to locate all installed client programs and update or install their application policy files, making publisher policy an easy solution.

Summary

The GAC is different from most other file systems you're used to dealing with, especially when it comes to updating assemblies. You looked at the differences between assembly versions and file versions and the effect these have in the GAC. Configuration files—publisher policy files in particular—are useful tools to redirect client programs to use different assemblies. Traditional deployment of new versions of shared code means that existing files are necessarily replaced, but you don't need to use this paradigm in .NET when policy files can redirect to new versions of assemblies.

As the saying goes, this is not your father's deployment model. .NET doesn't need you to follow this traditional sharing model, and actively discourages it in the GAC. This chapter should help to show you that you should be using the side-by-side model, which means that you should be installing assemblies together with the applications that need them in their nonshared private application folders. If you think you need to install assemblies into the GAC, go back and read the sections "Why Use the GAC?" in this chapter and "Why Use the GAC at All?" in Chapter 8. If you're convinced that you do need to use the GAC, you should still follow the side-by-side model and avoid sharing—and therefore needing to update—the same assembly in the GAC. If after that you're still convinced that a single copy of an assembly in the GAC needs sharing between multiple client products, look at policy redirection instead of in-place updates to get your clients to use the latest version.

CHAPTER 12

Updates Using Patches

You can update installed applications by using Windows Installer patch files. You choose a patch when the difference between one version of a product and the next is small, because only a few files have changed. The main advantage of Windows Installer patch files is exactly that: They're small and well suited to delivery over the Internet.

This chapter will show an example of creating a patch file using the tools in the SDK, because there's no support for producing patches with VS setup projects.

What Is a Patch?

At its most basic, a patch is the delta—the difference—between one version of a package and another, expressed in terms of tables that change and files that change. Conceptually, this is easy to understand. A package file is a database, and a comparison between one database and another to generate a new package containing the differences is a simple concept. Once you have the patch, you deploy it with Msiexec.exe using a command-line install naming the patch. You don't need to name the target product because that's described in the patch itself.

A patch contains three major pieces of data. The first is a transform that describes the differences between the original package and the new one, the second is the file update information (another transform and a CAB file containing changes), and the third is target information describing the product(s) that will be patched.

Creating a Patch

You'll go through the creation and application of a patch to the sample Notepad product. Creating the patch requires the following steps:

1. Create administrative install images for both the original version of the product that's already installed on client systems, and for the updated version containing new versions of the files. In reality, what's required to create a patch is a fully uncompressed image so that the SDK tools can

determine more easily the changes between the original and the update. An administrative install image is the easiest way to go from a compressed MSI package to an uncompressed collection of the files.

2. Create a Patch Creation Properties file (PCP) file, with the .pcp suffix. This is a database package similar to an MSI package that contains parameters to the patching process.

3. Run the patch program Msimsp.exe from the Windows Installer SDK, which produces a patch file—an MSP file—from the "before" and "after" administrative images and the PCP file.

The scenario you're using is that a text file in the package is being updated, so the only content difference between the old and new packages is this updated file and the resulting changes, such as the File table column for FileSize. You're also changing the ProductVersion of the product, as defined in the Property table, from 1.0.0 to 1.0.1, although this isn't a requirement for a change to a single file. First, you create a product that users install, then some time later you make a new product package containing a fix, the updated text file, that you want to make a patch for. You make the patch from administrative images of both old and updated products, then apply the patch to the users' systems.

Creating the Administrative Install Images

An administrative image of a package consists of the package itself, together with the files separate from the package in the same folder. You might be familiar with the idea of an administrative image on a network share for users to install from. However, in this context, you're creating two administrative images of the package, because this is a necessary part of the patch-creation process; the patching tool must be able to work out the differences between the old and new versions and create the delta between them. You produce administrative images with a command line like the following:

```
msiexec /a  "path to MSI file" /qn+ TARGETDIR="path to destination folder"
```

That /qn+ option is there simply to make the process relatively free of UI, and the end result is that the package file and its content files are created in the specified folder. So to create a patch, you create two administrative images, one for the base version of the product and one containing the updated version.

Creating the PCP File

This is where the fun starts: the definition of what it takes to create a patch. This file is a database package that you can edit with Orca. There are two examples in the Windows Installer SDK: Example.pcp from an example of how to create a patch and Template.pcp, with a few of its tables populated.

There are four tables that are the minimum essential to be populated: Properties, ImageFamilies, TargetImages, and UpgradedImages. I'll go through them all and describe their contents.

When I use the term "target" in this patching context, it refers to the base package: the original MSI file that a patch is being created for. I use the term "upgraded" to describe the new package—the updated one—where the patch being created is the difference between old and new. The patch-creation process uses these terms.

TargetImages

This table describes the original base package (see Figure 12-1).

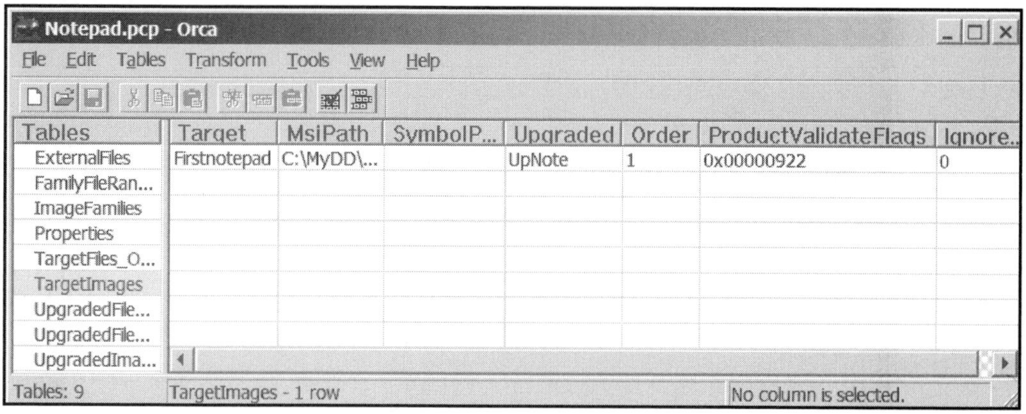

Figure 12-1. TargetImages table in the PCP file

- **Target** is a name you can choose.

- **MsiPath** is the path to the administrative image of the first MSI file. This doesn't need to be an absolute path; it can be relative to the PCP file, such as .\Admin1\Your.msi.

- **Upgraded** is the key of the corresponding new version of the product in the UpgradedImages table.

- **Order** is in case you have multiple targets that apply to a new upgraded version, so you need to specify the order in which the targets are processed.

- **ProductValidateFlags** is a set of validation flags that you use to avoid unnecessary generation of transforms, the value shown being the default. This default is the recommended value that patch authors should use.

- **IgnoreMissingSrcFiles** can be set to a nonzero value, indicating that the patch generation process shouldn't terminate if there are missing files in the administrative image—the uncompressed files. This allows you to create a patch from just the files that have changed—you don't need all the files from the entire package.

Properties

Figure 12-2 shows the Properties table in the PCP file.

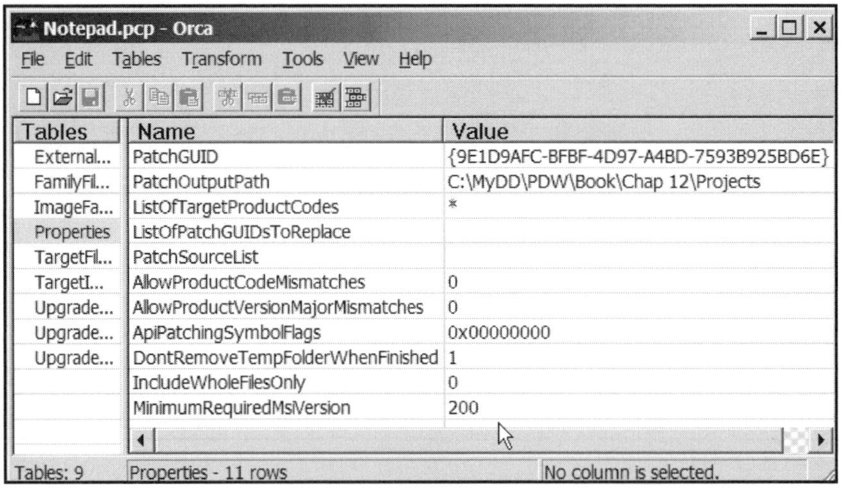

Figure 12-2. Properties table in the PCP file

The options here determine how the patch is created. The SDK documents these, so I'll be brief here.

- **PatchGUID** is a GUID for the patch. Every patch is required to have its own unique GUID.

- **PatchOutputPath** is where the patch file is to be created.

- **ListOfTargetProductCodes**, as the name implies, is the list of product code GUIDs that this patch applies to. An asterisk means that this list will be derived from the actual MSI files referred to in the TargetImages table.

- **AllowProductCodeMismatches** allows product codes to be different between the target MSI file (the base, defined in the TargetImages table) and the new package (the MSI file names in the UpgradedImages table). You'd need this to have a value of 1 if the patch effectively results in a major upgrade of one product code to another, but using a patch to generate a major upgrade definitely isn't recommended. This example shows 0 because you're doing a minor update.

- **AllowProductVersionMajorMismatches** can be set to 1 to allow the major version of the ProductVersion properties in the target and upgraded MSI files to be different. It's 0 here because you aren't changing the major version of the ProductVersion between target and upgraded versions of the packages.

- **IncludeWholeFilesOnly** with a value of 1 means that the resulting patch will contain the entire file if the file has changed between the target and upgraded versions. Otherwise, 0 means that the patch generation process will attempt to create a binary patch to the updated files. More accurately, the zero value here means that the patching process will attempt to minimize the size of the patch, and this includes the possibility that a binary patch will be created that's the delta between the old file and the updated file. However, if the resulting delta turns out to be larger than the new version of the file, the patch process will build the patch containing the new file instead of the delta.

- **MinimumRequiredMsiVersion** is set to 200 to indicate that a minimum Windows Installer version of 2.0 is required. (This numbering scheme works in the same way as the Summary Information Word Count property that also denotes the minimum version of Windows Installer needed to install the package.) It's set to 200 in this example because it allows you to omit some values from the ImageFamilies table that make this patching process a bit easier for you. This value isn't in the SDK examples so you need to add it manually.

- **DontRemoveTempFolderWhenFinished** causes intermediate temporary information to be saved in the file ~PCW_TMP.TMP system's or user's Temp folder. This can be useful in troubleshooting the patch-creation process.

Incidentally, if you do add new name and value pairs to this table, as I did with MinimumRequiredMsiVersion, be sure that you don't inadvertently add trailing spaces, otherwise the patch-creation process won't recognize the name.

UpgradedImages

This table points to the upgraded version of the package: the updated MSI file (see Figure 12-3).

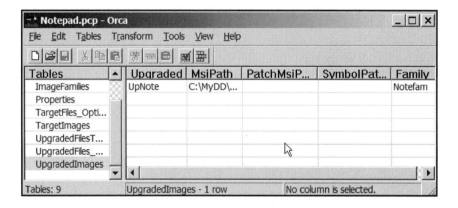

Figure 12-3. UpgradedImages table in the PCP file

- **Upgraded** is the table key. Note that this must match the corresponding target entry, so this is the value in the Upgraded column in the TargetImages table (see Figure 12-1).

- **MsiPath** is the path to the upgraded package: the new MSI file. Like MsiPath in the TargetImages table, this too can be a path relative to the PCP file instead of an absolute path. For example, .\Admin2\Your.msi.

- **Family** is a reference to the ImageFamilies table.

ImageFamilies

When you create a patch containing new or updated files, the patching tool creates a new internal CAB file to contain them. You must coordinate this CAB file with existing media tables and CAB files and also with the sequences in the package's File table (see Figure 12-4).

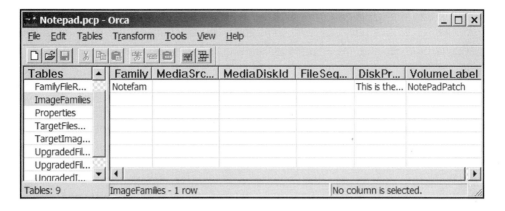

Figure 12-4. ImageFamilies table in the PCP file

- **Family** is the table's key, and it must be the same as the Family value in the UpgradedImages table (see Figure 12-3).

- **MediaSrcPropName**, **MediaDiskId**, and **FileSequenceStart** can all be left empty because you specified a MinimumRequiredMsiVersion of 200 in the Properties table. This saves you from working out file sequencing manually.

- **DiskPrompt** and **VolumeLabel** are added to the new Media table in case an explicit prompt is required for different media volumes during an install. You'd use these values if the patch file were shipped on a CD or removable media. If Windows Installer ever needs to prompt for the media containing your patch file, it will use these values, so they must accurately reflect the patch media volume label.

Those tables are the minimum that need populating to create a patch, which you perform by running MsiMsp.exe from the Windows Installer SDK.

Both the TargetImages and UpgradedImages tables contain an entry I haven't mentioned: the SymbolPaths entry. In both tables, this is the path to the debug files (PDB files) for code files that have changed. Although the patching process takes longer, the debug files are used internally to reduce the size of the binary patch. I haven't used them here because this patch example changes a text file. If your goal is the smallest possible patch package and you're patching code files, you should use this technique.

Running MsiMsp.exe

You produce the actual patch file by running MsiMsp.exe with these command-line options:

```
msimsp -s C:\MyDD\Patching\Notepad.pcp -p notepad.msp -l notey.log
```

The -s option is followed by the path to the PCP file; the -p option names the patch being created, and is required despite the existence of the PatchOutputPath value in the PCP's Properties table (see Figure 12-2). The path that's actually used is the one you pass into MsiMsp.exe with this -p option. This is just the way that MsiMsp.exe works; if you were to use the Win32 API UICreatePatchPackage in PatchWiz.dll, you could code this API call so that it uses the value in PatchOutputPath by passing NULL as the szPatchPath value.

The -l option creates a log. You'll need this in case of failures, and even in successful cases it's useful to take a look at:

```
***** Log starting: 2004-02-29 12:42:08 *****


Input-PCP path        = 'notepad.pcp'
Patch-MSP path        = 'notepad.msp'
Temp Folder = 'C:\DOCUME~1\PHIL~1.H1Z\LOCALS~1\Temp\~PCW_TMP.TMP\'
Patch GUID  = '{9E1D9AFC-BFBF-4D97-A4BD-7593B925BD6E}'
ListOfPatchGUIDsToReplace        = '<none>'
ListOfTargetProductCodes         = '*'
PatchSourceList                  = '<blank>'
AllowProductCodeMismatches       = '0'
AllowProductVersionMajorMismatches = '0'
OptimizePatchSizeForLargeFiles   = '<blank>'
ApiPatchingSymbolFlags            = '0x00000000'
MsiFileToUseToCreatePatchTables  = '<blank>'
SqlCmdToCreatePatchTable         = '<blank>'
SqlCmdToCreatePatchPackageTable  = '<blank>'
SqlCmdToCreateMsiPatchHeadersTable = '<blank>'
DontRemoveTempFolderWhenFinished  = '1'
IncludeWholeFilesOnly             = '0'
MinimumRequiredMsiVersion         = '200'


Using internal SQL cmd to create 'Patch' table.
Using internal SQL cmd to create 'PatchPackage' table.
Using internal SQL cmd to create 'MsiPatchHeaders' table.


User supressed error for ProductVersions not matching between Target and
                        Upgraded images.
```

```
      Files differ: 'C:\MyDD\PDW\Book\Chap 12\Projects\Admin2\.\SomeTextFile.txt',
                    'C:\MyDD\PDW\Book\Chap12\Projects\Admin1\.\SomeTextFile.txt'.
    Patch API could not create a small patch; using whole upgraded file.
  Including entire file:
    'C:\MyDD\PDW\Book\Chap12\Projects\Admin2\.\SomeTextFile.txt';
          FTK=_8267E0FDCD374FB891E8BAC45218DB0B;
                      temp location=Notefam\00002.FLE.


***** Log finishing: 2004-02-29 12:42:13 *****
```

Most of this is confirmation of the content of the Properties table. The text saying "User supressed (sic) error for ProductVersions . . ." results from MsiMsp.exe issuing a message box asking for confirmation of the change from 1.0.0 to 1.0.1 in this example. The log also confirms the file that has changed and that MsiMsp.exe included the entire file instead of creating a patch to it.

The end result is a patch file—an MSP file—that you can apply to the installed product. Before applying the patch, it's worth looking at the changes the patch made when compared to the original package. If you open the original MSI package with Orca, the Transform menu has a View Patch choice. Browsing to the generated patch and opening it results in Orca highlighting the areas that have changed. For example, if you look at Figure 12-5 you'll see the File table entry showing that the updated file has a different size, and the Attributes value now includes the msidbFileAttributesPatchAdded bit.

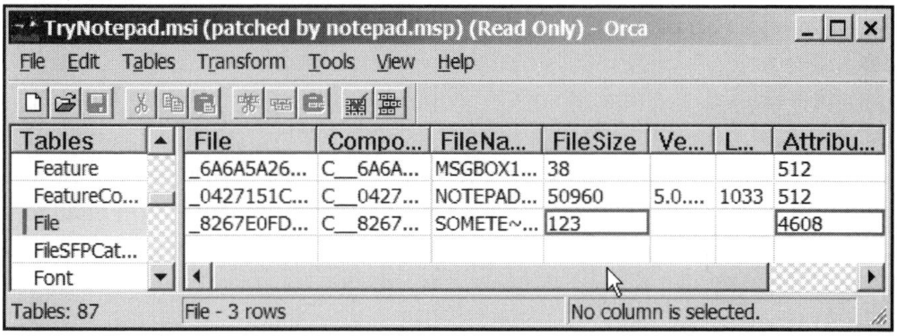

Figure 12-5. The File table showing patch differences

Applying the Patch

You apply the patch to the product installed on the client system using this command line:

```
msiexec /p  <path to patch> REINSTALL=ALL REINSTALLMODE=omus
```

When you do this with a package generated with VS, this shows the UI giving you a choice of Repair or Remove; Repair applies the patch. You can use a /q choice on that command line if you want the patch to be applied silently.

One of the issues you might have when working with MSI packages generated with VS concerns the Media table in the package. You might find that you can apply the patch to the product installed from an uncompressed administrative image (where the files are separate from the MSI package and not in a CAB file), but not from the original MSI package containing all the files (internally in a CAB file) because you get error 2356. This error is due to a mismatch between the internal CAB files of the base and updated packages. You might find that VS changes the name in the Media table's Cabinet column between generating your first MSI package and when you generate the updated package containing your patched files. In other words, the Cabinet value in the Media table of the original MSI package, and therefore in its administrative image, isn't the same as in the updated MSI package (and therefore not the same as the administrative image you generated from it). This Cabinet value might be something like #_EADEB8C6E423AA23F8C68691F63F5F7F. If this error 2356 occurs, go and check the Media table and correct the table in the updated MSI package to have the same Cabinet value as the original MSI package.

It's convenient to be able to double-click the patch and have Windows Installer just apply it without needing to specify REINSTALL=ALL and REINSTALLMODE=omus as you did in the preceding command-line install of the patch. You can do this by adding two Type 51 CAs that set these two properties when the patch is being applied. You need to author these CAs and corresponding changes to the InstallExecute sequence table in the updated MSI package so that they're present in the generated patch file. Alternatively, if you need to preserve the updated MSI package, you can just make a copy of it with these changes and refer to this copy in the PCP file. Here are the changes you need to make to the MSI package to allow the resulting patch to be double-clicked to install it:

1. Create a Type 51 CA (call it SetReinstall) and set the Source value to be REINSTALL and the Target to be ALL. If you know exactly which features are being updated, you could put the feature list in here instead of ALL.

2. Create a Type 51 CA (call it SetReinstallmode) and set the Source value to REINSTALLMODE and the Target to omus.

3. Insert these two CAs into the InstallExecuteSequence before CostFinalize.

4. For the SetReinstallmode CA you should use a Condition value of Installed AND PATCH AND NOT (REMOVE~="ALL"). This condition means that the REINSTALLMODE property is set only if the product is already installed, a patch is being applied, and the product isn't being uninstalled.

5. For the SetReinstall CA, you should use the same condition, although you might want to add an extra condition AND REINSTALL="". The reason for this is that the patch might apply to several features, but you might want to use it to correct a specific client issue with a single feature. So, you can name the feature with a REINSTALL specification on a command-line install and this CA condition won't override it.

You might have to tweak these conditions for specific cases. For example, if you were targeting a patch for a specific feature, you'd use the SetReinstall CA to set REINSTALL to the specific feature name(s) instead of to ALL, as mentioned in the preceding point 1. However, you then need a way to identify that the patch you're applying is the patch for that feature. You can do this by naming the patch in the MediaSrcPropName column in the PCP file's ImageFamilies table. If you have a MediaSrcPropName value such as FEATURE_HOTFIX1, this names the patch. So, instead of just AND PATCH, your condition would add AND PATCH=FEATURE_HOTFIX1, giving you a patch condition of this:

AND PATCH AND PATCH=FEATURE_HOTFIX1

So, you're testing that you're patching and that the patch is the appropriate one. This means that REINSTALL and REINSTALLMODE only get set to the appropriate values when the patch targets the specific feature.

Patching Multiple Products

The Properties table of the PCP file has a value for the ListOfTargetProduct Codes property. As the name implies, you can create a patch that targets multiple installed products. The TargetImages and UpgradedImages tables in the PCP file allow you to specify multiple MSI packages. Although I've not described it here, this might be a useful technique to update a product suite of several separately installed MSI packages or even multiple versions of a product, including the base release and later versions.

Patching Tips

Prior to Windows Installer version 2.0, applying a patch always required access to the source medium. Version 2.0 helps eliminate this requirement, but the biggest complaint you see in patching is still that the installation of the patch might ask for the original product package, such as the CD or perhaps the network install source. Sometimes this might be a deliberate choice you can make—you might decide that your clients shouldn't be able to install patches without verifying that they have the original install medium. The ResolveSource action is one thing that causes Windows Installer to go to the original source, so your condition on the ResolveSource action should include AND NOT PATCH to eliminate source resolution during patching.

Another thing that can cause a prompt for the source install medium is when unversioned files are in the original installation. Windows Installer cannot tell whether an unversioned file on disk is the same as the one originally installed with the product, which is the file that the patch might apply to. Therefore, Windows Installer goes to the original source medium to get the original file. Windows Installer 2.0 (MSI 2.0) does this copy from the source medium whether it needs to patch the file or not. You can prevent the possibility of Windows Installer copying these unversioned files from the source by using the MsiFileHash table. This table in the MSI package contains one entry for each file in the package that you compute the hash for using the MsiGetFileHash Win32 API call or the SDK tools MsiFiler.exe and WiFilVer.vbs. The point of the file hash is that it's stored in the cached MSI package for the product on the client's system. When a patch install needs to determine whether the unversioned file has changed, Windows Installer can compute the file hash for the unversioned file on the client's system and compare it with the corresponding hash in the MsiFileHash table of the cached MSI package, instead of retrieving the file from the original source medium. If the two file hashes are identical, the file hasn't changed and can be patched because it's identical to the one installed as part of the product. In MSI 3.0, this behavior has been enhanced: It goes to the source medium to copy the file if there's no MsiFileHash entry for it *and* if the patch affects the file. MSI 3.0 tries to avoid going to the source install location at all costs. A file is only considered in the patch application if the patch has touched it. Then, it'll only go to the source if the file uses a delta patch (not Full-File update), and if the file on disk or any one of the caches that MSI 3.0 maintains cannot be patched using the current delta.

In addition, you should follow these recommendations:

- Don't change the sequence numbers of files between the original and the update packages.

- You can add new files in a patch update, but you must add them at the end of the file sequence. This wasn't something you looked at in this particular example because you didn't add files. Also, you used MinimumRequiredMsiVersion of 200 in the Properties table of the PCP file and consequently didn't need to set the FileSequenceStart value in the ImageFamilies table.

- Use the default ProductValidateFlags value in the TargetImages table of the PCP file.

- Use patches for minor and small updates, not for major upgrades.

Uninstalling Patches

One of the useful features of MSI 3.0, which is scheduled for release in mid-2004, is the ability to uninstall patches and restore the product as it was before the patch was installed. Internally, this is accomplished by caching a minimum set of files (the original product and the latest baseline) before the patch is applied to the client system so that the files can be restored if the patch is uninstalled. One of the results of this is that Windows Installer doesn't need to go back to the source install location to obtain previous versions of files when a patch is uninstalled. Chapter 16 describes some of the other features of MSI 3.0 .

Transforms

I mentioned at the start of this chapter that a patch package consists of the difference between the original database and the new one in terms of updated files, plus the difference in terms of database table changes. A transform describes this database table difference; transform files have an MST suffix. As an example of creating a transform, you can open a base package and edit it with Orca or some other means, then save it as a different name. Then you can use the following VBScript to generate a transform describing the difference between the two packages:

```
option explicit
dim wi, basedb, newdb
const msiTransformValidationLanguage = 1
const msiTransformErrorNone = 0
set wi = CreateObject("WindowsInstaller.Installer")
set basedb = wi.opendatabase("trynotepad.msi", 0)
set newdb = wi.opendatabase ("modifiednotepad.msi", 0)
newdb.GenerateTransform basedb, "thetransform.mst"
newdb.CreateTransformSummaryInfo basedb, "thetransform.mst",_
    msiTransformErrorNone, msiTransformValidationLanguage
set wi=Nothing
```

This example should be self-explanatory, but note that the summary information stream for the transform file is applied to the file separately from the creation of the actual transform file.

You can generate a transform without using a script such as this; Orca can generate a transform for you. You do this by opening the original MSI package with Orca and then using the Transform ➤ New Transform menu choice. You can turn any changes you apply to the package after this into a transform by using the Transform ➤ Generate Transforms menu choice.

The point of having a transform is that you can apply it to the base package at install time, resulting in an install that behaves like the modified package. In fact, you can *only* apply it at first install of the product. One of the often-quoted uses of transforms is localization. Starting with a base package, you can translate the UI and its messages into some other language and then generate a transform. Then you can install the base plus the transform instead of the modified package. The advantage of this is that you can ship a single package for a product together with a number of transform files, each containing a specific language. The resulting collection of files is smaller in total size when compared to a number of MSI packages, each with its own language. Another scenario is a transform that deletes one or more features from a package for some set of users. This is commonly referred to as a customization transform because it's useful when system administrators want to tailor some set of product features to end users.

Summary

The primary advantage of patches is that they're much more compact than the other servicing choices you saw in Chapter 6 (major and minor upgrades). This makes them ideal for Internet downloads. Although generating a patch is nontrivial, you'll probably find that third-party tools can hide a lot of the detail I've covered here using the SDK tools.

Installation Environments

IN THIS CHAPTER, you'll look at some of the different ways you can install your product, and also examine the impact of Terminal Server and Windows 64-bit.

Advertised Installations

One of the ways to install a product is for you to advertise it to the extent that the user can see the visible part of the product (usually a shortcut), and using that shortcut causes the product to be fully installed onto the user's system. Although an advertised install is most closely associated with advertised shortcuts, advertisement is also related to the Windows Installer repair mechanism, and is associated with installed items that have an MSI descriptor attached to them (which includes file extension and COM registration entries).

This might be stating the obvious, but you must mark shortcuts as advertised in the MSI package so they can perform an automatic installation when the client uses them. If they're advertised, this also means automatic Windows Installer repair activities will use them, so the downstream effect of an advertised shortcut is that the components and features it refers to are health-checked and missing components reinstalled if necessary. This is usually a good thing, but occasionally setup programs install files that are then manually removed. Sometimes it's a surprise to see them reinstalled when a shortcut is used that causes a repair.

Advertised installs in this context are usually "no touch" because, as you'll see, the end user isn't shown dialogs or choices; using the shortcut causes the installation to occur showing only a Windows Installer progress bar. To a developer who might like the concept of tweaking every possible option during the installation process, perhaps the idea that the user has no choices appears unfair. However, many users or corporate environments don't need these choices and prefer that the install just do the right thing, work properly, and not bother them.

VS, as you saw in Chapter 2, creates advertised shortcuts, which means you can advertise a product setup created with VS and have it install on demand. Here's a way to install a product in advertised mode:

```
Msiexec /jm <path to MSI package>
```

The "j" in the command line is what installs the product in advertised mode, and the "m" is the per-machine option. This means that the product is advertised to all users on the system. To advertise to the current interactive user, use the "u" option instead. However, this won't allow a non-Administrator interactive user to install the product, because you don't want non-Administrator users to be able to advertise the package to themselves and install it with elevated privileges. The key notion of installing with elevated privileges is that the application install is managed; that is, blessed by the system or domain administrator with Administrator privileges.

If you do this, for example with the MSI package from Chapter 2, you'll see that not only is there no UI during the user's install, but there also isn't one when you advertise the product with the /j command-line option. Furthermore, that msiexec /j command line ignores any properties entered on the command line. So in the absence of a UI and specification of property values, how does the user get to modify something such as the application folder where the product is to be installed, or the per-user and per-machine choices? The short answer is that the user doesn't get to choose, and that's because this type of installation is intended primarily for situations where the user doesn't get a choice. This is common in corporate managed networks where the Total Cost of Ownership (TCO) can be reduced by having all workstations configured the same way with the same products. An administrator can set up the advertised install so that the product is installed from a common share on a server when first used.

Because the advertised install has no UI, there's potentially an issue if the MSI package is deployed with behavior that differs from the default behavior that exists in the package, such as the installation folder, per-machine or per-user, and features being installed. This is where transforms are useful (see Chapter 12). You can make a copy of the package and edit its properties, altering the tables to change its behavior, and then generate a transform that's the difference between the two packages. You can apply this transform at the same time that the product is advertised:

```
Msiexec /jm <path to MSI package> /t sometransforms.mst
```

These transforms are applied when the product is installed.

You've seen in earlier chapters that you can perform an install silently by using the command-line option /q, and that you can specify properties on the command line. Advertisement is another way to accomplish a silent install. The advertised install is perhaps somewhat less error-prone when you use transforms because you create the required property values (or other changes) once as a transform file and then specify them once when the product is advertised.

The other thing to notice is that any CAs happen when the product is installed as a consequence of using the shortcut. In other words, this is when the InstallUISequence and InstallExecuteSequence tables are processed.

Figure 13-1 shows the sequence of actions that occur during the creation of an advertised install. This sequence is interesting because it shows which items in the package are associated with advertisement such that their use causes full installation of the advertised product. The CreateShortcuts action is there, as you would expect, but also other actions that create COM registration entries and file extension entries. You can therefore expect that not only shortcuts, but use of COM classes, ProgIDs, and file extensions cause an advertised product to be installed. Remember also that advertisement and repair are closely connected in that they use the same general mechanism (the Windows Installer MSI descriptor) to locate installed components and features and repair or install them. So, a repair can occur automatically in the same ways that an advertised product can be installed. Repair can occur when shortcuts, ProgIDs, COM classes, and file extensions are used.

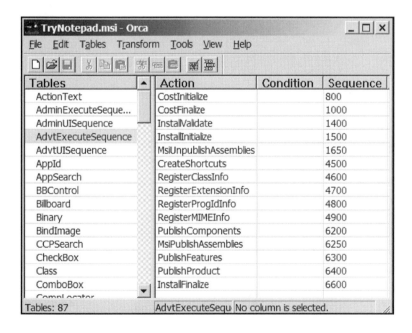

Figure 13-1. The Advertise sequence

Advertisement isn't automatically available for every feature in a package. At the feature level, you can explicitly disallow advertisement by setting the msidbFeatureAttributesDisallowAdvertise bit in the Attributes value of the Feature table. It's also still the case that the INSTALLLEVEL property determines whether a feature should be installed or not (see the section "Features and Components" in Chapter 9).

There's another type of installation that's similar to advertisement, although strictly speaking it's more a preadvertisement. You can publish products with Group Policy by configuring Group Policy Objects (GPO), but it's not a topic I'll cover in this book.

Privileges and Managed Applications

Advertisement is an important tool because it plays a large part in allowing nonprivileged users with user-level privileges to install products that would otherwise require them to have Administrator privileges. A managed application is one that an administrator has "blessed" in some way. An administrator can bless a package by advertising or installing the product to a user or a machine, or by assigning or publishing it using Group Policy or related tools.

Why is this important to the author of an MSI package? Primarily because of the effect it has on any privileges you need to install your product. If your product is being installed in a managed mode, it's allowed to run with elevated privileges because an administrator has enabled it to do so. There's no way that you, the author of the package, can declare that you'll run with elevated privileges. You can do so only if you're installing while running with Administrator privileges or otherwise have been allowed to install in a managed mode.

You might be aware that you can set a policy called AlwaysInstallElevated at the machine and user level in the Registry to enable elevated privileges during an install. Note that this policy is a machine policy and applies to every MSI package that you install, as opposed to managed installations where individual products and their MSI packages have been marked to run with elevated privileges. Using AlwaysInstallElevated is a security risk because any install will run with elevated privileges. You can never know if your machine is secure because of what a malevolent MSI package might have installed. You would never give every user the right to run any program on your system with Administrator privilege, but this is effectively what the AlwaysInstallElevated policy amounts to.

The difference between an ordinary and a managed install shows up in the properties you use if you need your install to run with elevated privileges: the AdminUser and Privileged properties. The AdminUser property is true if the installing user is a member of the Administrators group. The Privileged property is true if the install is running with elevated privileges, either because the user is a member of the Administrators group *or* because it's a managed install that an administrator has blessed. This means that Privileged is probably the most appropriate property to use in a Launch Condition.

The design of your installation also has a major effect on the privileges that users need in order to install it. Although some changes to the system, such as installing Services, require Administrator privilege, there's no need for a design that requires this privilege only as a consequence of your choice of folders or Registry keys. Some Registry entries (such as HKLM) and folders (such as the Windows System folder) are more secure than user-oriented folders. In other words, don't get yourself into the situation where you perhaps made an arbitrary decision to install a file in the Windows System folder that consequently requires the installing user to have more than just user-level privileges.

Installing from the Internet

You can do a direct install from the Internet with a command line that runs Msiexec.exe referring to a URL for the package:

```
msiexec /i  http://somedomain/setups/trynotepad.msi
```

This behaves in the same way as an install from any other location: The source install location of the package is stored locally and used for any subsequent repairs or modification of the installed product. To perform a major upgrade to a newer version, put the updated version of the MSI package at a different URL and prompt the user to repeat the installation from that new URL, which replaces the older version with the newer version. A new location is preferable in order to avoid confusion with the prior version, which might still be required for repairs.

A correct install from the Internet has the characteristic that the cached source of the package is the URL. Beware of installing packages from within a browser by double-clicking an MSI file. The issue here is that you'll be downloading the package into the folder for temporary Internet files and installing it from there. You don't want the source install folder to be a temporary folder (see the section "Bootstrappers and Temp Folders" in Chapter 14 for a similar situation).

Advertisement also works from the Internet. Instead of delivering the entire MSI package to your clients, you could deliver a way to advertise the product. This doesn't necessarily mean that your clients need to run Msiexec.exe commands as you did in the previous section. There are APIs for this functionality, primarily MsiAdvertiseProductEx, so you can ship a program to perform the advertised install. Note that this API allows you to specify transforms.

For an example of advertising from the Internet using the Notepad installation, use this command:

```
msiexec /jm http://localhost/instasp/setups/trynotepad.msi
```

An issue to be aware of is that of advertised Internet installs from an administrative image. An administrative image consists of the MSI package with the constituent files stored separately in the same folder. If you advertise this, the actual installation will attempt to retrieve the files from that URL, and consequently you'll be trying to copy (for example) executable files from the Internet to the target system. Most reasonable security schemes don't allow this.

Security and Advertising with Transforms

A command line that advertises an application can also add transforms to be applied to the installed product. In the preceding example of installing from the Internet, you can use this command, using the example transform from Chapter 12:

```
msiexec /jm http://localhost/instasp/setups/trynotepad.msi
    /t http://localhost/instasp/setups/thetransform.mst
```

This causes the package to be advertised such that the transform file is applied when the product is installed.

There are security considerations with transforms. For example, you don't want users to be able to alter the contents of a transform file that's about to be installed. Because of these concerns, you can use options and properties to tell Windows Installer how to deal with using transforms at advertisement time and what to do if the transforms need to be reapplied (for example, during a repair or modification of feature content).

For example, in a command-line install, you can use the following command as an alternative to the preceding one:

```
msiexec /jm http://localhost/instasp/setups/trynotepad.msi /t @thetransform.mst
```

The @ character means that the transform is secure-at-source. In other words, the physical location is required to be in the same folder as the MSI package (the same URL folder in this example). More importantly, Windows Installer caches the transform in a secure location on the client system where users have no write access. There's also a secure-full-path choice (prefixing the transform location with a vertical bar) that differs from the secure-at-source option in that the full path (which is required) can be a different location. That is, you can have your MSI package and your transforms at a different location.

Properties and policies affect the treatment of transforms. You can set the TRANSFORMSSECURE property to 1 in the package to cause caching of transforms on the client system in a location where the user has no write access. In addition, Windows Installer retrieves the transform from the specified source path during maintenance activities, such as repair or feature modification.

You can also set the Windows Installer policy TransformsSecure to produce TRANSFORMSSECURE behavior for every product.

SDK Internet Tools: MsiStuff.exe and Setup.exe

The Windows Installer SDK has a couple of tools to help with installing from the Internet: MsiStuff.exe and Setup.exe. The SDK supplies source code, and the code content for this chapter contains the tools converted from Makefile builds to a VS 2003 solution.

Setup.exe is a customizable program that installs an MSI package from an Internet URL. The customization consists of data—such as the URL—stored inside the resource section of the code file, and MsiStuff.exe is the program that puts those resources there. The general idea is that you customize the Setup.exe program to your specific requirements using MsiStuff.exe, and then distribute Setup.exe to perform the install from the Internet, or more likely provide a link on a Web page to perform the bootstrapping. Because the source is supplied to both of these programs, you can do either of these options:

- Compile them and use them in "SDK mode," as described in the SDK documentation. This means that you run MsiStuff with a command line that specifies the parameters for the setup.

- Go into "developer mode" and use the source to construct your own custom download.

Among the items you can configure are the base URL for the MSI package, the name of the package, the type of the installation (allowing an advertised install of the package), and the minimum level of Windows Installer. If your target system isn't at that level, the program can download and install the redistributable installs for Windows Installer (InstMsiA.exe for the 9x systems and InstMsiW.exe for the NT series). It would be a useful extension to add a .NET Framework version to these capabilities, but you'd need to code that yourself.

Apart from the built-in features for installing from the Internet, there's a UI, a Cancel capability, and better error reporting than if you were to use Msiexec.exe installing from a URL. See the SDK documentation and the source for details.

MsiStuff.exe reads its command-line options and parses them for accuracy. It then opens the resource section of the target code file (Setup.exe) and adds the command-line specifications into the resources. (This also makes MsiStuff.exe an interesting example of how to use the resource APIs such as UpdateResource to modify code files.) By default, the behavior of MsiStuff.exe is accumulative, so you can run it several times to add items. You can remove existing items by specifying that item with no data following it.

When Setup.exe runs, it reads its embedded resources and follows these general steps:

1. Parses its command-line options.

2. Checks to see if another MSI-based installation is already in progress. If you're curious about the name of the mutex used to implement this, look here or in the documentation.

3. Checks that the requirements for the minimum Windows Installer level are met. If they aren't, it uses the specified URL to download and install that version.

4. Downloads the MSI package using the URLDownloadToCacheFile function.

5. Performs trust checking.

6. Queries the MSI package for its ProductCode and checks whether ProductCode is already installed. If the product isn't installed, Setup.exe does a first-time install. If the product is already installed, it performs an automatic minor upgrade using the REINSTALL=ALL REINSTALLMODE=vomus command line.

7. Performs a reboot if the upgrade to the new Windows Installer version returns a result saying a reboot is required.

Installing on Terminal Server

Quite a few articles that discuss installation of products on Terminal Server (TS) talk about using the CHANGE USER command with the /install option to put TS into "install mode." Similar articles talk about performing installations using the Add/Remove Programs applet to browse for setups because this also puts TS into install mode. The idea of install mode is that you should distinguish whether you're installing a product per-machine or per-user. However, Windows Installer already has the notion of per-user and per-machine installs, and you don't need to be in install mode to install per-machine products. In fact, it's a bad idea to install a product in per-user mode while you're in install mode, because then you've installed a per-user product in a per-machine mode. This places advertised shortcuts on other users' profiles. Needless to say, these shortcuts won't work correctly.

The other area to beware of is mapped drives. These are specific to user accounts, so if you install a product from your mapped drive that's specific to your environment, you can bet it won't be available to other user accounts on the system with their own unique mappings. If you install from a network, use a universal naming convention (UNC) name, naming the server and the share name. This isn't a specific issue with TS systems because it's also true of any install for all users from a mapped drive.

A similar drive-mapping issue occurs in reverse if you try to use a share on a TS system that's based on a particular user's TSClient shares, because they too are relative to the user.

Starting with Windows Server 2003, CAs on TS have the option of the msidbCustomActionTypeTSAware bit in the Type of the CA. If a CA is impersonating the installing user (in other words, the msidbCustomActionTypeNoImpersonate bit is *not* set), the CA will correctly impersonate the installing user on a TS system. If you don't have this bit set, per-machine CAs run with no user impersonation on TS systems. In other words, deferred CAs are running in the context of the local system account unless you set the msidbCustomActionTypeTSAware bit. If this situation is an issue because you're installing on a pre-Windows Server 2003 OS, here are a couple of alternatives:

- See if it's appropriate for your CA to be an immediate CA instead of deferred, but sequenced at the same place in the execute sequence. However, remember that immediate CAs shouldn't update the system.

- You could sequence an immediate CA after InstallFinalize. This means that you can't roll back if your CA fails. Also, the installation process won't roll back if your CA fails.

Installing on Windows 64-Bit

Windows Installer is likely to be the only way to install 64-bit applications onto Windows 64-bit systems. Although the 32-bit world has a history of non-Windows Installer setup tools and programs, it's not likely that you'll see the vendors of those products offering 64-bit development tools that aren't Windows Installer–based. I'll do a brief outline of Windows 64-bit OS behavior and its effect on installations and the tools used to build them.

When an install package runs code as part of the installation of a 64-bit product, you must consider three main issues:

- **Processes:** 32-bit processes run in an emulation layer on a Windows 64-bit OS, and have a 32-bit view of the world.

- **Registry:** 32-bit processes have a 32-bit view of the Registry. When they read and write the Registry, they read and write the 32-bit view, and they cannot directly access the 64-bit part of the Registry. If your applications are mixed 32- and 64-bit programs that share Registry entries, the programs will be looking in different places, so you probably need to have the 64-bit program explicitly access the 32-bit view of the Registry. This also means that non-Windows Installer 32-bit installation programs can install Win32 applications, but 32-bit programs cannot install 64-bit applications.

- **DLL calls:** A 32-bit process cannot call a 64-bit DLL, and vice versa. This has implications for the tools that build 64-bit packages, and for CAs at install time.

The point of these views is to allow 32-bit MSI packages and the products they install to run within the 32-bit environment of the 64-bit system, known as Windows on Windows 64 (WOW64). Keep these behaviors in mind as you look at packages and running code from them.

64-Bit Installer Packages

Installation packages—MSI files—are just files. The Windows Installer Service on 64-bit systems is a 64-bit process that installs the package, and together with its associated 64-bit and 32-bit processes and DLLs, it can install products to both the 32-bit and 64-bit parts of the system. Looking at some of the tables makes it apparent that nothing is specific to the 32/64-bit nature of the platform. For example, the UI is constructed from the Dialog and Control tables at run time by the installer Service; no 32-bit code is in the package to show these dialogs. The same is true of the Service tables—there's nothing specific to 32/64 bit systems.

Setting the msidbComponentAttributes64bit in each 64-bit component makes an installer component a 64-bit component. This isn't simply the component that contains the 64-bit executable, but everything associated with the installation of it. For example, if you have an installer component that creates Registry entries for 64-bit applications, you must also mark that component as a 64-bit component so that the Registry entries are created in the 64-bit part of the Registry. If you don't mark a component as a 64-bit component, it will be a 32-bit component, and actions taken on behalf of that component will affect the 32-bit part of the system.

At the package level, the Intel64 Summary Information property (the Template Summary) marks the package as an Intel 64-bit package, starting with the Itanium chip. The effect of this is that the package cannot be installed on 32-bit systems but can be installed in 64-bit mode on 64-bit systems. For the AMD family of 64-bit processors, use the AMD64 value.

64-Bit Custom Actions and Searches

If you use a Type 1 CA—a call to a CA DLL—you can write this code as a 64-bit DLL or a 32-bit DLL. Because Windows Installer fires off a process (Msiexec.exe) with the appropriate bit-ness to host the DLL, you don't need to tell it whether you're calling a 64-bit or a 32-bit DLL.

CAs based on scripts require an extra bit to be set in the type: the msidbCustomActionType64BitScript bit. A script needs to tell Windows Installer whether it's a 32-bit or 64-bit script because it might contain calls to CreateObject. Without some bit-ness context, the OS cannot know whether you intend to instantiate the object from a 32-bit DLL or a 64-bit DLL.

For any code that affects the target system, you need to consider which part of the system it's supposed to change or view. If a CA is being called on behalf of a 64-bit part of the install, it can run either as 32-bit or 64-bit code because either can make changes to the 32-bit part of the system. But if you're changing (or need to query) the 64-bit part of the system, you'll need to run a 64-bit CA.

Because there's a 32-bit view of the system and a 64-bit view of the system, you need to tell AppSearch which view of the system your searches should be directed towards by using the msidbLocatorType64bit value in the Type of the RegLocator table. Other AppSearches don't need this setting because they search for installed Windows Installer components by component GUID (the CompLocator table) or files (the DrLocator and IniLocator tables). In the case of a file-related AppSearch, you can use 64-bit folder properties in addition to the 32-bit folder properties.

64-Bit Folder Properties

A few folder-related properties describe path locations on a 64-bit system. For example, on a 32-bit system the ProgramFilesFolder property describes the actual location of the Program Files folder on the target machine. When you install a package that uses the ProgramFilesFolder property onto a 64-bit system, it refers to the 32-bit Program Files folder, typically C:\Program Files (x86). If you want to install a file into the 64-bit Program Files folder, you use the ProgramFiles64Folder property. You need both of these properties because you might install a 64-bit package that contains both 64-bit and 32-bit executables, and it's good practice to put each in its appropriate Program Files folder. Similarly, there's a CommonFiles64Folder property that returns the location of the Common Files folder on 64-bit systems.

COM Registration and Packaging Tools

COM registration performed from the class tables in the installation package is easier if the tools you use can populate these tables automatically. You saw in Chapter 3 how you can mark COM servers with a Register property of vsdrfCOM in VS to do this. Tools typically work by spying on the Registry entries that get created by calling DllRegisterServer, or the entries created by running Regasm.exe on a class library assembly. However, most installation development tools are 32-bit desktop applications. You know that a 64-bit DLL won't run on a 32-bit platform, so if all you have is a 64-bit version of a COM server DLL, you're stuck with the question of how to populate the COM tables with 32-bit tools that can't automatically collect that data.

One approach is fairly straightforward if you're also building 32-bit versions of your COM DLLs. The COM interfaces being exposed are the same for 32- and 64-bit servers, so you build your installation as a 32-bit package, extracting the COM registration from the 32-bit DLLs. Once you have a 32-bit installation project, you then substitute the 64-bit versions of the files and mark the installer components as 64-bit components with the msidbComponentAttributes64bit bit. This time you build with IDE settings that don't attempt COM extraction. The ease with which you can do this depends on the tools you're using, but you can do all this on a 32-bit development platform.

If you're never planning to ship 32-bit versions of the COM servers, you have some difficulties. At the time of this writing there appear to be no tools that can extract COM registration data from 64-bit COM DLLs on a 64-bit system. The methodology I've been advocating is to populate the COM tables (Class, ProgID, and so on) so that you don't require self-registration when the DLL is installed. I also advise this because of the resilience and advertisement features, together with the side-by-side COM behavior described in Chapter 3. However, in an automated build process, you compile the code and then build the MSI package from the generated code files, so your organization might have difficulties modifying this process when there are no tools that dynamically extract COM registration data from 64-bit DLLs. You could perhaps fall back to using self-registration until the tool situation improves, but be aware of the limitations and issues that this causes; self-registration is absolutely not recommended. I'll reiterate comments I've made elsewhere in this book: It's a bad idea to run registration code at install time. The Class table-driven approach to COM registration is the right way to go.

Embedded DLLs

It's not unusual to find that installation development tools have embedded a DLL in the installation, usually for CAs. In Chapter 10 you saw that VS adds a helper DLL called InstallUtilLib.dll to manage various parts of the installation. This DLL isn't a .NET DLL of managed code; it's a 32-bit DLL, so if this DLL performs installation tasks for you, there's a question of whether it will do the right things for a 64-bit package.

Similarly, InstallShield setups package a COM server to process InstallShield's proprietary InstallScript language. If this server is a 32-bit process, the InstallScript code you write will affect only the 32-bit part of the target system.

In .NET Services installed with .NET Framework Installer classes, you might suspect that there are similar potential issues, but if you look at the types of these Installer classes and what they install, you'll see that the classes all target areas of the operating system that are required to be 64-bit. Windows Services, event logs, Perfmon counters, and so on make little sense as 32-bit parts of a 64-bit system, so there's no conflict here: You'll be installing to the 64-bit system, not the 32-bit subsystem. However, note that the helper DLL in these packages (InstallUtilLib.dll) is a 32-bit DLL, so if that current design is continued into the 64-bit world, I'd expect to see a 64-bit version of InstallUtilLib.dll in the package when you target a 64-bit system.

The same should be true of ASP.NET and Web Services installed with VS Setup and Deployment Projects. These contain a DLL called MSVBDPCA.DLL that provides support for .NET Framework version checking and the installation of IIS virtual directories, so expect to see a 64-bit version of this DLL in 64-bit packages.

What About 64-Bit .NET Assemblies?

A .NET assembly compiles to intermediate language (IL) which, if you've written it with portability in mind, is Just-In-Time (JIT) compiled to native processor code when it runs. But what if you made it either 32-bit or 64-bit dependent because of some P/Invoke call? Also, you might get into the situation where a running 64-bit process needs to load your assembly from the GAC but your assembly is designed to run in 32-bit mode. Because of these edge situations when assemblies are being loaded, it's likely you'll see something in Windows Installer describing what an assembly is capable of.

Summary

Advertisement is a key technology for deployment, and should be given serious consideration in corporate networks and other managed environments. As a package author, you should decide whether your product supports advertisement as an installation method. It's also the case that you should test your install package in the appropriate deployment scenarios to make sure it behaves as expected. This chapter describes some of these environments: installing advertised products, installing on TS and on 64-bit systems, and from the Internet. Windows Installer integrates well with the Internet, including advertisement, and the SDK has sample code to assist in installing from the Internet.

Over time, 64-bit systems will get more important. Although the Windows Installer SDK has documentation for this, the tools for development of 64-bit packages for the most part appear somewhat incomplete as of spring 2004.

CHAPTER 14

How-Tos, Tips, and Gotchas

THIS CHAPTER IS A grab bag of tips, tricks, and advice. When you have a problem building or installing a package, take a look here. The advice is arranged into sections called "How To," "Advice," and "Warning." The "How To" section is a collection of tools and code that you might find useful, and the "Warnings" section tells you about some of the traps lying in wait when you're building and running your installs. The Advice section offers recommendations for good practices that I believe will make your installs easier to build and maintain.

How To . . .

Some questions about debugging or building installs crop up regularly. To choose one example that touches two of the following items, I'm surprised at how often repair turns up in discussions, and how to disable it. Repair issues are often the consequence of an installer repair dialog while someone is using the application. I must admit that it's crossed my mind more than once whether someone is asking how to disable the repair so that the pesky installer dialog goes away, despite the fact that something might well be broken. If it happens to you, I hope this book helps you diagnose the problem instead of hiding it.

Find Dependent DLLs

You can find out what DLLs a file is linked to by using a dependency walker program. There's one called depends.exe in the Platform SDK tools, and another at http://www.dependencywalker.com. Be aware that a dependency walker program cannot know about any COM servers that might be required when a program runs because there's no reference to them in the linking section of the code file. It also cannot know of any files loaded by calling the Win32 API LoadLibrary(Ex).

Prevent Repair with a Null Component GUID

One of the ways you can prevent an installer component from being repaired is by not giving it a GUID. This prevents the installer component from being registered with Windows Installer, so it won't be repaired. However, this needs care. For example, being registered is what makes shortcuts work, and an advertised shortcut won't work if its target isn't registered. If you don't want shortcuts to initiate repair, you can install them unadvertised (see the documentation for the Target column in the Shortcut table and the DISABLEADVTSHORTCUTS property). In addition, you cannot service the component with patches or minor upgrades if it isn't registered.

Show FilesInUse Dialog

Windows Installer detects when in-use files are being replaced. If a UI window is associated with the application using the file, Windows Installer prompts you to close the application. The way this works depends on a FilesInUse dialog being authored in the package. Most tools create this dialog to take advantage of this feature of Windows Installer. The issue is whether you can use a UI window to close down the application. If there isn't one, the install will silently mark the file to be replaced and require a reboot at the end.

However, you can use the installer APIs to show this dialog if you're willing to do your own detection of in-use files and to prompt the user to do whatever is necessary to release them.

You can use a VBScript CA to invoke the FilesInUse dialog. The assumption here is that you can detect your in-use situation with VBScript. The way it works requires that the script return a value that tells the installer how to proceed, and this in turn requires that the script CA be a function. As I noted in Chapter 5, VS doesn't let you name the function to be called in the script. With that in mind, this is the basic CA script code to cause a FilesInUse dialog to be invoked:

```
option explicit
Function DoFilesInUse
dim inst, rec, res
const tryagain=4
const DoExit = 2
const Docontinue =1
set inst = Session.Installer
set rec=inst.CreateRecord (2)
rec.StringData(1) = " "
rec.StringData(2) = "Please use Task Manager to terminate the program MyFile.exe"
```

```
Do
res = Session.Message (&H05000000, rec)
' check for the program terminated
loop until res <> tryagain
DoFilesInUse = res
end function
```

This function uses the Windows Installer automation interface to create a record containing information that's shown to the user, and repeatedly calls the Session.Message method to show the dialog until the user no longer replies with the Try Again button. The &H05000000 parameter is the value of msiMessageTypeFilesInUse, sending the record to the FilesInUse dialog. Note that in silent installs this dialog isn't shown.

Figure 14-1 shows the CustomAction table for a VS Install CA, modified to have the function name in the Target column.

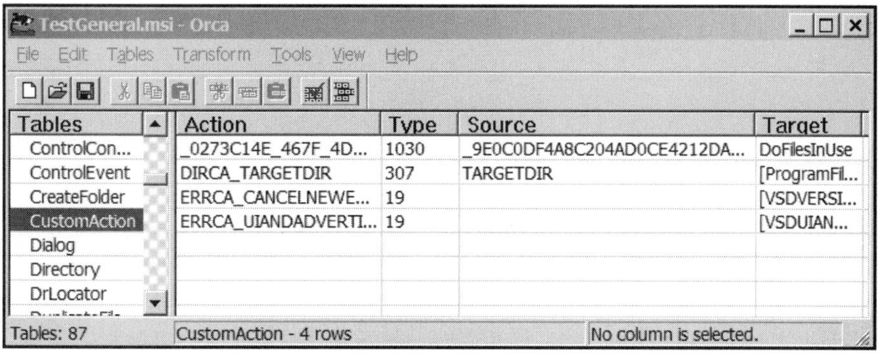

Figure 14-1. CustomAction table with target showing function name

If you want more flexibility, you can do the same in a CA DLL function, and use C++ to detect the in-use situation and report it to the user:

```
UINT __stdcall ShowFilesInUse (MSIHANDLE hInstall)
{
PMSIHANDLE hRec = MsiCreateRecord(4);
MsiRecordSetString(hRec, 1, TEXT(" "));
MsiRecordSetString(hRec, 2, TEXT("Please use Task Manager to Terminate these
     programs:"));
MsiRecordSetString(hRec, 3, TEXT("someprogram.exe"));
UINT res = 0;
do
{
res = MsiProcessMessage(hInstall, INSTALLMESSAGE_FILESINUSE, hRec);
}
```

```
while (res == IDRETRY);
if (IDOK==res) // 1 is the Continue button in VS
    return 0;
if (IDCANCEL ==res) // The Exit button in VS
    return ERROR_INSTALL_USEREXIT;
return 0;
}
```

Find In-Use Files in the Log

You can detect when in-use files are causing a reboot by taking a log and searching for the string "in use" (without the quotes), or 1603. The log notes which files are in use at the time of an install or uninstall and that would require a reboot to replace. You can also look for 1903, an error number indicating that a restart is being scheduled. (Internally, you can use the ReplacedInUseFiles property to detect that a file being replaced during the install was held in use, but note that this property isn't set until the InstallExecute or InstallFinalize actions.)

Uninstall Broken Packages

If you have an installed product that won't uninstall because it calls a broken Uninstall CA or has a ResolveSource action that wants to access an original package that you don't have anymore, it's sometimes possible to hack your way out of the problem. The package being processed is one of the cached MSI files with obscure names in the Windows\Installer folder. If you have enough privileges, you can open the MSI file with Orca and fix whatever is breaking. If it's a ResolveSource or a CA that's causing the problem, just make the condition false and save the file, then try the uninstall again. You can identify which cached MSI package belongs to your product with the MsiGetProductInfo Win32 API call (Installer.ProductInfo in the automation interface, passing LocalPackage as the second parameter).

The other method that you can use is the Msizap.exe utility. This has a number of command-line options that you can use to remove all the Windows Installer data (Registry entries) for a product. It doesn't remove the product's files. There's also a UI program called the Windows Installer CleanUp Utility that's described mostly in Microsoft Knowledge Base articles associated with Microsoft Office. There were two versions at one time: one for the Windows 9x systems and one for the NT series. This cleanup utility is a UI wrapper around Msizap.exe, and often isn't appropriate to use. For example, prior to March 2004, Knowledge Base article 238413 described the cleanup utility as not supported on MSI 2.0 and later, until Knowledge Base article 290301 announced a new version

How-Tos, Tips, and Gotchas

that applies to 9x and NT series and new versions of Office. Msizap, on the other hand, is current with each release of MSI.

List Windows Protected Files

On the newer OS versions, most OS files are protected from replacement with a scheme that restores them from a cached location on disk, or from the Windows OS installation CD if the file needing replacement isn't in the cache. This is called Windows File Protection (WFP). You can replace these protected files only in Microsoft-approved ways, which include service packs, hotfixes, and other setups that update OS components such as MDAC and the Windows Installer engine. The bottom line is that you cannot replace these protected files, so if your application requires some minimum level of an OS feature, you'll need to ask the user to install a service pack. Although Windows Installer is integrated with WFP so as not to replace protected files, the file protection applies to all types of setup programs except the Microsoft-approved ones that I just mentioned. There isn't a list of which files are protected, but one way to create a list is to run the following program on the OS in question:

```
#include "stdafx.h"
#include <windows.h>
#include <stdio.h>
#include <sfc.h>

PROTECTED_FILE_DATA aFile = {0};
FILE *stream;
int main(int argc, char* argv[])
{
    BOOL res = true;
    long i=0;
    stream = fopen( "sfcfiles.txt", "w" );
    while (res)
    {
      res = SfcGetNextProtectedFile (NULL, &aFile) ;
       if (res)
            fprintf(stream, "%S\n", aFile.FileName);
     }
    fclose (stream);
    return 0;
}
```

This program requires linking with sfc.lib. The key API here is SfcGetNextProtectedFile, which enumerates each protected file. If you want to

245

know if a specific file is protected, you can use the SfcIsFileProtected API, passing the full path to the target file.

You shouldn't replace protected files using some brute-force approach because Windows replaces them. If it can't find them in the cache, it will prompt the user for the CD to replace them.

Install Performance Counters

The .NET Framework has the PerformanceCounterInstaller class to install custom performance counters. This works in the same general way as the other installer classes: as CAs that call those specialized classes during the install.

However, don't overlook the other existing methods of installing performance counters, although they're more appropriate for C++ providers. The utility programs Lodctr.exe (to install) and Unlodctr.exe (to uninstall) are part of the OS; they're protected files in the System folder. You can use them in Type 50 CAs, where the Property table has an entry naming Lodctr.exe

Use Properties in the Standard Dialogs

You can add your own text, as well as properties, to VS's setup dialogs to be more informative.

Figure 14-2 shows the text in the final dialog of the install, altered to report the name and the version of the product and where it has been installed.

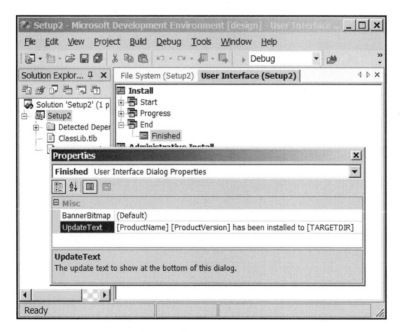

Figure 14-2. Properties in VS's UpdateText

Log an Uninstall

Sometimes an uninstall doesn't work and a log would be useful to find out why. You can create a log with a command line such as this:

```
msiexec /x {ProductCode Guid} /l*v arp.log
```

The /l*v option is what creates the log, named arp.log in this example.

Stream Data from the Binary Table

Sometimes it's useful to have a file in the Binary table that you want to copy to the target system yourself during the install. The following code shows the basis of how to accomplish this in C++ code. Although this program is written as a separate executable, the only major difference if this were in a CA is that MsiGetActiveDatabase would be called instead of MsiOpenDatabase to get a handle to the database.

```
int main(int argc, char* argv[])
{
    PMSIHANDLE hDatabase;
    PMSIHANDLE hView;
    PMSIHANDLE hRecord;
    UINT res = MsiOpenDatabase
        ("trynotepad.msi", MSIDBOPEN_READONLY, &hDatabase);
    char Query [] = "SELECT * FROM Binary WHERE Name='DefBannerBitmap'";
    res = MsiDatabaseOpenView(hDatabase, Query, &hView);
    if (ERROR_SUCCESS !=res)
        return 1;
    res = MsiViewExecute(hView, NULL);
    if (ERROR_SUCCESS == res)
        res = MsiViewFetch(hView, &hRecord);
    if (ERROR_SUCCESS ==res )
    {
        char bname [100] = {0};
        DWORD bnamelen = 100;
        // Name shows up in field 1 of record, assumed <100 chars
        res = MsiRecordGetString (hRecord, 1, bname, &bnamelen);
        char FileName [] = "bitmap.bmp";
        char Stream [2048] = {0};
        BOOL stillok = TRUE;
        HANDLE hFile = CreateFile(FileName, GENERIC_WRITE, 0, NULL,
```

```
                    CREATE_ALWAYS,
                    FILE_ATTRIBUTE_NORMAL, 0);
      if (INVALID_HANDLE_VALUE ==hFile  )
         res = -1;
      else
      {
        DWORD lenwritten=0, len=0;
        do
          {
            len=sizeof(Stream);
            res = MsiRecordReadStream(hRecord, 2, Stream, &len);
            if ((ERROR_SUCCESS == res) && (len > 0))
              {
                res = WriteFile(hFile, Stream, len, &lenwritten, NULL);
                stillok = (res==1);
              }
            else
            if (ERROR_SUCCESS !=res )
                stillok = FALSE;
          }
        while (stillok == TRUE && (len > 0));
        CloseHandle(hFile);
    }

  }
return res;
}
```

This code uses the same kind of SQL query you've used before, together with MsiDatabaseOpenView to open a view to the database for the query, MsiViewExecute to perform the query, and MsiViewFetch to get each record associated with the query. The data is streamed out of the record using MsiRecordReadStream and written to a file.

Find Updated Files in the Log

A log of the install tells you whether files have been replaced or not, and the reason why. Here's the kind of entry you'll see:

```
MSI (s) (CC:9C): File: C:\Program Files\Phil\TryNotepad\SomeTextFile.txt;
             To be installed; No patch;  No existing file
MSI (s) (CC:9C): File: C:\Program Files\Phil\TryNotepad\NOTEPAD.EXE;
          Won't Overwrite; No patch;  Existing file is of an equal version
```

There's an entry just prior to these types of entries showing the file version that's a candidate for installation.

Disable All Advertised Shortcuts

The shortcuts produced by VS are advertised shortcuts. This has advantages because they cause repair when a component is damaged, and are essential for advertising features for install on demand. A shortcut is an advertised one when the Target column in the Shortcut table refers to an entry in the Feature table. You could use Orca to make it into a nonadvertised shortcut by replacing this feature with a reference to the actual shortcut, using [TARGETDIR] and the file name; for example, [TARGETDIR]Notepad.exe. You can also disable advertised shortcuts by using the DISABLEADVTSHORTCUTS property. If you add this to the Property table with a value of 1, all the shortcuts that Windows creates from the Shortcut table will be nonadvertised.

Check for Privileges and Administrative Rights

When checking for privileges to perform an install, it's tempting to check whether the installing user is a member of the Administrator's group, typically with a Launch Condition for AdminUser, a standard Windows Installer property that tells you this. However, policies can allow a non-Administrator to act with elevated privileges for the duration of an install. When this is happening, the installing user is still not a member of the Adminstrator's group, so AdminUser doesn't tell you if the user has the privileges to perform the install. For that, you should be testing the Privileged property.

Having said all that, it's important to realize that the elevated privilege applies to the standard actions that are applied to the system from the database tables in the package. You saw in Chapter 5 that CA code runs with the privileges of the installing user. This doesn't change just because the install is running with elevated privilege; CAs are still performed while impersonating the installing user. The user's rights aren't elevated during an install with elevated rights. Elevated rights do allow CAs to run with the LocalSystem account, if the CAs are of that type (the msidbCustomActionTypeNoImpersonate bit is set). So, in the cases where a CA absolutely requires Administrator privilege, it's the right answer to require AdminUser, but remember that your product is then undeployable to non-Administrator users.

Validate a CD Key Serial Number

VS offers a default set of dialogs for use during the install. In addition, if you select the setup project in Solution Explorer and choose View ➤ Editor ➤ User Interface, you'll see a set of additional dialogs that you can add to the install. You'll add the Customer Information dialog, and I'll show you how it interfaces with the rest of the install and its properties. After adding it, the appropriate place to show it is after the InstallWelcome dialog.

The Customer Information dialog is useful because it's where you can ask users to supply a serial number, the CD key if you like, to validate that they're authorized to install the software. As shown in Figure 14-3, the ShowSerialNumber property must be True for this serial number box to be shown during the install.

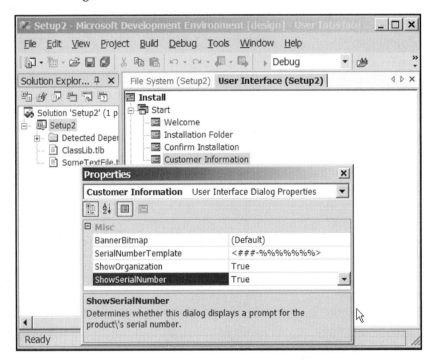

Figure 14-3. Customer Information dialog in VS

The SerialNumberTemplate property corresponds to a standard Windows Installer property that you can use to verify the format of the entered serial number: the PIDTemplate property. The Windows Installer Platform SDK documentation describes the allowed formats of this MaskedEdit control, and this specific value in VS breaks down as requiring a group of three numbers and a group of seven numbers, separated by a dash. If you run the install on Windows XP, you'll see a balloon error message if you try to type a non-numeric character in these spaces.

VS generates packages that use the built-in Windows Installer properties and actions relating to serial numbers:

- The **PIDKEY** property is the raw form of the serial number entered by the user. You can specify this on a command line or type it into a serial-number MaskedEdit field during the install.

- The **PIDTemplate** value determines some of the structure and content of PIDKEY, and this checking occurs when the ValidateProductID action occurs.

The output from validation of PIDKEY is the ProductID property.

You can see this in the package. The Property table contains the value of PIDTemplate transferred directly from the SerialNumberTemplate property shown in Figure 14-3, and Figure 14-4 shows the MaskedEdit control with PIDKEY as the property content.

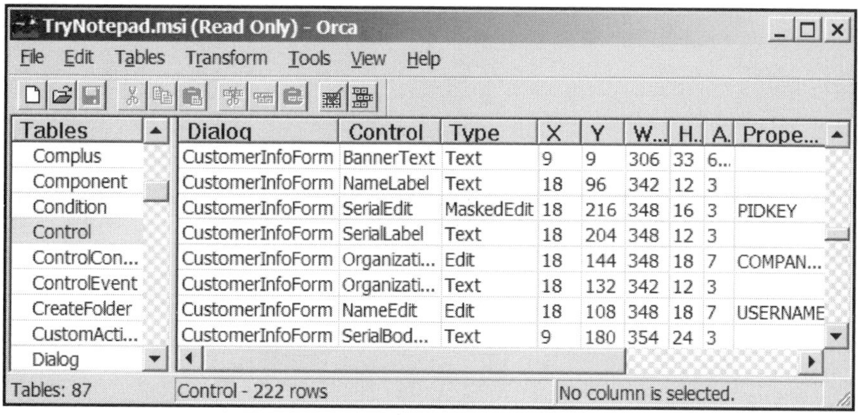

Figure 14-4. MaskedEdit control applied to PIDKEY property

Figure 14-5 shows ValidateProductID being called when the Next button on the form is clicked.

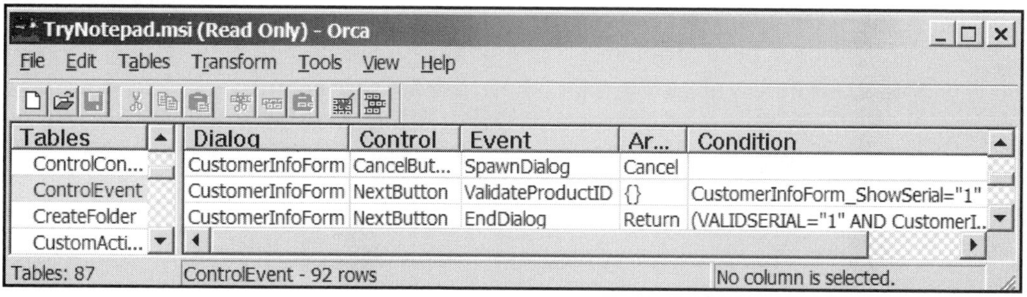

Figure 14-5. ValidateProductID ControlEvent from the Next button

These internal details are interesting if you want to perform your own serial number checking, because you need to replace this checking with a call to your own validation code. The strategy for this validation depends on how useful ValidateProductID is to you, because if you don't care about the built-in ValidateProductID action you can replace it with a call to your own CA that validates the PIDKEY property. However, if you believe that ValidateProductID serves a useful purpose, you'll want to add further validation that looks at the ProductID property. You'll use this latter route as an example, adding further validation to the ProductID after ValidateProductID has been done.

It turns out that the mask that VS uses for PIDTemplate isn't useful for the truly arbitrary string of numbers you'll use here. That's because the second part of the mask, the seven "%" characters, disallows two consecutive identical numbers, so this needs changing to a mask of <###-#######>.

You'll use a VBScript CA to validate the contents of the ProductID. You could do this equally well with a CA call to a DLL (see Chapter 5), but the example can be illustrated in a more compact form with VBScript. Here's the validation code:

```
option explicit
dim ser
Function ValidateSerial
ser = Property("ProductID")
if ser <> "123-1234567" then
    Property ("VALIDSERIAL") = "0"
    msgbox "Please enter the correct key"
    ValidateSerial = 1
else
    Property ("VALIDSERIAL") = "1"
    ValidateSerial = 1
end if
end Function
```

This is the entire CA script, a function that gets the value of the ProductID property and compares it to a fixed string. If it's successful, it sets the value of the VALIDATESERIAL property to the string "1."

You first need to add this script to the setup project as an Install CA. This is just a short way of getting it into the install package before you start editing it with Orca. After you build the package, the CA table contains an entry looking something like this:

Action	Type	Source
_DBE15EC1_1BE6_40E7_8B37_782B0E743D2A	1030	_C2BFC8BD4E4D8BA2F9A5C0FAD1E713FF

The Target column is empty. This is a Type 6 CA (a VBScript) set to run in deferred mode. First, delete all occurrences of that CA from the sequence tables, set the Type to be 6 (immediate), and rename it to something friendly such as CheckSerial. In the Target column, add the function name, ValidateSerial. This completes the CA setup, and next the ControlEvent table needs modification.

In Figure 14-5, the ValidateProductID ControlEvent is called when users click the Next button. On the right of that figure, notice the ordering in which the ControlEvents happen. Adding your validation to this form requires a new row to call your CA after ValidateProductID has been done. Ignoring the Ordering column for now, this new row is

```
Dialog            Control    Event     Argument    Condition
CustomerInfoForm NextButton DoAction CheckSerial CustomerInfoForm_ShowSerial="1"
```

This means that the NextButton will perform a DoAction (call a CA) named in the Argument column if the condition is true. This particular condition is based on CustomerInfoForm_ShowSerial, which is set depending on the value of the ShowSerialNumber property in Figure 14-3. For the ordering, the ValidateProductID must come before the call to CheckSerial, followed by the EndDialog and NewDialog events (see Figure 14-5), so the Ordering column of the Events associated with the NextButton needs renumbering to achieve this. The ordering of events on the NextButton should be ValidateProductID, followed by the call to DoAction to validate the key, followed by EndDialog and NewDialog.

Finally, you must update the entries in the Condition column so that the UI can go on to the next dialog and complete the current one if the serial number has been successfully validated, which has happened if the VALIDSERIAL property has a value of "1." The conditions for EndDialog and RemoveDialog therefore need VALIDSERIAL="1" added to the Condition column. The resulting Condition for the NextButton to perform EndDialog or NewDialog is therefore

```
(VALIDSERIAL="1" AND CustomerInfoForm_NextArgs="") AND
(ProductID<>"" OR CustomerInfoForm_ShowSerial="0")
```

The resulting package behaves the way you'd expect. It has the validation expected of ValidateProductID, in that non-numeric entries result in a balloon pop-up message and an entry in the Application Event Log, and the message box in the VBScript CA code is shown if the text doesn't match the required string. Using the Back and Next buttons results in another validation of the serial number.

Should you rely on this as a complete solution to your licensing issues? Probably not—you must have noticed that MSI packages are easily altered (for example with Orca), so it's relatively easy for someone to disable the CA that validates the key or to otherwise subvert the key check. Although it's fairly common to see keys entered during an install, you should consider a solution where your application asks the user for a key when it first runs, encrypts the key and stores it somewhere, and then verifies that the encrypted key is present on subsequent runs. This isn't foolproof—it's still security by virtue of obscurity, and most technical solutions can be reverse engineered. (If you want an example of tight control over product use, look at Microsoft's product activation mechanism.) I'm not a lawyer, so this isn't legal advice, but in many cases the point of these license key mechanisms isn't to provide a foolproof, technically secure solution. The point is to provide enough of a mechanism that a bad person must take some overt deliberate action that's legally indefensible in order to circumvent your licensing mechanism.

Run a Program at the End of the Install

Chapter 5 described CAs and how to run a program from your install. In many cases the methods described require manual editing of the setup package. This is impractical in cases where you repeatedly test the install and then rebuild it. It's possible to automate the update of the package with a program, but perhaps the simplest way to run a program asynchronously from the install process is with VBScript. This type of VBScript CA works well:

```
Set WshShell = CreateObject("WScript.Shell")
WshShell.Exec <path to program>
```

By default, the Exec method doesn't wait for the initiated process to terminate, so the program runs separately from the install.

The main difficulty is likely to be knowing the location of the installed program. The solution to this is VS's CustomActionData property to pass the TARGETDIR property to this CA, so that Property("CustomActionData") is the folder where the application is installed.

Advice

When you're building or debugging an install, you get a lot of choices in design and implementation. For example, I've noticed that VS developers get stuck on the .NET Installer classes, and overlook the fact that they could perhaps achieve the same result with a lowly VBScript CA or a Type 1 call to a C or C++ DLL. There seems to be a reluctance to "go back" to something that's not C# or VB.NET. So I've added a reminder that the native CA calls haven't gone away in the .NET world, and are sometimes much easier and more versatile than those Installer classes. I hope the other topics here help you build and debug your setups more easily.

Use ARPINSTALLLOCATION to Save the Install Location

The best way to save the product's install location is to use a Type 51 CA that sets the ARPINSTALLLOCATION property from TARGETDIR. This is described in Chapter 5. The reason for this approach instead of your own custom Registry entry is that it integrates with the Windows APIs relating to installed products. Specifically, the Win32 API MsiGetProductInfo, when passed INSTALLPROPERTY_INSTALLLOCATION, returns the installation path. This is equivalent to the Installer object's ProductInfo property in the automation interface.

Strictly speaking, you should use a Type 307 CA, which is Type 51 to set the property ORed with 256 (msidbCustomActionTypeFirstSequence), so that the CA is performed only once even though it appears in both the InstallUISequence and InstallExecuteSequence tables.

Don't forget that component GUIDS are also useful for locating paths to individual components. Not only are there APIs to locate components, such as MsiGetComponentPath, but you can also search for components in an AppSearch (see Chapter 4).

Custom Action DLLs Are Versatile and Easy

The most versatile CA source is a C or C++ CA DLL, calling a function as an immediate CA. These have access to properties in the installation and have all the flexibility of C++ programming. They're equally useful as deferred CAs but need to use CustomActionData if they must use properties and states not available because of their deferred status.

Ignore Dialog Errors in Logs

When an install fails and you take a log and look at it, you might see a number of errors like this:

```
DEBUG: Error 2826:  Control Line1 on dialog MaintenanceForm extends beyond the
boundaries of the dialog to the right by 4 pixels
The installer has encountered an unexpected error installing this package. This
may indicate a problem with this package. The error code is 2826. The arguments
are:
MaintenanceForm, Line1, to the right
```

Although this example shows the MaintenanceForm dialog, you'll see this with other forms such as the error forms, and sometimes the error number is different. These dialog errors are never the actual cause of the install failure. What's typically happening is that the installer is setting up an error form to notify you of the failure and the form gets a few of these errors. The actual cause of the install failure is usually just before this type of dialog setup error, and it's probably a lot less verbose and easier to miss compared with the UI error. Seeing "Return Value 3" is a good indication of a CA failure. There's also a utility in the Windows Installer SDK called WiLogUtl.exe. You can run this on an installer log file, making it easier to see properties, errors, and so on.

VBScript Custom Actions Are Easy

Although CA DLLs are flexible, don't overlook VBScript. VBScript has access to properties and to any number of automation objects with CreateObject. The FileSystem object with ProgID "Scripting.FileSystemObject" is particularly useful for manipulating files and folders, and "WScript.Shell" for running programs, accessing environment variables, creating shortcuts, locating special folders, and so on. WMI can also be extremely useful. As a minor example, it can enumerate, and sometimes control, an astonishing area of a system, both hardware and software. The scripting model is consistent and much more compact than the corresponding C++ code would be.

Most WMI VBScripts start with something such as this:

```
Computername="."
Set WMIService = GetObject("winmgmts:\\" & strComputer & "\root\cimv2")
Set servicelist = WMIService.ExecQuery("Select * from Win32_Service")
```

This code uses Win32_Service as an example, but you could substitute Win32_Process, Win32_SystemDriver, and so on. Having collected the list, you can iterate through the items using For Each:

```
For Each item in servicelist
......
Next
```

Within the loop you can see the properties of each item, such as Name, State, and ProcessId.

Common Errors and Why You Get Them

Error 2762 is often caused by having a deferred CA sequenced after InstallFinalize. Make it immediate instead.

Error 1606 usually refers to a network location that can't be accessed. It happens when Windows Installer verifies the accessibility of potential installation folders during the CostFinalize action and finds an invalid one. The reason it sometimes refers to a network location is that a path that doesn't start with a drive letter is treated as a network path. One of the ways you can get this error is to have a property value that's the same as an entry in the Directory table. You can also get this error if one of your roaming profile locations is on a network share that's unavailable. Another way is rather more obscure, but sometimes the Windows folders at HKLM\Software\Microsoft\Windows\CurrentVersion\Explorer in the Shell Folders and the User Shell Folders keys can cause issues. For example, Knowledge Base article 330766 documents an instance of this error. Occasionally, users have reported incomplete folder names in these Registry keys that have caused problems. Windows Installer checks all the locations in the Directory table during the install, so you should ensure that this table doesn't contain invalid entries. In any case, you should only have Directory table entries that you are using during the install.

For error 1706, "No valid source could be found," see the "Warnings" section topic "Bootstrappers and Temp Folders," because the situation described there can cause this error. Windows Installer is looking for a copy of the original package. Error 1706 can also be a consequence of the ResolveSource action as described in the "Warnings" topic "ResolveSource and the Original Install Package."

Errors such as 1920 or 1921 usually refer to a problem with Services, and the text of the error gives a warning about having enough privileges to perform the associated Service action (such as start, stop, delete, and install). This privilege message is just a catch-all message; it doesn't mean that privileges are the problem, even though they might be. It can be difficult to deal with errors involving Services because they're dependent on the behavior of the Service itself, and consequently you can't tell whether your install is doing the wrong thing or the Service is. If the Service crashes or doesn't respond in a timely manner the install might roll back and appear to be broken, although the issue is actually in the Service.

Error numbers in the 1720-and-up range are typically associated with scripts or programs that fail to run correctly or fail to compile. In most cases of VBScript syntax errors, the log shows the error.

One of the problems you can get when running external programs is that of the exit code. Windows Installer considers a return exit code of zero to mean success, and any other values as failure. If you don't know what your executable's exit code is going to be, set the msidbCustomActionTypeContinue bit in the CA so that its exit code is ignored. It's bad practice to get into this situation because you'll have an incomplete install if external programs return zero even if they fail. As an alternative, you can write a CA DLL function in C/C++ that uses the CreateProcess API to initiate the executable and wait for it to complete, checking its exit code and returning a result back from your CA to Windows Installer to indicate success or failure.

Test the Install on a Clean System

After you build the install package, you'll probably test it on your development system, and if the application works you could fall into the trap of thinking that you've got an install that works on any system. The problem with development systems is that they pretty much contain every DLL that was ever needed to run any application. Maybe that's an exaggeration, but the point is that a development system is the worst possible place to test whether your install package works, primarily because of the dependencies that your application needs that your development system has, but that client systems and other versions of Windows don't have.

A thorough test requires testing on freshly installed Windows for each version of Windows that your application is supported on. If you can make the decision that your application will support only the NT range of systems (the later the better), you'll have a much simpler install because many Microsoft redistributable components are a standard part of the OS, and protected from replacement. If you don't support the Windows 9x range, you'll have the additional advantage of not needing to be concerned with ANSI versions of redistributables. For that matter, you don't need to be concerned with ANSI versions of your application—if you build a Unicode application you'll get some performance back because the OS won't be translating your ANSI strings to Unicode in the Win32 API calls.

But what exactly should the installation tests consist of? The vast majority of applications process data to return output that can usually be validated. Indeed, many programs and their functions are defined in terms of their inputs and outputs and the transformation of the data. An installation program uses well-defined input, but the output is rather opaque. Unless you're an expert in the Windows implementation of, for example, COM, the GAC, shortcuts, installer repair descriptors, and so on, it's difficult to inspect the system to determine whether the installation has done what you intended it to do. In practical terms, this means that the only effective tests you can perform are whether the application works correctly. If the application doesn't work correctly, then it must return diagnostics that tell you where it failed so you can determine if the installation is incorrect. It goes without saying that that the only application testing that ultimately matters is the testing performed on a clean machine after installing from the package that your customers will use.

Look at XML for User Settings

The conventional wisdom is that a per-machine installed product should store the personalized settings of users in the HKEY_CURRENT_USER hive of the Registry. Although this is convenient, it does raise the issue of what happens when the product is uninstalled and how to remove those user settings in user Registry hives that you cannot easily enumerate and remove. One of the difficulties that people have here relates to the Microsoft certification programs. These contain language implying you won't pass certification unless you remove all your application's Registry entries. For example, the Windows Server 2003 Application Specification says the application uninstall must remove "Registry entries except for keys that the application creates specifically for other applications to share and that might compromise those applications if it is removed." It's difficult to interpret that as meaning anything other than removing all the separate users' Registry entries. However, the language also says that user preferences can be considered as user data and can be left behind, together with a strong recommendation that you offer an option or document how to remove the preferences, perhaps because Microsoft recognizes the difficulties involved. A removal option during the uninstall might be rather difficult, given the usual silent behavior of Add/Remove Programs.

If you decide that uninstalling the product means uninstalling all user preferences from the Registry, this means that even if the same user reinstalled the product later, those entries wouldn't be there. You could argue that this uninstall loss is acceptable because the uninstall cannot know if the user ever intends to reinstall the product. You also need to consider who your customers are and what their reactions might be. Programmers might prefer that settings be preserved between an uninstall and a later install, perhaps because they know it's possible. A consumer client might have no such expectation. Note that I'm talking about uninstall here, not maintenance. You can design updates to the application, major or minor upgrades in particular, to preserve user settings.

If you're building applications based on the .NET Framework, you can hardly have failed to notice that XML is everywhere, and the Framework classes make it easy to create and manipulate data stored in XML files. This suggests the possibility of using a single XML file to store user settings for the application. If these settings aren't of a sensitive nature, the fact that the data is in plain text doesn't present much of a security or privacy issue. If the data is sensitive, it wouldn't be difficult to perform encryption to an extent determined by the amount of security or privacy required. The advantage of this approach is that you can install an empty version of this file, and therefore it's removed when the product is uninstalled. It's also useful in some support situations where you need to know the values of the user settings and it's easier to inspect a single file than collect data from multiple Registry hives in HKEY_USERS.

This approach isn't appropriate in all cases. You might need to worry about different users simultaneously accessing the file and be sure that the location of the file is accessible to all users. In other circumstances where a database is available, you could store user settings there, mark them for removal at uninstall time, and permanently remove them after some timeout of no activity. This is the kind of approach you see with "shopping baskets" in Web-based stores.

Warnings

Perhaps these are the bear traps. For example, I've lost track of how many times I've heard someone say they have a perfectly fine VBScript that works when they run it in WSH, but fails as a CA in an install. That, and others, are listed here in the hope that you'll avoid them.

VBScript Custom Actions Are Not Windows Script Host

It's a common assumption that VBScript CAs can use WSH constructs based on the WScript object model. But you cannot use script code such as WScript.CreateObject or WScript.Quit or WScript.Echo. The WSH environment provides the WScript object model, just as VBScript in a Web page uses an IE object model. Windows Installer scripting supplies objects such as the Session object for interacting with the install. You don't need WScript.CreateObject anyway—VBScript has a CreateObject method that does the same thing.

Msiexec Command Line Is Picky

When you're sure that the syntax of your command line is correct, but you still keep getting errors saying that the command line is incorrect, watch out for extra spaces that cause this error.

Public properties cause the most trouble. In a command line such as one of these, the extra space between the "=" and the value of the property causes the command line to fail:

```
Msiexec /I my.msi TARGETDIR= c:\MyPath
Msiexec /I my.msi TRANSFORMS= c:\trans.mst
```

Services and Environment Variables

The mechanism that distributes changes to environment variables doesn't work for Services because the Service Control Manager (SCM) doesn't respond to the notification messages that Windows broadcasts. Services pick up their environment variables from the SCM, which means that if you install a Windows Service that expects to see newly installed environment variables, it won't see them. The only way to make them visible is to restart the SCM, which means rebooting the system. Consequently, you shouldn't design Services that require environment variables to be assigned in the same install.

Changing the Product's Uninstall Behavior

You might have noticed Registry entries under the HKLM\Software\Microsoft\ Windows\CurrentVersion\Installer\UserData\Products key with an Msiexec command string associated with the name UninstallString. You might have tried to update this string to make your product behave differently during the product's uninstall, only to find it makes no difference to the behavior. You can't make a difference to the Add/Remove Programs behavior by altering this Registry string because the uninstall is initiated internally by calling APIs that are passed the ProductCode GUID, not by reading this UninstallString. If you look carefully at the Registry entries in this region, you'll notice that some products don't even have an UninstallString; that's because it isn't a requirement. In effect, you can't alter this behavior and neither should you try to; users expect common behavior from all uninstalls.

Services and Remote Computers

If you're installing Services on Windows NT 4.0, note that NT 4.0 Services that run with the LocalSystem account have restricted access to network shares and other resources on remote computers. This account has less access than the Guest account. It seems to be a common design practice to develop a piece of code that accesses remote computers, and then, when it works, to embed it in a Service only to discover it no longer works. The install process might get involved at this point because an obvious solution is to install the Service with a user account and password that does have access to the remote computer.

ResolveSource and the Original Install Package

The ResolveSource action determines where the package is running from (and accesses it), and sets the SourceDir property, the path to the package. This is useful when you have a CA that needs to find files in the same folder as the package being installed. If you add a ResolveSource action to your install

sequence, be sure to condition it on Not Installed. If ResolveSource is unconditional, it will get called every time the sequence is processed. The most inconvenient example of this is if you're trying to uninstall a product and it asks you to
insert the product CD or otherwise locate the original package. See the section
"Uninstall Broken Packages" for a way around this.

There's an alternative to the SourceDir property. The OriginalDatabase property contains the path to the package being installed, including the name of the
actual MSI file, and is always available. However, this is useful at install time but
not in subsequent maintenance installs because OriginalDatabase often points
to the cached MSI file, not the original installation path.

Your Custom Action Won't Run As System Account

You can run deferred CAs with no impersonation by using the
msidbCustomActionTypeNoImpersonate bit in the CA Type. Sometimes you'll
find that CAs that were intended to run with no impersonation will run with the
installing user's account and behave unexpectedly. This can happen if the install
isn't managed. The UI is typically where the user gets to choose between a per-
machine and a per-user install, and this UI choice sets the value of the
ALLUSERS property. But if there's no UI there's nowhere to set per-user or per-
machine, and the default Windows Installer setting is per-user, so you need to be
careful that your installs don't become per-user and unmanaged when you
install them silently. See Chapter 13 for a discussion about privileges and managed installs.

The way to ensure that your install defaults to the required behavior is to
hard-code the value of ALLUSERS in the Property table, giving it a value of 1 if
you want the default to be a per-machine install.

Bootstrappers and Temp Folders

Many install development tools let you build a bootstrap executable that first
makes sure the Windows Installer engine is on the system (the Windows 9x or NT
versions) and then extracts the embedded package—the MSI file—and installs it.
One of the problems with this scheme is that the MSI file sometimes gets
unpacked to the system's Temp folder where it can be removed all too easily. If
the file is needed for repair or modification of the product, it's gone, and you
might see error 1706 and dialogs asking you for the location. The moral of this
story is to try to control where the unpacked MSI package is stored, and don't
use the Temp folder.

Raising Privileges During Custom Actions

A process can normally raise its privileges to perform actions that require those privileges. The Windows security model doesn't automatically assign all allowed privileges to a process. Instead, the process is allowed to assign them to itself if necessary. The API that does this is AdjustTokenPrivileges.

If you do this during a CA in the InstallExecuteSequence (such as a deferred CA DLL call from a VS setup project), it doesn't work. You won't necessarily see any failures reported from the security APIs, but the action requiring the privilege returns error 1300, meaning that "Not all privileges referenced are assigned to the caller." However, you *can* make this work by having the CA run deferred in the system context, so a Type 3073 CA DLL call succeeds (a Type 1 call to a CA DLL function + 3072, msidbCustomActionTypeInScript + msidbCustomActionTypeNoImpersonate).

The issue is related to the local DCOM calls that are occurring internally within the installation processes. Your deferred CA running as the installing user is being called via a local DCOM call from the installer's Service process. DCOM removes disabled privileges during this call sequence, so your CA code is running in an environment where the only privileges you can use are those that are already enabled. You don't have access to the disabled ones that you want to enable. You can make AdjustTokenPrivileges calls during the UI sequence because your immediate CA code is running from the calling Msiexec user process (or from the program invoking your install through an API call) and no DCOM calls are involved.

There's example code in Chapter 5's CA DLL sample of acquiring the SE_BACKUP_NAME privilege in order to create a backup of a Registry key using the RegSaveKey API call.

Use Unique Property Names

When you choose names for your custom properties, be careful that you don't inadvertently choose an identifier name that's the same as a standard but perhaps undocumented property. For example, Windows Installer uses the DATABASE property to name the working package file name. Not only do you need to avoid these kinds of names, you also need to avoid any properties that the development tool added to your package. So, for example, you see property names that VS created, which are usefully prefixed with VS in all the cases I could find.

Perhaps the best place to see these properties, apart from the documentation, is in a log of the installation.

Summary

Although I could have scattered some of these topics throughout the book, I thought it would be more useful to collect these together in one place. It's fair to say that these topics mostly deal with how you can successfully integrate your setup design with Windows Installer and debug it, avoiding some frequently encountered problems.

CHAPTER 15

Exploring the Installer APIs

IN THIS CHAPTER, you'll look at some of the ways you can find out about products installed on the system and their components, locations, and so on. These are useful if you're interested in an inventory of the system; they can also be useful in CAs, or in any situation where you need to find out if specific products are installed on the system.

WMI

The WMI APIs can be helpful for querying or configuring the provided Windows Installer classes, partly because of WMI's remoting capabilities and perhaps also because you're used to its architecture and code.

The WMI classes include Win32_Product, which, like many classes, you can retrieve as a collection that can be enumerated to examine each item in the collection and its properties and methods. That's just a long way of saying that you can use this kind of VBScript code to see each product:

```
option explicit
public computername, objwmi, coll, prod, msg, fso, a
computername = "."
Set fso = CreateObject("Scripting.FileSystemObject")
Set a = fso.CreateTextFile("listproducts.txt", True)
Set objwmi = GetObject("winmgmts:\\" & computername & "\root\cimv2")
Set coll = objwmi.ExecQuery("Select * from Win32_Product")
For Each prod in coll
    msg = prod.name & " " & prod.version & " " & prod.identifyingnumber
    a.writeline(msg)
Next
```

The IdentifyingNumber property is the ProductCode of the installed product, and other properties tell you more about each product. A typical result of this script showing one product is this code:

```
Orca 2.00.3790.0000 {63A68338-16A3-4763-8478-A45F91A61E7A}
```

Other WMI classes return information about installer components, most notably the Win32_SoftwareElement class, which describes each Windows Installer component installed on the system. The virtually identical VBScript code that follows lists each installer component.

```
option explicit
public computername, objwmi, coll, comp,msg, fso, a
computername = "."
Set fso = CreateObject("Scripting.FileSystemObject")
Set a = fso.CreateTextFile("listcomps.txt", True)
Set objwmi = GetObject("winmgmts:\\" & computername & "\root\cimv2")
Set coll = objwmi.ExecQuery("Select * from Win32_SoftwareElement")
For Each comp in coll
    msg = comp.InstallDate & " " & comp.path & " " & comp.IdentificationCode
    a.writeline(msg)
Next
```

The results of this script are something like this, showing the install date of the component , followed by the KeyPath of the component, followed by the component GUID:

```
20031026000000.000000-000 C:\Program Files\Orca\Orca.exe
                  {BE928E10-272A-11D2-B2E4-006097C99860}
```

The date here is in the WMI Date and Time Format (look for this heading in the WMI Platform SDK documentation for a complete description). You can probably figure out that the first four digits are the year, followed by two digits each for month and day of month.

Sometimes you'll see this type of result:

```
20040111000000.000000-000 C:\Program Files\Microsoft Office\
                  {0525EB1B-7F16-4E64-9068-065A8B42B833}
```

In this case the KeyPath is a folder name rather than a file name, and that's because in the absence of an explicitly named KeyPath file, Windows Installer uses the component's destination folder as the default KeyPath.

KeyPath items can also be Registry entries. Some KeyPath items look like the following, where the number preceding a Registry key denotes the actual key using the same values as the Root column in the Registry table of a package (except that on 64-bit systems you'll see other values to distinguish between the 32-bit and 64-bit parts of the Registry).

```
20031026000000.000000-000 01:\SOFTWARE\Microsoft\Win32SDK\Directories\Install Dir
                  {3737E81B-7A88-4F89-B80A-EECC7CF805E3}
```

Using WMI to Install a Product

You'll look at a couple of ways that you can use WMI to install a product on a remote system, from the administrative point of view. The safest way to do this is probably to advertise the product, because this requires no user interaction. When running processes on remote computers (or indeed on your own with a user account that's not the current interactive user), you must beware of UI activities taking place within an invisible window station.

The first way you'll look at is a VBScript example that runs a command line to advertise a product. This runs Msiexec.exe in command-line mode using the Win32_Process class:

```
option explicit
public wloc, winst, remsys, aduser, adpass, wproc, wserv, wcom, wstat, wid
remsys= "remotesystem"
aduser= "Administrator"
adpass = "thepassword"
wcom = "msiexec /jm D:\PDW\Trynotepad.msi"
Set wloc = CreateObject("WbemScripting.SWbemLocator")
set wserv = wloc.ConnectServer (remsys, null, aduser, adpass)
wserv.Security_.ImpersonationLevel = 3 ' impersonate
set winst = wserv.Get("Win32_Process")
wstat = winst.Create(wcom, null, null, wid)
msgbox "Process id " & wid
```

This uses the generic Win 32_Process class to initiate a process on the named remote computer, and assumes that the user account and password (aduser and adpass in the preceding code) are valid on the remote system. The assumption here is that the named package has already been copied to the remote system, perhaps using an administrative share.

Although this works, it's probably more correct to use the WMI Win32_Product class to advertise the product on the remote computer. The following C# example uses the .NET Framework's management classes to perform advertisement using the Advertise method of the Win32_Product class.

```
public void WinProd()
{
ConnectionOptions coptions = new ConnectionOptions();
coptions.Username = "Administrator";
coptions.Password = "some password";
coptions.Impersonation = ImpersonationLevel.Impersonate;
string msilocation = @"D:\pdw\trynotepad.msi";
string remsys = "remotesystemname";
```

```
ManagementScope scope = new ManagementScope ("\\\\"+remsys+"\\root\\cimv2",
      coptions);
try
 {
 scope.Connect();
 ManagementPath mp = new ManagementPath ("Win32_Product");
 ManagementClass mc = new ManagementClass (scope, mp,
        new ObjectGetOptions(null, new TimeSpan(0,0,0,60, 0), true) );
 object [] args = {msilocation, null};
 object getback = mc.InvokeMethod("Advertise", args);
 }
catch (Exception e)
 {
  MessageBox.Show (e.Message);
 }
}
```

In this example, everything up to the call on scope.Connect() is one of the standard ways to connect to WMI on a remote system. After that, the code sets up a call on the Advertise method of Win32_Product, and the result is returned into "object getback" as the Win32 API error number, either success (zero) or one of the Windows Installer error codes.

Once again, there's the requirement that this runs with an account that has the required privilege on the remote system. In practice, this usually means that the remote system is part of a domain and the account used is that of a domain administrator.

Sometimes these uses of WMI can provide a timely solution to a deployment problem. For example, Microsoft Knowledge Base article 305702 describes a couple more ways to use Win32_Product in the install and uninstall context. But you shouldn't view these examples as complete solutions to installing software onto remote computers. Anecdotal reports suggest that in practice much more code is needed to manage properly the installation and maintenance of installed products on remote computers.

Listing Products with WMI and the .NET Framework

As you see in the preceding example, WMI functionality is available in the Framework classes in the System.Management namespace. Once you've got the idea of these classes, the programming model is consistent and uses the usual text interfaces (such as Select statements), as in this C# code:

```
public void WhatProds ()
{
string servername =".";
ObjectQuery oq = new ObjectQuery("select * from Win32_Product");
ManagementScope scope = new ManagementScope("\\\\"+servername+ "\\root\\cimv2");
scope.Connect();
ManagementObjectSearcher sea = new ManagementObjectSearcher(scope, oq);
foreach (ManagementObject proc in sea.Get())
{
   Console.WriteLine ("Name {0} Cache {1} Guid {2} Version {3}\n", proc["Name"],
      proc["PackageCache"], proc["IdentifyingNumber"], proc["Version"]);
}
Console.ReadLine();
}
```

This example enumerates products, analogous to the VBScript example earlier. The ManagementScope class provides the ability to name a WMI context—a computer name—and then to connect to it. ManagementObjectSearcher lets you associate a query with a ManagementScope and use the Get method to retrieve a collection that can be enumerated. You can obtain the properties of each item in the collection by using the string property name (such as "Name") as a C# indexer into each returned instance.

This pattern is flexible in the sense that you could use Win32_Service, or any number of other classes, instead of Win32_Product, and you only need to change the names of the properties.

WMI or the Installer APIs

Perhaps the three most useful features of the WMI interfaces to Windows Installer are these:

1. You get the same information from remote computers for free. The preceding examples both show a computer name of "." referring to the local system, but you can put another computer name in there and, for example, inventory products installed on that remote computer.

2. You get the ability to make specific queries by adding conditions to the Select statement. For example, this Select statement returns all installed products with "Microsoft" in the name:

   ```
   Set coll = objwmi.ExecQuery("Select * from Win32_Product where Name
   LIKE '%Microsoft%' ")
   ```

3. You have the same general programming and scripting pattern as the rest of the WMI classes. Familiarity with the programming pattern of other WMI classes could save you some time if you need, for example, an ad-hoc VBScript to enumerate installed products on a remote computer.

There are four major disadvantages when using WMI:

1. The Windows Installer WMI provider isn't always installed. For example, a default installation of Windows Server 2003 doesn't include it.

2. Its performance can be slow compared with using the native APIs. This is mainly a result of its architecture, using out-of-process COM. It's also slow depending on the data you return. For example, the Win32_SoftwareElement class has a Name property that's the name of the installer component in the MSI package. The WMI provider can return this only by going into the cached MSI package to retrieve it, which might in turn cause registered transforms and patches to be applied so that the information is up-to-date with patches and transforms that aren't part of the cached MSI file. There are also security constraints to reading the cached MSI package.

3. A system administrator might have applied extra security restrictions to WMI, in particular with respect to accessing remote computers.

4. Not every API in the Windows Installer functionality has an equivalent WMI property or method, so if you start using the WMI classes, you might find that you need to use the installer APIs anyway.

In an administrative context where you "own" the systems in question, you could perhaps arrange to install and configure WMI appropriately, and use the Windows Installer classes. Otherwise, you cannot guarantee that the Windows Installer classes are available or that you have the privileges to use them.

Although WMI is a useful and consistent programming model, you'll find that the native Windows Installer APIs provide better performance and more predictable behavior than using WMI.

The Installer APIs

Windows has a set of Win32 APIs, and instead of using them directly you'll use some .NET P/Invoke code to call them.

The basis of the example here is the static class used to call the Win32 APIs:

```
public class CallMsi
{
public const string INSTALLPROPERTY_LOCALPACKAGE          = "LocalPackage";
public const string INSTALLPROPERTY_INSTALLEDPRODUCTNAME =
"InstalledProductName";
public const string INSTALLPROPERTY_VERSIONSTRING         = "VersionString";
public const string INSTALLPROPERTY_INSTALLDATE           = "InstallDate";
// This MsiOpenDatabase signature works only with a filename in "persist"
[DllImport("msi")]
public static extern int MsiOpenDatabase (string dbpath, string persist,
  ref IntPtr msihandle);
[DllImport("msi")]
public static extern int MsiDatabaseOpenView(IntPtr handle, string query,
  ref IntPtr viewhandle);
[DllImport("msi")]
public static extern int MsiViewExecute (IntPtr viewhandle, IntPtr recordhandle);
[DllImport("msi")]
public static extern int MsiViewFetch (IntPtr viewhandle,
  ref IntPtr recordhandle);
[DllImport("msi", CharSet=CharSet.Auto)]
public static extern int MsiRecordGetString (IntPtr recordhandle, int recno,
    StringBuilder szbuff, ref int len);
[DllImport("msi")]
public static extern int MsiCloseHandle (IntPtr handle);
[DllImport("msi")]
public static extern int MsiViewClose  (IntPtr viewhandle);
[DllImport("msi", CharSet=CharSet.Auto)]
public static extern int MsiEnumProducts(int index,   StringBuilder guid);
[DllImport("msi", CharSet=CharSet.Auto)]
public static extern int MsiEnumComponents(int index, StringBuilder guid);
[DllImport("msi", CharSet=CharSet.Auto)]
public static extern int MsiEnumClients(string compguid, int index,
    StringBuilder prodguid);
[DllImport("msi", CharSet=CharSet.Auto)]
public static extern int MsiGetProductInfo (string guid, string propertyname,
    StringBuilder retprop, ref int szbuf);
}
```

The more complete list is in the code examples for this chapter.

These APIs are all in Msi.dll (as in the DllImport specification), with parameters shown here mapped from the Win32 types. I'll show their use by enumerating the products on a system, and by going into the Property table to retrieve the UpgradeCode value.

```
public void ListProducts ()
{
int ix = 0;
StringBuilder guid = new StringBuilder (64);
int res=0;
while ( (res=CallMsi.MsiEnumProducts(ix, guid)) == 0)
{
  ix++;
  int len = 512;
  StringBuilder cachedmsi = new StringBuilder(len);
  int getprop = CallMsi.MsiGetProductInfo(guid.ToString(),
      CallMsi.INSTALLPROPERTY_LOCALPACKAGE, cachedmsi,  ref len);
  if (0==len)
    continue;
  len = 512;
  StringBuilder productname = new StringBuilder (len);
  getprop = CallMsi.MsiGetProductInfo(guid.ToString(),
      CallMsi.INSTALLPROPERTY_INSTALLEDPRODUCTNAME, productname, ref len);
  len=50;
  StringBuilder versionstring = new StringBuilder(len);
  getprop = CallMsi.MsiGetProductInfo(guid.ToString(),
      CallMsi.INSTALLPROPERTY_VERSIONSTRING, versionstring, ref len);
  len = 50;
  StringBuilder installdate = new StringBuilder (len);
  getprop = CallMsi.MsiGetProductInfo(guid.ToString(),
    CallMsi.INSTALLPROPERTY_INSTALLDATE, installdate, ref len);
  GetMsiData mi = new GetMsiData (cachedmsi.ToString());
  string ucode = mi.DoQuery ("SELECT `Value` from `Property` WHERE
      `Property`.`Property` = 'UpgradeCode' ");
  mi.Dispose();
  }
}
```

MsiEnumProducts is an index-based API that returns a ProductCode GUID for each increment of the first parameter, an integer. MsiGetProductInfo is a general-purpose function that returns a variety of data about installed products, and one of these items is the location of the locally cached package. The preceding code collects other product attributes, but perhaps more interestingly, opens the locally cached package to return the product's UpgradeCode, which can't be discovered any other way.

I should point out that this example doesn't deal with some possible situations, for example, products that are advertised but not yet installed. In addition, the cached MSI package used in this example might be for a product that has been patched or has had transforms applied. Patches and transforms aren't stored in the cached MSI package—they're separate files. So this example that retrieves the product's UpgradeCode GUID should work fine in most circumstances because a transform or patch that altered the UpgradeCode would be rare but not impossible. However, you shouldn't rely on data from a cached MSI package that might have been subjected to patches or transforms.

This example uses the GetMsiData class to wrap the calls into a package. You pass the class's constructor the path to the package; it opens the package and saves the handle.

```
.....
string thepath = null;
IntPtr dbhandle = IntPtr.Zero;
public GetMsiData (string package)
{
  thepath = package;
  int nres = CallMsi.MsiOpenDatabase (thepath, null, ref dbhandle);
}
.....
```

You can retrieve the UpgradeCode by passing the appropriate query to the DoQuery method:

```
public string DoQuery(string query)
{
IntPtr viewhandle = IntPtr.Zero;
IntPtr nothing = IntPtr.Zero;
int nres = CallMsi.MsiDatabaseOpenView (dbhandle, query, ref viewhandle);
nres = CallMsi.MsiViewExecute (viewhandle, nothing);
IntPtr rechandle = IntPtr.Zero;
nres = CallMsi.MsiViewFetch (viewhandle, ref rechandle);
if (0!=nres) // No data
{
  CallMsi.MsiCloseHandle(viewhandle);
  return null;
}
int outlen = 255;
StringBuilder outbuff = new StringBuilder(outlen);
nres = CallMsi.MsiRecordGetString (rechandle, 1,  outbuff, ref outlen);
int rel = CallMsi.MsiCloseHandle(viewhandle);
rel = CallMsi.MsiCloseHandle (rechandle);
```

```
if (0!=nres) // No data
  return null;
return outbuff.ToString();
}
```

The code in this method follows the same path as the other examples you've looked at, such as the VBScript in Chapter 2. It shows you how to query the database package using MsiDatabaseOpenView to pass the query. MsiViewExecute returns a view handle, and MsiViewFetch returns a record handle that you can use to return# each of the items in the record. This class uses the IDisposable model of releasing the handle to the package, where clients call the Dispose method when they've finished with the object.

You can enumerate the installed components and the products that use them with the MsiEnumComponents call to retrieve the components, and then call MsiEnumClients to list each of the client products for that component:

```
public void ShowCompsAndClients()
{
int cix = 0;
int res=0;
StringBuilder cguid = new StringBuilder (40);
while ( (res=CallMsi.MsiEnumComponents(cix,  cguid)) == 0)
{
  cix++;
  int pix=0;
  int cres=0;
  StringBuilder prodguid = new StringBuilder (40);
  while ( (cres = CallMsi.MsiEnumClients (cguid.ToString(), pix, prodguid)) ==0)
  {
    int plen = 256;
    StringBuilder pname = new StringBuilder (256);
    int pires = CallMsi.MsiGetProductInfo (prodguid.ToString(),
              CallMsi.INSTALLPROPERTY_INSTALLEDPRODUCTNAME, pname, ref plen);
    int len = 512;
    StringBuilder pth = new StringBuilder (len);
    CallMsi.MsiGetComponentPath (prodguid.ToString(), cguid.ToString(), pth,
              ref len);
    pix++;
  }
}
}
```

This C# code enumerates each installer component. For each component, it uses MsiEnumClients to enumerate the products using that component (which returns the ProductCode GUID of each client product); then the code gets the name of that client product by calling MsiGetProductInfo. Finally, the code uses MsiGetComponentPath to get the component's KeyPath as used by the client product. If the code presented all that data, you'd see a complete inventory of all the components on the system and where they're located, together with the products that are using them. Note that the MsiGetComponentPath call (and the equivalent ComponentPath method of the automation interface's Installer object) can trigger a request for the source medium if the component is installed to be run from the source. You can call either MsiQueryComponentState or the automation interface's ComponentState property of the Product object to determine if this is the case.

Types of Installer APIs

Some of the Win32 MSI APIs have similar names and seem to provide equivalent functionality. For example, both MsiOpenDatabase and MsiOpenPackage seem to have the same functionality, so which do you use and when? The difference in this particular case is that you use MsiOpenDatabase when you're treating the MSI package like a database, a file that you want to perform queries against and perhaps modify. That's the way the code uses MsiOpenDatabase in the preceding section "The Installer APIs." You use the handle rather like a file handle. However, the handle returned by calling MsiOpenPackage (or MsiOpenPackageEx) is a handle to an install, and you can use this returned handle to call functions such as MsiDoAction that perform installation tasks. As you might expect, a call to MsiOpenPackage requires security rights associated with installing products on the system and is also subject to the system's Windows Installer polices. MsiOpenProduct also has the same semantics as MsiOpenPackage—it returns an install handle.

You can get an idea of which functions you should be using from the organization of the SDK documentation. Although you can use some API functions in a number of different contexts (particularly those dealing with database records and views), the documentation lists Database functions in a separate section from the Installer functions. For example, MsiQueryFeatureState is in the Installer Function Reference, not the Database Function Reference. You call MsiQueryFeatureState to determine the state of a feature associated with a product that's installed on the system; it returns a value denoting the state of the feature. But MsiGetFeatureState is in the list of database functions, and the documentation describes the parameter handle as being provided through MsiOpenPackage or having been passed to a CA DLL function. In other words, MsiGetFeatureState is referring to the state of a feature during an active install.

Similarly, if you look at MsiGetComponentPath, it's in the installer function list, and (as you saw in the preceding section "The Installer APIs") returns the path to a component that's installed on the system. However, the similar-sounding MsiGetTargetPath is in the list of database functions, it takes a handle to an install, and it returns the target path associated with a Directory table entry in the running install referenced via its handle parameter. MsiGetSourcePath has similar semantics to MsiGetTargetPath—it applies to a running installation.

This means that the first distinction you should make when deciding which APIs to use is between accessing products that are installed on the system and a particular product that's the subject of an install.

The type of handle you need is also crucial here; in particular, note the difference between a database handle and a handle to the current install. For example, if you're in CA code you have a handle to the install, not to the database, and you get a read-only handle to the current installing database by calling MsiGetActiveDatabase. If you look at the SDK documentation, you'll see that the handle you pass into an API is sometimes called an installation handle. This is another clue that the API applies to a running install, not to a product on the system or a database. For example, MsiGetComponentState uses a handle to the installation, and it tells you whether a component is marked for installation or not in this current install. However, MsiQueryComponentState takes no handle and is a general query about a particular component that's installed on the system.

To summarize these APIs based on their use of handles, the functions can be generalized in several ways:

- Functions without a handle generally query or manage the state of the system and its installed products through product codes, features, and component GUIDS.

- Functions that take an installation handle, usually called hInstall in the SDK, query or alter the state of a running active installation.

- Functions that take a database handle, usually named hDatabase in the SDK, are the basis for queries or updates to a database (notably MsiDatabaseOpenView), whether the database is one you opened on disk or whether you got the handle from MsiGetActiveDatabase.

Summary

One of the major advantages of Windows Installer and its integration into the Windows APIs is that you can find an amazing amount of detail about the products installed on the system. It's only a partial exaggeration to say that you can discover nearly everything about the products on the system, their files, and their versions.

CHAPTER 16

Tools and Futures

I'VE LOOKED EXCLUSIVELY AT VS as a tool for developing installation packages, but it should be apparent that VS doesn't take advantage of many of the features of Windows Installer that I've covered in this book. In this chapter, I'll look at alternative tools and talk in general terms about their capabilities.

One of the effects of a standardized Windows Installer technology is that you can use a growing number of tools to build MSI packages. In fact, given the Windows Installer SDK and knowledge of how to use it, it's perhaps easier than ever to build your own tool from scratch if you're so inclined.

Development Tools

The big companies offering installation development tools are InstallShield, Wise, OnDemand Software's WinINSTALL, and Zero G's InstallAnywhere. By "big" I mean the most well-known in the industry through sales, books, advertisements, and so on. (This isn't a complete list by any means, and I encourage you to visit http://www.installsite.org for a wealth of information on Windows Installer, including a list of the available tools for building MSI packages.) Some of these companies offer two general types of tools:

1. A tool that you use to build an MSI package from scratch, like you can in VS.

2. Repackaging tools, which let you build an MSI package in a couple of ways. First, you can open an existing MSI package and effectively convert it to use the new tool. This is almost reverse-engineering of an existing package. Second, some tools take a snapshot of the system before and after an installation (usually non-MSI) and build an IDE view of the process that you can use to generate an MSI package. Sometimes they monitor the system to capture these changes.

Of these choices, the first is preferable because it's more deterministic as well as safer. The main issue with the snapshot-based approaches is that anything that happens to the system between the before and after snapshots can end up in the installation package. Even something as seemingly innocent as moving a Windows Explorer window and closing it generates a flurry of changes to the Registry.

You can get specific details about the features these products offer by visiting their Web sites or using evaluation versions of the products. In general, many of them have the following characteristics:

- They have an expert view of the installation at the detail level. For example, you see a component-based view of the installation. These products let you add files to installer components and choose which file or Registry item is the KeyPath for the component. You can have multiple files in a component.

- They can organize components into multiple features and subfeatures. You can condition these features and the user can also choose whether to install them or not.

- They have IDE support for designing dialogs that integrate into the Windows Installer standard dialogs in the MSI package. You can design buttons on these dialogs—perhaps most usefully on Next buttons or their equivalent—to call CAs.

- They might have support for troubleshooting or debugging the installation.

- They have support for immediate and deferred CAs and you can explicitly sequence them in the UI or execution sequences.

- They make it easier to create installer patches. You can usually point the IDE at different packages and the tool creates a patch for you. Many let you create transforms in the same way.

- They provide dynamic file linking. You can point the IDE at a folder of files and the tool adds them all into the package instead of you having to add them all explicitly one by one.

- They have IDE support for Windows Services, for what will ultimately be the content of the ServiceInstall and ServiceControl tables.

- They often support a large number of localized languages.

- They often make some "routine" tasks easier with CAs or wizards in the IDE. For example, they can simplify deploying COM+ applications, creating IIS virtual directories, running SQL scripts, and digital signing.

Apart from the larger companies, individuals and small groups have built tools to create MSI packages. It's almost becoming a cottage industry. Note that you don't need to be locked into one vendor. For example, if you were to make extensive use of Merge Modules to build packages, you might find that some of these tools are more convenient (or cheaper) for this task, and you can use a fully featured product to build an install package that uses those Merge Modules.

What About Visual Studio?

It should be clear from this preceding feature list and from what you've seen in this book that VS has limitations. This isn't necessarily a bad thing—VS lets you build a basic installation package without you needing to worry about the issues relating to components, features, sequencing CAs, and so on. Aside from the fact that the preceding list describes additional Windows Installer functionality that VS doesn't have, my guess is that the following areas are where you'll find VS most limited as you get more adventurous with installations:

- VS has no support for building a package containing multiple features. VS generates a single feature in the MSI package. You can make something similar by inserting some of the available dialogs and associating radio buttons with properties, and then using those properties as conditions on files, but this is limited. Products that use features also have the ability to modify the installed features (Add/Remove Programs and a Modify choice), and you can't get that with a VS setup.

- CAs are always deferred and always in the execute sequence. For example, you can't run code to initialize properties to use in the UI or in a Launch Condition. If you have a custom launching program (perhaps a bootstrapper), one approach you can use is to create entries in the Registry in your launcher program. These are relatively easy to find in VS with its Search Target Machine feature.

- You cannot choose the place during the install (the sequence) where your CA is called.

- There's limited functionality for building UI forms. VS lets you insert some forms in the UI sequence and associate form content with properties, but you can't design your own forms or link CAs to buttons on the form.

- .NET installer classes provide the support for installing Services written with the .NET Framework. There's no VS support for Win32 Services in setup projects. In other words, VS setup projects don't make use of the standard ServiceInstall and ServiceControl tables. See Chapter 10 for details.

- VS isn't designed with minor upgrades in mind. Although you can perform minor upgrades with VS setup packages, you need to be careful that, for example, you don't break the rules about component GUIDs. See Chapter 6 for details on servicing installed products and Chapter 12 on updating products with MSI patches.

Futures

In early 2004, the beta 2 version of Windows Installer 3.0 was released. The main focus of this release is on servicing applications, especially patches. As of that beta date, the main features of 3.0 are in the following areas.

- Patch Uninstall: Native support for uninstallation of patches that were installed using MSI 3.0.

- Patch Sequencing: Ability to sequence patches in their logical order (whereas before sequencing was always chronological, and thus not always correct).

- Delta Compression Updates: Easier authoring of patch (MSP) files that use deltas rather than full files for servicing. This significantly reduces the payload size of the patch, resulting in a smaller download. Another advantage of this is how smart Windows Installer is with respect to applying the deltas and in minimizing source requirements (see the "Patching Tips" section in Chapter 12, which explains why access to the source medium might be required).

- Multiple patching: Ability to apply more than one patch to the product in a single transaction with integrated progress and rollback.

- Elevated patching: Support for application of "approved" patches by non-Administrators to a managed installation.

- New APIs: There are new APIs for management of the sources of installer packages and patches. Management of the source installed location of packages is a frequent issue, and the new APIs can alter the location of the installed source and its volume label. Refer to the documentation for the MsiSourceList* set of API functions. There are also new or enhanced functions that enumerate products and patches.

- Extra installer log features: The installer log has some extra features. In particular, the time is shown, and an entry is made when a property value changes.

Where Are Improvements Needed?

These are the areas in which developers often run into difficulties because there's no simple solution in most cases.

- XML configuration: .NET XML configuration files are flexible in being able to redirect assembly versions and change other policies of an application or the system. It's easy to install a configuration file, but it's difficult to update an existing one. This means you'll be writing relatively complex CAs to do this. As more applications use .NET, it would be ideal to have Windows Installer support for adding, updating, and removing (at uninstall) sections of private and system-wide configuration files. As an alternative to XML (or other types of files) where you want to supply variable data into CAs, don't forget that you don't need a plethora of properties; you can have custom tables and data in the MSI package that can be extracted at install time.

- Assemblies in the GAC: These behave differently from other files, as you saw in Chapters 8 and 11, not only in regards to the visibility issue when they're first installed, but also when updating them later. Their behavior is a strong encouragement to avoid the GAC in your application design.

- Embedded MSI files: These can be difficult to manage and update. Where you have a choice, it's better to build Merge Modules that can be added to your package, but sometimes you don't have a choice. The fact that COM+ exports MSI packages instead of Merge Modules means that you'll need to use a tool that makes embedding easy, if you choose to go this way. You also need to understand the limitations and restrictions of embedded MSI packages, most importantly in the area of updating them with minor upgrades. However, embedded MSI files are really just a way to get more than one MSI install happening at the same time, so if Microsoft were to remove this restriction you wouldn't need to think about embedded MSI files. The best recommendation for now is to use a launching program where appropriate to install multiple MSI packages.

Summary

Don't expect VS to satisfy all your installation needs. It wasn't intended to use all the features offered by Windows Installer, so for more flexibility look at other tools. Even if you choose other tools, the content of this book will still be useful, because underneath it all there are still the basics of installer tables, CAs, sequences, and all the functionality of Windows Installer.

Index

forums.apress.com

JOIN THE APRESS FORUMS AND BE PART OF OUR COMMUNITY. You'll find discussions that cover topics of interest to IT professionals, programmers, and enthusiasts just like you. If you post a query to one of our forums, you can expect that some of the best minds in the business—especially Apress authors, who all write with *The Expert's Voice*™—will chime in to help you. Why not aim to become one of our most valuable participants (MVPs) and win cool stuff? Here's a sampling of what you'll find:

DATABASES
Data drives everything.

Share information, exchange ideas, and discuss any database programming or administration issues.

INTERNET TECHNOLOGIES AND NETWORKING
Try living without plumbing (and eventually IPv6).

Talk about networking topics including protocols, design, administration, wireless, wired, storage, backup, certifications, trends, and new technologies.

JAVA
We've come a long way from the old Oak tree.

Hang out and discuss Java in whatever flavor you choose: J2SE, J2EE, J2ME, Jakarta, and so on.

MAC OS X
All about the Zen of OS X.

OS X is both the present and the future for Mac apps. Make suggestions, offer up ideas, or boast about your new hardware.

OPEN SOURCE
Source code is good; understanding (open) source is better.

Discuss open source technologies and related topics such as PHP, MySQL, Linux, Perl, Apache, Python, and more.

PROGRAMMING/BUSINESS
Unfortunately, it is.

Talk about the Apress line of books that cover software methodology, best practices, and how programmers interact with the "suits."

WEB DEVELOPMENT/DESIGN
Ugly doesn't cut it anymore, and CGI is absurd.

Help is in sight for your site. Find design solutions for your projects and get ideas for building an interactive Web site.

SECURITY
Lots of bad guys out there—the good guys need help.

Discuss computer and network security issues here. Just don't let anyone else know the answers!

TECHNOLOGY IN ACTION
Cool things. Fun things.

It's after hours. It's time to play. Whether you're into LEGO® MINDSTORMS™ or turning an old PC into a DVR, this is where technology turns into fun.

WINDOWS
No defenestration here.

Ask questions about all aspects of Windows programming, get help on Microsoft technologies covered in Apress books, or provide feedback on any Apress Windows book.

HOW TO PARTICIPATE:
Go to the Apress Forums site at **http://forums.apress.com/**.
Click the New User link.